CLYDE STUBBLEFIELD

MUSIC OF THE AMERICAN SOUTH

Clyde Stubblefield
Rhythms of the Funky Drummer

D. Leah Steinberg

THE UNIVERSITY OF GEORGIA PRESS ATHENS

Published by the University of Georgia Press
Athens, Georgia 30602
www.ugapress.org

Designed by Erin Kirk

Set in Miller Text

Printed digitally

EU Authorized Representative
Easy Access System Europe—Mustamäe tee 50, 10621 Tallinn, Estonia, gpsr.requests@easproject.com

Library of Congress Cataloging-in-Publication Data
Names: Steinberg, D. Leah, 1952– author
Title: Clyde Stubblefield : rhythms of the funky drummer / D. Leah Steinberg.
Description: Athenbvgghbjgs : The University of Georgia Press, [2026] | Series: Music of the American south | Includes bibliographical references and index.
Identifiers: LCCN 2026017560 | ISBN 9780820377704 hardback | ISBN 9780820377711 paperback | ISBN 9780820377735 pdf | ISBN 9780820377728 epub
Subjects: LCSH: Stubblefield, Clyde | Drummers (Musicians)—United States | Funk musicians—United States | LCGFT: Biographies
Classification: LCC ML419.S829 S74 2026 | DDC 786.9092 [B]—dc23/eng/20260501
LC record available at https://lccn.loc.gov/2026017560

To the memory of Clyde Austin Stubblefield and the singular polyrhythms and joy he brought to the world

"Clyde leaves a mark on your soul."

—**FRED WESLEY**, trombone player for James Brown

"Clyde plays the way that Clyde plays. . . . Nobody's gonna play like Clyde."

—**JOHN "JABO" STARKS**, drummer, Clyde Stubblefield's rhythm partner, and collaborator with James Brown and The Famous Flames

PROGRAM

Set Break

SET 3. Madison, Wisconsin: The Rhythms of His Time

ENCORE

WHO'S WHO

Joey Banks Clyde's friend, musician, Madison-area drummer

Trevor Banks Film director, *Give the Drummer Some*

Joe Burke Chattanooga drummer for the Blue Shufflers, the Cascades

Adam Deitch Record producer, drummer for Lettuce

Pee Wee Ellis Jazz saxophonist

Robert "Slim" Eppinger Chattanooga bass player, the Whirltones, the Cascades

Lenell Glass Chattanooga bass player, the Blue Shufflers, the Cascades, the Playboy Club House Band

Jody Hannon Clyde's wife

Wally Ingram Clyde's friend; drummer for Timbuk 3, the David Nelson Band, the Bob Weir/Phil Lesh tour; played with Bob Weir in many settings

Robbie Kowal DJ

John **Medeski** Keyboardist, Medeski, Martin, & Wood

Cris Plata Clyde's friend; guitarist, songwriter, Tex-Mex band Cris Plata and Extra Hot

Pauli Ryan Clyde's percussionist and friend

Ben Sidran Clyde's friend, jazz keyboardist

David Stanoch Clyde's friend, drummer, educator

Tom Strader Clyde's friend, instrumental in getting Clyde's honorary PhD

Fred Thomas Bass player for the JBS

Rickey Vincent DJ, teacher, radio host of *The History of Funk*, KPFA, Berkeley, California.

Fred Wesley Trombonist, band director, James Brown and The Famous Flames, JBs, Parliament Funkadelic, Fred Wesley Band

Kathie Williams Clyde's manager in Madison, Wisconsin, from 1999–2017

"MY OWN RHYTHMS"

I just played what I felt. It was different rhythm patterns I played on different songs. I used to listen to a drummer named Joe Burke. He was a hot jazz drummer. No one taught me anything. I can't read music either. He said, 'Just sit down and play your rhythms and enjoy yourself.' I did that and came up with my own rhythms. I really loved my rhythms, too. I was playing mainly rhythm and blues, but occasionally jammed with a jazz band. I played in Nashville at the Grand Ole Opry. I like playing country music, too. I didn't play the same drum pattern rhythm behind Marva Whitney on 'It's My Thing.' I played mainly what the guitar player was playing—the straight 'chop, chop, chop.' I put a 4/4 rhythm behind it with a backbeat. I didn't add any extra beats. I was playing what Marva was saying and singing. I'm just a drummer who plays what I feel. I don't know what I'm going to play until I hear the song.

—**CLYDE STUBBLEFIELD**, "The Clyde Stubblefield Interview" (2020), *Jake Feinberg Show*

BACKSTAGE

"James who?"

This was Clyde Stubblefield's playful but pointed way of deflecting the inevitable questions of having played drums for one of the most preeminent musicians of the twentieth century: James Brown.

Unlike many other people, I came to know Clyde not because of his longtime connection to the legendary Godfather of Soul. In fact, I met him when I wandered into a small, almost empty bar late one night in the mid-nineties during the dead of winter in Madison, Wisconsin. As a result of that chance encounter, we became friends. We stayed in touch for years, off and on, until his death in 2017.

Clyde's music was a refreshing and thrilling change from the music I had listened to for decades. As a child growing up in the Midwest, I was surrounded by classical music: I took piano lessons and accompanied my sister on the flute and my father on the clarinet. Growing up in a Midwestern liberal Jewish family, I attended classical concerts and learned dozens of songs while my father practiced his clarinet for musicals he played in with other musicians from the Argonne National Laboratory in Illinois where he was a nuclear physicist.

Like countless other children of the 1960s, I was introduced to the folk music of Peter, Paul and Mary, Judy Collins, the Kingston Trio, and many others. I knew many tunes as folk songs, but I was unaware as a child that their rhythms and lyrics were born among Black people who were held in bondage in slavery. My horizons expanded in high school: I veered toward rock and roll and the blues, which I related to, and was drawn to the melancholy sadness of Bob Dylan's poetry, and later the soulful ballads of the Grateful Dead. Through their poetry and music, I found understanding and connection to my personal experiences. Over the years, there were certainly plenty of other reasons to seek solace in the blues—everything from the Cold War, the Vietnam War, and the invasion of Iraq, to perpetual racism and sexism in our culture and the looming threat of climate change.

I grew up comfortably in a middle-class, mostly white community, yet I'm grateful for the times I had my eyes opened to the world that existed beyond my suburb. One such moment came in 1969 when, during a summer program for students sponsored by my friend's Lutheran church, we learned about the inner city. We attended Jesse Jackson's Operation Breadbasket meetings on the Chicago South Side. There, I was introduced to the power of uplifting Black gospel music. Years later, I had a similar revelatory experience when taking part in a day of Black spirituals in Oakland, California.

Funk, though, was different, a world of its own, and I discovered it thanks to Clyde Stubblefield.

As a student at the University of Wisconsin, I attended the occasional concert and jazz show in Madison. My musical vocabulary didn't change much, however, until one night in the mid-1990s when I first heard Clyde play at the The Chamber on King Street, which was later renamed the King Club. Funk, as I found out, had its own unique rhythm. It might have had its roots in the blues and soul but it was powered by an energetic and intricate beat that reached me at a deep level. It felt uplifting and, at the same time, grounding and thoroughly intoxicating. Listening to it, I felt that this was the rhythm that was missing from my life. The beats that Clyde played took me down a new road, which included buying my own drum set and taking lessons. I was only too happy to have Clyde lead the way.

I loved Clyde's music, but I came to realize that more people needed to know it—and know him. Who was this man who had lived in the shadow of James Brown and who was now performing modest gigs in Madison, Wisconsin, far from the celebrated clubs of New York, Chicago, and Los Angeles? And so, a few years after I first heard Clyde play, I asked him if I could write his story. He readily agreed.

But after gathering pictures and stories from his early band members in Chattanooga, Tennessee, that formed the foundation for Clyde's early, pre–James Brown years, I was not up to the task of fulfilling my promise. Time passed. Life got in the way. And the details of a vibrant musical heritage from Chattanooga sat stacked in a cardboard box, moving from place to place, waiting for me to take notice once again.

While visiting Madison in 2014, I heard Clyde play at an upscale venue, a more sanitized club than where I had first heard him play his funky rhythms. But the musical quality was at the same high level. I took Clyde's photo—the last one I have of him. His hair was now short and gray, and he was recovering from his bout with bladder cancer a few years earlier. But he persevered. A half-century of drumming had maintained his strength and will to live. And, as always, his broad, warm smile radiated kindness.

After he finished his set, I went up to say hello. "You were going to write a book about me," he said with a serious tone and a disappointed look. I felt a deep sadness that so many things had gotten in the way of that promise.

But I was determined to fulfill my promise to Clyde and tell his story. A year later, back home in the Bay Area, I told my friend Alice that I was finally reviewing the interviews I had done in Chattanooga so many years earlier when trying to get this book started. "You better write it soon," she said. "You never know how long Clyde will be around."

In 2017, only a few weeks after I rededicated myself to the project, however, I received some terrible news: Clyde was in the ICU at a hospital in Madison. A few days later, at age seventy-three, Clyde passed away from kidney failure.

I was heartbroken and couldn't bring myself to reopen the box I had labeled "Clyde's Stuff." And then, two months later, I had a dream. Clyde showed up as I had last seen him, with his short graying hair and wide smile. A serious look came over him, and in a determined but friendly tone—a distinctly Clyde voice—he said this: "Do it anyway." And that was it. That was all the motivation I needed. I woke up and got to work. Reinforcement continued when I told Fred Wesley, trombonist and fellow James Brown band member, I was writing a book about Clyde and he said, "I appreciate it because Clyde was my good friend and anything you can do for him you are doing it for me too."

I dove into the musical history of the Delta that stretched back to Africa. I traced some of the rivulets that spread to all branches of American music. As Clyde's polyrhythms resettled into my own internal rhythms, I got a sense of how Clyde's musical journey reached back to the South and its traditions and, further back, across the Atlantic to Africa. This book is organized as a progression of Clyde's life, beginning when he first moved to Madison where he lived for most of his life, but then looking back to paint a portrait of the world he came from and who and what formed his foundation and influenced his early music career. I also look further back to the roots of African and African American music and rhythms where almost all American music was derived and that evolved through many iterations, eventually to funk.

Clyde Stubblefield will always be remembered as the "Funky Drummer"—after his famous drum solo that James Brown introduced by announcing, "Give the drummer some!" But Clyde never got his full due. His drum breaks from "Funky Drummer" and "Cold Sweat" are among the most frequently sampled rhythms in hip-hop and popular music. But that was not the only thing, or even the most important thing he wanted to be remembered for. Clyde once told jazz pianist Ben Sidran, one of Clyde's friends and collaborators in Madison, Wisconsin, "You and I brought R&B to southcentral Wisconsin. There was none there. We invented that." In fact, he became the most sampled drummer of all time and yet was never compensated for these samples. He told me what bothered him more than the lack of money from his work was the lack of recognition. Rarely was he given the credit he was owed. With this book, I hope to change that.

A MEDLEY OF MUSICIANS

My first musical journey to the roots of American music and into the South and Clyde's past took place in an old vw van, rambling down part of the old "Blues Highway" from near Madison to Chattanooga in 1996. I had a list of names on a crumpled piece of paper in Clyde's handwriting in my purse. On the list were the people he said I should speak with. Even though he wanted me to write a book about him, he was a private person and mainly kept his views to himself. So, I took his advice and hit the road where I thought I would learn more in the place Clyde was born and started his musical journey.

Clyde did not talk often about his past, either his time with Brown or his growing up in the segregated poorer section of Chattanooga. Many people who knew him a long time said they did not know much about his early years. I often puzzled about why he didn't talk to me directly about his life. I think he wanted others to tell his story; he was a drummer, he was rhythm, he did not say it with words. Clyde was conflicted about Brown, fame, and his past—both his personal and musical career history. In his later years he opened up slightly.

While in Chattanooga I spoke with Clyde's sister Vivian and with his mentors and band members from his early teenage years. So, after a long drive through the Midwest to the South, I stood in a hotel lobby inside a phone booth in downtown Chattanooga. I put a quarter in the slot, punched the buttons on the rectangular silver phone, picked up the black earpiece, and pulled the door shut. After a few rings Robert "Slim" Eppinger picked up. We had spoken in Madison and we agreed on a time to meet the next day. The next day I was in Slim's car, driving around the Big 9 where blues, rhythm and blues, jazz, and soul music poured out from the clubs into the streets. Chattanooga's musical heyday lasted from the early 1900s through the 1960s. I used a small cassette recorder to capture Slim's words as well as those of the other Chattanooga musicians I spoke with. I later transcribed the tapes, word by agonizing word, backing up and going forward with a slow Southern summer's pace. The other musicians from Chattanooga that I was not able to reach while I was in town I spoke to later by phone.

A couple of decades later, I interviewed musicians from James Brown and The Famous Flames after Clyde left the band and lived in Madison. It was after Clyde had passed and I felt he was guiding me to the people he wanted to speak for him. My interviews of the musicians during Clyde's time with James Brown and later in Madison took place during the Covid pandemic that began in 2020. It was easy to reach people—no one was touring, the internet made it simple to find people, and connecting was mostly a matter of looking up their web pages and setting a time to talk. All seemed to be happy to revisit some of the most exciting and, for some, interpersonally challenging, musical times of their careers. I also think many were happy to have something else to think about rather than an invisible virus that was messing with all our lives. Some interviews were done over Zoom, others on the phone, depending on the interviewee's preference.

Setlist

Set 1

Chattanooga and the Roots of the Heartbeat

I'm just a drummer.

—**CLYDE**

The drummer is the heartbeat—everything comes from him. The beat, the time—he is the heartbeat. It's like the heart pumping blood to the rest of the body; he is the heartbeat of an orchestra of a band, of a group. He is the heartbeat.

—**JABO STARKS**, *Soul of the Funky Drummer* (2004)

1

The Darkest Hour

It was past midnight on July 26, 1970. The singing, the dancing, and the twenty-one-piece orchestra had gone silent. James Brown's show was over, and a cleanup crew was picking up after a crowd of thousands who had vacated the Dane County Coliseum in Madison, Wisconsin. Across town, on the northeast side of the city, Clyde Stubblefield knocked softly on the door of a nondescript, ranch-style house. His hands were sore from hours of drumming. Mosquitoes were buzzing around his head, making music of their own in the midsummer heat. A muted "Who's there?" came from inside. Clyde's answer drew a smile from the man—Clyde's older brother, Frank—as he opened the aluminum door. Frank was happy to see his younger brother and delighted they would once again be living in the same town. But Frank also had concerns, as he knew it was possible Clyde's future might not be smooth.

Stubblefield's unlikely journey to Wisconsin had been long. He had circled the world on back roads and interstates, traveling on endless bus rides and flights, and playing for American troops in Vietnam. It had all started when he was a teenager, learning the street sounds of Chattanooga, Tennessee, under the tutelage of old Black men. Decades later, standing outside his brother's house in Madison, he was now about as far removed from his native Tennessee as he could get—culturally and racially, to say nothing of being one of the coldest climates—while remaining in the continental United States.

Madison, for James Brown, was just another stop on yet another tour—a place to play a gig, collect money, then move on to the next show.

Clyde, though, had arrived in the capital of Wisconsin with a plan. He had left Brown's band when the singer had fired most of his musicians the year before, but rejoined the group with several other musicians who had difficulty making it on their own. In Madison that night, Clyde dutifully played his funky rhythms, yet he had other things on his mind: he was ready to begin the escape he'd been planning for some time. From what his brother Frank told me, Brown had no idea of Stubblefield's plan to leave that day. Clyde was weary but determined, even if the future that lay ahead of him was uncertain.

Once and for all, Stubblefield made the difficult choice of parting ways with the bandleader for whom he had laid down his signature rhythm of funk, helping make the Godfather of Soul world-famous. In crossing the doorstep of his brother's home, he was taking his first steps away from an abusive boss, away from grueling practice and studio sessions, away from impossible standards of perfection, away from paychecks that were withheld. Here, in this urban but scenic isthmus surrounded by four lakes, Clyde knew there was much that appealed to many: beautiful sunsets, boating and swimming in the summer, ice fishing in the winter, a state university with a storied history of radical politics. But, for him, it was a new start. And, most importantly, his brother lived there.

Folklore says the Midnight Special was the name of a steam train that originated in Houston, Texas, and then left from Jackson, Mississippi, just after midnight, at 12:05 a.m. It brought friends and family to visit prisoners at the Parchman Farm Prison—the Mississippi state prison 130 miles north of Jackson.[1] Other tales say it passed by the Louisiana State Penitentiary and still others the Sugar Land Prison, in Texas. But the staying power of the legend is that the light from that train would shine into prison cells. Over time, a kind of superstition developed among the prisoners that if you were cast in that train's light, you would gain freedom and good fortune.[2] Huddie Ledbetter—aka "Lead Belly"—recorded "The Midnight Special" while in prison in 1934.[3] These stories are just some of the tales that wind their way through the South and the history of the blues. Such stories are hard to validate; they are as elusive as the backstories of all the innumerable artists who have shaped the mosaic that is Black music in America. And yet these stories have staying power; they resonate through the ages.

In my mind's eye, when I picture Clyde standing on his brother's doorstep, I imagine the glow of a porchlight as his own Midnight Special beacon. He has just walked away from fame but has gained his long-earned freedom, his brother's light leading the way. Clyde is standing in the town he will live in for the rest of his life. He is home.

2

Africa, the Musical Delta, and Beyond

The Roots of Rhythm

> The curious beauty of African music is that it uplifts even as it tells a sad tale. You may be poor, you may have only a ramshackle house, you may have lost your job, but that song gives you hope.
> —**NELSON MANDELA**

Long before Stubblefield ever played with James Brown, his music was suffused with the sounds of Africa. Understanding the roots of these rhythms—and how they developed into uniquely American musical forms—is essential to understanding his story. In *Rock & Roll: An Unruly History*, author Robert Palmer quotes Fela Sowande, a Nigerian musicologist, as saying, "If we seek to discover the foundations of traditional music in Africa, I think we have to look for them . . . in the traditional African's predilection for the esoteric and the occult, in religion and magic."[1] The Ashanti of West Africa "believe 'the man in the moon' to be a drummer."[2]

Africans brought both their oral traditions and music with them when they were captured and enslaved in what is modern-day Benin. Matthew Montfort chronicles the rhythmic traditions of Africa, as well as of Bali and India, in *Ancient Traditions—Future Possibilities*, writing, "In West Africa, societies such as the Yoruba, the Ewe, the Akan and the Ibo possess a music rich in rhythmic vitality. It is a music of multiple layers of rhythms. While European classical music has developed complex harmonies of tones, West African music has developed a complex interweaving of contrasting rhythmic patterns. The African musician strives for the occurrence of at least two different rhythms at once, and it is precisely this juxtaposition of opposing rhythms that creates the vital spark of African music."[3] Unlike traditional European music, the sounds of Africa rested on cross-rhythms, also known as "polyrhythms," each with separate starting points and meters that contrasted and emphasized unaccented beats. These intertwined rhythms created new sounds that had not yet been heard in Western music, and they wound their way through the Mississippi Delta, in time cross-pollinating across several genres, becoming new, uniquely American forms of music: jazz and blues.

Music is integral to the African experience. LeRoi Jones discusses African contributions to American music in his book *Blues People*. "The most apparent survivals of African music in Afro-American music are its rhythms: not only the seeming emphasis in the African music on rhythmic, rather than melodic or harmonic, qualities, but also the use of polyphonic, or contrapuntal, rhythmic effects. Because of this seeming neglect of harmony and melody, Westerners thought the music 'primitive.' It did not occur to them that Africans might have looked askance at a music as vapid rhythmically as the West's."[4]

In "Funk and James Brown," Rob Bowman writes that "rhythm is intrinsic in the way Africans communicate, thus the drum became crucial in communal expression, both political and musical. Rhythm is so connected to the African way of life, that art is life, not a removed foreign entity as defined in the Western world."[5] After adopting Stubblefield's funk rhythms, James Brown encompassed this idea when he made the sounds of the drum paramount not only with its rhythms but when he directed all the instruments of the band to reflect the sounds of the drum.

This focus on the drum had its beginnings when Stubblefield joined the band. It also became an intrinsic part of the musical and political changes of the '60s and early '70s. Bowman continues, "The concept of rhythm, translated through the drum is highly important in African culture. To Africa, rhythm replicates the endless beat of breath and life, allowing use to improvise with the changes of life."[6] Stubblefield echoed this deep connection when he said, "My music is my life—my music is my breathing."

Ben Sidran writes in *Black Talk*, "Capturing the rhythms of African or modern Afro American Music with western notation is a lot like trying to capture the sea with a fish net."[7] Sidran explains why it is difficult to notate African and African American music: "These were attempts at describing rather than notating this rhythm. . . . The complexity of this rhythmic approach is in large part due to the value placed on spontaneity and the inherently communal nature of oral improvisation."[8]

Africa is the root of funk, Rickey Vincent explains, it is how people react to the rhythms on an emotional, body and soul level, as opposed to a typical Western way of individualism.[9] He further states, "In the African musical experience, everyone is included, for everyone's individual's rhythms are essential to the total vibe."[10]

As has been well documented, enslaved people used melodies and lyrics when singing work songs, using call-and-response singing to pass the time as they labored in fields. Singing occurred often as they worked in their own fields, but the content and tone were vastly different when being forced while enslaved in a foreign land.[11] Sometimes the music communicated encoded messages that went unnoticed by their enslavers. One example is the African American spiritual "Follow the Drinking Gourd," which included secret instructions about the Underground Railroad: "For the old man is a-waiting for to carry you to freedom if you follow the drinking gourd." The drinking gourd referred to the big dipper, the North Star, the road out of slavery. There were specifics: "The riverbank makes a very good road; the dead trees will show you the way," and "the river ends between two hills . . . there's another river on the other side."

Over the course of the eighteenth and nineteenth centuries, the hums and cries of old Negro spirituals laid the foundation for blues music. Songs like "Go Down Moses" and "Sometimes I Feel Like a Motherless Child" are songs that many people associate with church.

After emancipation, beginning in 1863, formerly enslaved people who became sharecroppers continued to sing the songs that had been passed down to them. They sang them in the fields, and they sang them as they built roads, railroads, and levees on rivers. Musicians also carried on the traditions. Their rhythms and melodies rang out in the South on streets, in bars, at house parties, and in music halls—the places where Stubblefield played in his teenage years while growing up in Chattanooga.

Alan Leeds, former road manager for James Brown, bridges the beats of rhythm across time and continents when he says, "One can trace the same fundamental rhythm patterns from Yoruba to Afro-Cuban ritual, to the 'ring shouts' of Southern backwoods churches, to the 'shout' rhythms of sanctified musicians such as Whirling Willie, and on into rhythm and blues, rock and roll, soul, funk, and hip-hop."[12] One day Lionel Hampton, who popularized the backbeat that became R&B and, later, rock and roll, went to a church revival and saw Whirling Willie, who became his muse. Hampton said, "I started working on my musicians, getting them to play with that kind of inspiration. And I think I was the first to bring all that music from the Holiness church—the beat, the hand clapping, the shouting—out into the band business. When rock and roll came in, they took a whole lot of things from us."[13]

African American music is at the heart of much of American music. From its roots in West Africa came the backbone of the spirituals, the foundation of slave songs, the heartbeat of the blues, the innovative sounds of jazz, the infectious spirit of rhythm and blues, the soul of gospel, the dance moves of rock and roll, and, ultimately, the contagious rhythms of funk. The accented beats of these old African rhythms remain vibrant today; one can easily hear them in hip-hop, the rhythms of Clyde's funky drum that became looped over and over. These sounds are tied together by ghost notes, the invisible threads bridging the musical forms together. They're the notes and rhythms that I believe were coded in Clyde's DNA, written in his heart and soul from when he first picked up a pair of drumsticks.

3

The One Heartbeat

Musical Branches of the Mississippi Delta

It's a few hundred miles from Tunica, Mississippi (in the northeast of the Delta, considered the Gateway to the Blues), to Chattanooga, where Clyde was born and began his musical journey. Eighty-seven miles wide and two hundred miles long, the Delta extends all the way to the Gulf of Mexico, its winding shape suggesting an ancient creature that's finding its way to the sea. It's here that the blues was born, spreading over time throughout the South, then moving north to St. Louis and Chicago. The music was played by mostly self-taught musicians who, over time, refined its basic form into a twelve-bar chord progression, often accompanied by guitar and harmonica.

The roots of jazz go back to New Orleans. It's in the city's old downtown marketplace, in Congo Square, where most people believe jazz began. In this spot, from the mid-eighteenth to the late nineteenth century, enslaved people congregated weekly to sing, play music, and dance to the songs of their home countries. They accompanied each other on bells, drums, and other instruments. Congo Square's key role in musical history is honored in a plaque that stands in this hallowed space. It reads: "By 1803, Congo Square had become famous for the gathering of enslaved Africans who drummed, danced, sang, and traded on Sunday afternoons. By 1819, these gatherings numbered as many as 300 to 600 people. Among the most famous dances were the Bamboula, the Calinda, and the Congo. These African cultural expressions gradually developed into Mardi Gras Indian traditions, the Second Line, and eventually New Orleans jazz and rhythm and blues."[1]

Today the Mahalia Jackson Theater for the Performing Arts proudly stands in Congo Square. It is a testament to a long tradition of honoring the history of the square and its role in New Orleans music. Just three blocks away, Preservation Hall is dedicated to nurturing the early jazz tradition. On the three hundredth anniversary of the city of New Orleans, the renowned jazz musician Wynton Marsalis said, "Every strand of American music comes directly from Congo Square."[2]

Likewise, in Chattanooga, the Bessie Smith Cultural Center celebrates that city's Black history, much of it tied to musical pioneers, including Bessie Smith, the "Empress of the Blues," who was born in Chattanooga. Here, too, of course, is where Clyde was born and raised, as were his early bandmates, Lenell Glass, Robert "Slim" Eppinger, and Joe Burke.

The story of race in the emergence of jazz is as divergent as the music is revolutionary. While the blues arose in agricultural areas, jazz was born in New Orleans, the Crescent City, where Caribbean, African, and European influences merged. However, some claim Mississippi is the true birthplace of all American music, including gospel, country, jazz, bluegrass, and rock and roll.[3] This theory maintains that Black people went to New Orleans from the Delta, bringing their blues music with them.

The Creole people of New Orleans were the offspring of relationships between Blacks and French settlers; their skin was lighter in color than those whose parents were both native Africans. Creole musicians learned music through more formal means from their European neighbors and relatives. They trained in classical music and saw themselves as separate from darker-skinned Blacks, who were often self-taught, couldn't read or write music, and played music that Creoles thought less refined. "In 1894, the infamous 'White Act' was passed, forcing Creoles, since they also had African ancestor, to lose their privileged status," according to the Soul of America.[4] The enactment of restrictive Jim Crow segregation laws in the late 1800s and early 1900s caused Creole people to be considered Black, mandating them to live and work with darker-skinned people on the other side of town. They lost the privileges they had been afforded. Creole musicians began playing with African American Blues musicians, who mainly lived and worked in Faubourg Treme.[5]

Out of this mix emerged many musical styles in the twentieth century. Some had beats in equal divisions called "straight rhythms," while others had more complicated and elaborate polyrhythms, popular in African

American culture and adopted from African traditions. Southern forms influenced and merged, creating an increasing diversity of sound: New Orleans Street processional/marching music with their Second Line rhythms, shuffles, swing, blues, jazz, gospel, boogie-woogie, rhythm and blues, country, bluegrass, and rock and roll. And then came funk, a potent and irresistible mixture of soul, jazz, and R&B.

A critical new direction in the expression of jazz came from the early bebop music of Miles Davis. Later in his career, as more elaborate forms of jazz developed, Davis left bebop behind to search for his authentic funky roots. This resulted in his album *Get Up With It*, which included jazz-funk, jazz-rock, experimental jazz, and funk fusions with tracks like "Honky Tonk" and "Red China Blues." Davis found fresh inspiration and vitality in blues and funk, but the new styles he developed did not replace the traditional Delta style, and the blues continued. The variety of these genres resulted in unique interplays and new versions of expression, such as jazz-funk and blues-funk, which Stubblefield utilized, along with straight blues music as the foundation of his music in his post–James Brown era.

Stubblefield's drumming style was undeniably innovative. Yet its roots go back to the early twentieth century, and the musical ripples of the Mississippi Delta extend throughout the South and across the country. Henry Roeland Byrd, better known as Professor Longhair, was born in Bogalusa, Louisiana, on the outskirts of New Orleans, in 1918. He developed a percussive, hard-driving method of drumming called rumba-boogie, which became popular in the 1930s. As he played an upright piano, Byrd would rhythmically kick its soundboard, foreshadowing the development of the kick drum. His style became popular with Black laborers who heard the hard-driving nature of their repetitive work in Byrd's kicking. These were sounds that Clyde also heard early in his life on the streets of Chattanooga and picked up in his own rhythms—the pounding of a grain elevator, the rolling of train engines. In 1909, William Ludwig invented the bass drum pedal for the kick drum. A half-century later, Stubblefield's mastery of that drum peddle was the engine that powered the hard-driving funk sound of James Brown.

Dixieland was an attempt by white musicians to take traditional jazz out of New Orleans and market it to larger audiences, with Kansas City and Chicago being the primary spots. Eventually, white and Black solo musicians and bands traveled north and east out of New Orleans, creating and playing their unique musical styles and establishing themselves in new cities and towns. All-Black and all-white big bands were also migrating out of New Orleans during the 1930s and '40s, and this music became the soundtrack of the swing era. This music influenced the sounds of the Chattanooga bands like the Blue Shufflers and the Cascades—the bands Stubblefield played with as a teenager.

Ultimately, the big bands, some as large as fourteen musicians, became integrated, helping lead the way for interracial audiences and laying a blueprint for cultural change in society. It was also during this time, in Kansas City, that Charlie Parker was developing bebop utilizing smaller bands, including a saxophone, trumpet, piano, double bass, drums, and soloist. These bands were about half the size of the big bands.

In the 1940s, many Southern Blacks traveled north to find work in cities, bringing their music with them. One crucial place that advanced the proliferation of the blues was the South Side of Chicago. Chicago became a mecca for blues music, and "Chicago Blues was one of the most significant influences on early rock music."[6] Muddy Waters, Chuck Berry, Etta James, and scores of others recorded at the Chess Recording Studio on the South Side.

At the turn of the century, on Chicago's West Side, Jewish merchants who had escaped persecution in Russia and Eastern Europe created open markets on Maxwell Street. Black musicians were welcome on Maxwell Street. Just as Congo Square is considered the place where jazz began, Maxwell Street is known as the birthplace of the Chicago Blues.

After World War II, a more percussive style emanated from musical rhythm sections, while amplification made music more easily heard—and electrifying—for audiences. The Southern bluesmen brought with them a variety of blues styles; some of its hard-driving sounds led to the birth of rock and roll. Rhythm and blues also grew out of the blues of the 1930s and '40s. With the emergence of bebop in the '50s, many Black jazz musicians such as Miles Davis, John Coltrane, and Thelonious Monk began reclaiming the Afro-American heritage of their music.

Ultimately, Charlie Parker moved to New York and, with Dizzy Gillespie and later Miles Davis, changed the face of jazz. With smaller bands, the movement to bebop allowed for virtuoso performances in time-honored venues such as the Blue Note in Manhattan. While Blacks were reclaiming jazz, the path for the future of rock and roll, still called rhythm and blues, was taken up by white groups and singers, bringing it to white suburbia. Elvis Presley, Jerry Lee Lewis, the Rolling Stones, and others acknowledged their debt to African American music but capitalized on its rhythms and sounds. Rock and roll offered a sense of freedom to rebellious white teenagers. For the cost of a 45, an album, a concert ticket, a joint, and some torn jeans, the boredom of suburbia could be transformed, epitomized by the Who's 1965 song "My Generation," the ultimate anthem to teenage rebellion. Despite the road this music paved out of apathy, the recognition and success of blues and rhythm and blues musicians, like many of those who played with Clyde in his early days in Chattanooga, were left behind. Many seemed to float down the Mississippi River, unsung, back into the Delta.

As discussed earlier, many tributaries of American music can be traced back to the blues and across the ocean to West Africa. The rhythms that developed in the twentieth century by a handful of drummers defined the backbeat of everything from R&B, rock and roll, funk, and hip-hop. There were many influential and prominent drummers of Stubblefield's day, having all contributed exciting but distinct rhythms to several genres of African American music. The drummers' backgrounds and popularity were vastly different. Stubblefield joined Brown in 1965 and created the rhythms of modern funk, which later became adapted and sampled by thousands of hip-hop and rap musicians. He had no formal training, was casually mentored on the streets of Chattanooga, and never learned to read music. Earl Palmer (1924–2008), who had formal musical training at the Gruenwald School of Music, created the backbeat of rock and roll when he played with Fats Domino. Earl Palmer's drumming on "The Fat Man" "featured the backbeat that has come to be the most important element in rock and roll." Palmer said, "That song required a strong afterbeat throughout the whole piece. With Dixieland you had a strong afterbeat only after you got to the shout last chorus. . . . It was sort of a new approach to rhythm music."[7] Elvis called Fats the real king of rock and roll. Benny Benjamin, or "Papa Zita" (1925–69), helped defined the Motown sound as part of the Funk Brothers rhythm section with James Jamerson, on bass with a focus on R&B-funk, Southern soul, and Memphis soul, which powered the Detroit sound from 1959 to 1972. Albert J. Jackson Jr.

was a member of Booker T. & the M. G.'s, a group of session musicians who worked for Stax Records in Memphis.

While rock and roll was exploding, Motown was emerging from urban Detroit, with highly choreographed music and steps, proper suits, and "Sunday best" dresses. As white teenagers tried to drop out of the suburbs and society, many African Americans tried to find a way in. Two posters of the same concert from the time typify this contrast. Organized by famed concert promoter Bill Graham, the Labor Day weekend shows at San Francisco's Fillmore West, from September 2–5, 1966, featured Martha and the Vandellas, as well as Jefferson Airplane, the Grateful Dead, and Quicksilver Messenger Service. Graham created two posters to attract different kinds of audiences: one mainly white hippies, the other mostly Black Motown fans. One poster shows the three Vandellas standing together, smiling, resplendent in matching cocktail dresses, their poofy hair curled in perfect flips. The band's name is in bold black lettering, and the Fillmore's letterings and Labor Day stand out in red. The other poster, by contrast, depicts a naked white woman in graphic form, her long hair draped around psychedelic lettering announcing the most popular bands of the San Francisco scene.

James Brown insisted that his band members be impeccably dressed. This was just one of the points of contention between him and his band. Deviations from Mr. Brown's rules resulted in fines if the musicians did not comply. Brown expected perfection in all ways—every shoe that shared the stage with his had to be shined to a buffed polish. After leaving the James Brown band for life in Madison, Clyde adopted a freer lifestyle in clothes and musical genres. As the jazz keyboard player and composer John Medeski told me, Clyde had his own attitude toward formal wear for gigs. When Clyde was with Brown, he and the other band members had to conform or be fined, but later in Madison, away from the almost military rigidity, his approach to such matters was: "Fuck it."

4

Chattanooga

Clyde Austin Stubblefield was born in the segregated Southern city of Chattanooga, Tennessee, to Frank D. Stubblefield and Vena Southers Stubblefield on April 18, 1943, in Carver Hospital, an all-Black facility. Carver, formerly Ellis Hospital, admitted only whites until a newer all-white hospital in East Chattanooga was built. Stubblefield took his first breaths a few blocks from West Ninth Street, already an important center for blues and jazz. In a few years, the area became an important home for R&B and soul.

The blues were alive and thriving in the Black community from the blues' early days through vaudeville, but by the early 1930s the blues were just another cultural avenue that was impacted by the Great Depression. Clark White writes, "The majority of successful performers up to this time had been Black women [including Bessie Smith]. It would be another decade before the blues regained its economic vitality."[1] That next decade included the time Stubblefield grew up learning and playing music on the burgeoning musical streets of Chattanooga, Ninth Street, the Big 9. White continues, "In the world of the juke, the people of the juke in Chattanooga continued to preserve, present and perpetuate blues culture and the Black experience with elegance and style."[2]

Clyde had two older siblings, Vivian Yvonn Walton (1940–97) and Frank Jr. (1936–2016). Their mother, Vena, born in 1917, also had two stepchildren from when she later married TK Simmons. Clyde lost his mother after a short illness on Sunday, October 21, 1956, a mild but rainy fall day. Rev. Robert Richards officiated Vena's funeral the following

Friday at Hardwick's Memorial Chapel. Clyde's mother was laid to rest at Greenhill Cemetery in Chattanooga, leaving behind a thirteen-year-old boy who was already forging his unique rhythmic sounds to share with the world.

After their mother died, Clyde and his older sister Vivian continued to live together in a small apartment near the center of town. Frank Jr. was in the Air Force at the time, with the whereabouts of their father unclear. Frank Sr., born in 1912, had served in World War II. Robert "Slim" Eppinger, a friend and early bandmate of Clyde's, suggested alcohol may have been involved in Frank Sr.'s absence. Like his mother, Clyde's father died young: Frank Sr. was fifty-two when he passed away on July 13, 1964. When Slim heard the news of Frank Sr.'s death, he went searching for Clyde, tracking him down at the local pool hall. Upon hearing the news, Clyde told the bartender, "Pour me another one."

Growing up in poverty in the segregated South, Stubblefield never graduated from high school. Free to wander through Chattanooga at a young age, he'd sit on corners and walk the streets, absorbing the sounds of the city. He had a keen mind and remembered complicated rhythms. He quit school to hang out with older Black men who gave him his first drumsticks. At the age of fifteen, he joined his first band, the Cascades, consisting of bandmates Robert "Slim" Eppinger, Lenell Glass, and Joe Burke. It wasn't long before Stubblefield became a part of the city's burgeoning music scene. Situated on the Tennessee River, which narrowly snakes its way through town, Chattanooga lies only twenty-three miles from the border with Georgia and Alabama. On its southern side is Lookout Mountain, or, in the Cherokee language Tsatangui, which means "rock coming to a point" or "end of the mountain," from which Chattanooga takes its name. It was shaped by a shallow sea that covered eastern Tennessee 240 million years ago. From the limestone peak, one can peer down on Chattanooga and into Georgia. To quote Martin Luther King Jr.'s "I Have a Dream" speech, "Let freedom ring from Lookout Mountain of Tennessee." Clyde may have heard that ring come down from that mountain and echo throughout the rhythms of the city.

During World War II, Chattanooga became a business hub connecting the South, East Coast, and Midwest. The Southern Railways Birmingham Special, another train of musical folklore known as the Chattanooga Choo Choo, rolled through town at the height of the war, stopping at the elegant red-brick Terminal Station that won architect

Donn Barber first place at the 1900 Paris Beaux Arts competition. Sixty to eighty trains arrived and departed daily from the station, helping boost the city's economic base. In 1942 Glen Miller and his all-white band immortalized the train in "Chattanooga Choo-Choo." Despite its racist lyrics—"Pardon me, boy, is that the Chattanooga Choo-Choo? Track twenty-nine, boy, you can give me a shine"—it was the first gold record to put the city on the geographic and musical map. The train's route, though, did not include the Ninth Street neighborhood that was the hub of the city's Black music scene. The railroad provided some work for Black people, but segregation and poverty remained the foundations of most African Americans' lives. What the trains did offer the young Stubblefield was the sound of their whistles and grinding steel wheels that formed the backdrop and backbeat of his rhythmical patterns.

The Great Migration north for Black Americans began in 1915, when 10 percent of Black people lived outside the South. It ended in the late '70s, when 47 percent had gone north.[3] Just as Africans brought their music from Africa, Southern Blacks brought their music north. Miles Davis was born in Alton, Illinois, in 1926, after his family had moved from Arkansas. Thelonious Monk was born in 1917 in Rocky Mount, North Carolina, and went north when his family moved to Manhattan in 1922. And John Coltrane left Hamlet, North Carolina, for Philadelphia when he was sixteen, in 1943.[4] Stubblefield would eventually join these musicians and follow his own migration north.

Billboard charts first used the term "rhythm and blues" in 1942, one year before Clyde Stubblefield entered the world. R&B was a genre that would inspire a boy who was growing up a few hours' drive from Chattanooga, in East Tupelo, Mississippi: Elvis Presley. That same year, a Russian audience heard the premiere of Dmitri Shostakovich's Symphony No. 7 in Leningrad. Its persistent rhythms signaled the sound of war while the drum took the lead role, a first in the symphony. The drum was claiming a prominent place in music the year before Stubblefield was born.

Also in 1942, the first nuclear chain reaction was achieved underneath the soccer stadium at the University of Chicago, which would lead to the Manhattan Project. One hundred miles northeast of Chattanooga, in Oak Ridge, Tennessee, crucial secret tests of the Manhattan Project were being conducted to separate plutonium, the critical element in making the atomic bomb.

Like Beale Street in Memphis and Bourbon Street in New Orleans, Chattanooga's Ninth Street—the Big 9—is rich in musical history.[5] Blues, rhythm and blues, jazz, soul, and later rock saturated its clubs, spilling out into the streets, channeling and shaping the sounds of African American music. Some of the best music in the South from the 1900s to the 1960s found its way to Ninth Street. During much of the same time period, Moss writes that the Big 9 "was a mecca for black music and entertainment: Tennessee's very own Harlem. . . . When the 1950s came to an end, the big band and R&B sounds gave way to jazz. As the 1960s continued, jazz turned into soul."[6]

The Big 9 was the place to hear a cornucopia of sounds that spanned the '40s, '50s, and '60s. Ninth Street is where Clyde was given his first drumsticks by Joe Burke and where he was casually mentored, playing in his first bands with local musicians, and later Otis Redding. The Blue Shufflers, the Cascades, and the Inclines—all of whom Clyde played with alongside bandmates Robert "Slim" Eppinger, Joe Burke, and Lenell Glass—were deeply rooted in and around Chattanooga.

Many other Chattanooga musicians expanded the blues scene that originated with Bessie Smith. They include composer George S. Clinton; Sam Gooden and Fred Cash, who formed the Impressions; Jules Alexander, a founding member of the Association; Jimmy Blanton, a jazz bassist who played with Duke Ellington; Valaida Snow, known as "Little Louis" and "Queen of the Trumpet," who helped spread jazz across Europe and China after World War I; and Cora "Lovie" Austin, a top jazz piano player who performed with Louis Armstrong.

While visiting the city, I gazed at the gently sloping mountain and thought of all the history that unfolded in the valley below. I imagined seeing the stories of not only the life of an ancient sea etched into its stone but the history of the growth and struggle of its people after the sea retreated; from the centuries-long stain of slavery and lynching to the Underground Railroad, the Civil War, and the civil rights movement. This history and these struggles for freedom are woven into the music of the land, a music that has helped shape the history of the United States. And that musical history includes Stubblefield's rhythms and grooves. Beneath the gaze of the Civil War monument on Lookout Mountain lies a city that formed the bedrock for the unique rhythms of a sound that would be called funk.

In Chattanooga, I searched for the sounds and rhythms of Clyde's world—the train wheels on steel, the thump, thump, thump of the grain elevator on the Tennessee River. I sat by the river and imagined how the rhythms became a part of Clyde, the sounds emerging through his music. Clyde once told his friend and bandmate Ben Sidran:

> I was raised in Chattanooga, Tennessee. We had tick-tock clocks and wind-up clocks all through the night. It was pitch black and dark—you see nothing and just hit it. Tick tock, tick tock, through the whole night. That's time, and I'd go to sleep by that, then wake up to a factory that made wooden cases. They had a chimney that put out puffs of smoke, and we lived in an area surrounded by mountains and valleys. So, this thing would go pfft—and hit the mountains and go puff, pfft, puff—so that had a rhythm. Washing machines—slush, slush, slush—that had rhythm, and the train tracks. I was raised around all those rhythms. I'd walk into town with that, and that was it. That's how it happened. That's the way it started.

Chattanooga's population has grown slowly but steadily since the nineteenth century, and, in 1984, a nonprofit named Venture started what was called the Chattanooga Way, a process of civic renewal that brought together Black and white, and rich and poor, to discuss what they wanted their community to become by the turn of the century, with the aim to reduce city pollution, revive the downtown area, and build more housing. Smith and McClane write that, "instead of asking the perceived best and brightest to chart Chattanooga's future course, Venture leaders went to the general public without an agenda, records show, and asked every member of the community to build and refine the city's goals."[7]

When Stubblefield was born in 1943, roughly 130,000 people lived in the city.[8] By the time he died in 2017, the population had grown to about 180,000. A 2012 mural on one of the few remaining original buildings on the Big 9 honors, among other legends, Bessie Smith. Born in 1894, the future Empress of the Blues grew up singing the music on Chattanooga's streets. In 1923 she signed with Columbia Records, becoming the highest-paid Black performer of her day.

Like many of these musicians, Stubblefield eventually left town to make a bigger name for himself. In 1965, at the age of twenty-one, he traveled to Augusta, Georgia, to audition for no less than the Godfather of Soul. Stubblefield was leaving Chattanooga, and he was taking his sound and rhythms with him to James Brown and The Famous Flames and onto the world stage.

5

Heading South in Search of Clyde's Roots

We developed a feel for each other.
—**SLIM**

When Stubblefield left Chattanooga to play with James Brown, many of his early bandmates stayed home and continued to play music in and around town, finding day jobs and raising families. They watched from home as Clyde toured the country and the world, bringing his funk sounds wherever he went.

In the spring of 1996, my friend Norine and I hit the road in her Volkswagen van, traveling south with a crumpled piece of paper in my purse, on it the names of Clyde's early friends, first bandmates, and casual mentors. We left behind the snow and ice of Wisconsin and journeyed through Illinois and Kentucky, heading east in Tennessee, along Highway 61, the old blues highway. The road meanders 1,400 miles into the Delta, hugging the Mississippi River from Minnesota to New Orleans. It runs through Memphis and St. Louis, following the migration of blues music from its Southern roots to the North. The highway is also a legendary part of American lore, where Robert Johnson, at the fabled Crossroads—the intersection of Highway 61 and Highway 49—is said to have sold his soul to the devil for mastery of the guitar.

When we reached Chattanooga, the skies were blue, the grass was newly green, and flowers were blooming. I began my quest to learn about Clyde's musical roots. First on Clyde's list was Robert "Slim" Eppinger. He was the bass player for the Cascades, a band that brought on Clyde for his first stint as a drummer when he was just fifteen years old.

We arranged to meet Slim the day after arriving in the city. His nickname described him well—he was tall and lean with a welcoming smile, dark hair and eyes. He was eager to be our tour guide, driving us around town in his large blue Chevy. Together, we traveled back in time through Chattanooga's rhythm and blues past. In its musical heyday, Ninth Street, renamed East Martin Luther King Boulevard in 1981, stretched east-west for eight blocks. "We're getting to where it all happened," Slim said as we approached a large red-brick building that was under construction. "That's where the Bessie Smith Hall[1] will be, but the money keeps disappearing. B. B. King and Ray Charles came to help raise money, and they are still not through building it."

The original center was opened in 1983, but it took until 1996 to complete the new Bessie Smith Cultural Center and African American Museum now in the heart of the old Chattanooga music scene. It has the look of a school and a church, with red bricks forming a solid foundation and structure, holding its history and stories securely inside. Half a dozen blocks away, at 7863 East Martin Luther King Boulevard, is a "Big 9 Legends" mural that depicts thirteen musicians "whose sounds were once the musical soul of the city."[2]

"This is where we used to hang out," Slim said, pointing up and down the street. "There were clubs everywhere. Now they are all torn down." Slim nodded when spotting an old wooden door that looked as if it could tell a thousand tales. It fronted a building that had been vacant for many years. "That's the place we played behind Otis Redding," Slim recalled. "It was changed to the VFW [Veterans of Foreign Wars] and later called the Carousel Lounge.

"On any night, there would be six or seven bands up and down the street, four or five local groups like Jimmy Church and Bubba Suggs, who had an organ band. The lounge had a big Hammond B3 organ, which was the happening sound at the time. We had to claw our way in, and the older groups had a bit of a monopoly on the scene. But we had the sound, and we worked hard."

The music that Clyde and Slim played was ahead of its time, Slim said. "We used many types of rhythms and music and blended them. We sounded like they do today; everyone that knew our music said so. Some of the music we played then they are still playing now. Clyde's foundation came from what we did a long time ago in our band." Slim continued, "We had an openness to each other and our approach. Our saxophonist used to do ridiculous things. He would take themes from movies and TV like *Exodus* or the theme from 'Dr. Kildare' and play an arrangement on the piano. If we liked the arrangement, we'd each add to it. We played a variety of music—top 40, which back then they called soul. We played jazz, blues, and a mixture of styles, but no country. Some rock and roll. The audience loved it."

That mixture of styles is what appealed to a variety of crowds, he said.

> That's one reason why we had such an amazing group. Our theory was that nobody comes to clubs to boogie the first thirty minutes or hour of the show. People check to see who's there, what's up, and have a drink or two. We would ease into it, start with jazz, and by the time people were feeling good, we were playing what they came to hear. We continued with that until the end of the show. The last impression is always what people remember. We'd jam at the end, so they're still fired up the next time they come back. There were some white bands back then, the reality of white and Black musicians playing together in the same band was not as open as in some places.

Slim explained how at times a white musician would come and sit in with the Black bands, but the police would often show up and shut the place down.

"It wasn't about money," Slim said. "We were making money, but we could do more with twenty dollars than you can today with a hundred. We enjoyed playing and did whatever we could to make it happen."

Slim reminisced about the time when he and Clyde and their bandmates worked together as a cohesive unit. "We developed a feel for each other. You had to breathe the same music—that's the kind of connection we had. We would make a mistake and make it sound like it was supposed to be there—we covered for each other. We knew what the other man would do, with a slight emphasis on a note or beat. Everyone would feel it at the same time. Some guys would call me and say they had a gig in two or three days. Chances are we hadn't played together in a long time, but it would be fine because we knew each other. Today everyone is a unit unto themselves."

Clyde told me how he would never rehearse. He'd just show up and play, to the amazement of other musicians. He could feel what his bandmates would play at the moment it was happening. He knew it in his bones. Undoubtedly his ability to work with minimal rehearsals benefited from his early days playing in Chattanooga.

As we drove by Flynn Street, I imagined a confident fifteen-year-old ambling down the sidewalk, drumsticks swinging to his internal rhythms. In this narrow alleyway between Eighth and Ninth streets, Clyde would play music on corners with anyone who showed up. I picture him hanging out with older musicians who supported and encouraged him, sharing their world with this confident young man who had a friendly smile. Musicians who believed in him and casually mentored him, helping him on his path out of Chattanooga and into national music halls.

Some months later, I spoke with Joe Burke, an established drummer in Chattanooga when Clyde came on the scene. Joe was Clyde's first unofficial mentor. I asked Joe about teaching Clyde drum rudiments and patterns. "He watched me," he said. "I'd told him about paradiddles and flams, and he absorbed what he liked. He took advantage of what I did. I used to go to the auditorium and watch Count Basie's drummers. I'd watch them do unique rhythms with their sticks, then I'd come back and do them. Clyde did that with me. I'd put tiles in front of my drums and tune them. Other drummers, including Clyde, loved it and did it too. Clyde learned his good sense of timing from me."

Slim and another musician, Doc Covington, also gave Clyde suggestions, Joe said. "Clyde also picked up ideas from New Orleans musicians. That's why he could do so many unique rhythms."

Clyde likely heard that New Orleans sound when Crescent City marching bands came through town with their syncopated rhythms powered by improvisational drumming. Clyde embraced those rhythms, fueling his own unique sounds.

> Clyde always made the right move.
> —**SLIM**

Continuing on our tour of Chattanooga, and passing by several blocks of empty gravel lots in Chattanooga, with Slim guiding the way, I can almost hear lingering ghost notes sounding across the landscape.

"Bands from New Orleans, Chicago—they would come from all over and play blues in these vacant lots," Slim told me. "In June, there would be upward of ten thousand people—Black, white, blue, green, yellow, and street people would gather. People would put up small stands, barbecue, and all that jive and make money, money, money. Then no one would come back again until next year.

"There was an after-hours joint under the viaduct," Slim added, pointing to an old storefront. "We'd go there when we were done playing. We would find someplace like that after the gathering to jam."

I imagine a small, dark, smoky club filled with musicians and patrons indifferent to their rundown surroundings. People are dancing, shouting with glee, carousing with old friends until the early morning hours.

"I think Clyde went to school in that old building," Slim said, pointing to Joseph E. Smith Elementary School. "And he was born somewhere in this area. One of these buildings may have been the hospital." Slim gestured toward a small, mostly empty street. "Clyde lived there with his sister Vivian in a tiny two-room apartment. It had only a kitchen, living room, and bedroom combination."

Slim arrived in Chattanooga in 1956, when he was fourteen, and it wasn't until three years later that he met Clyde.

"Clyde, Little Junior Phillips, and Emmet Barnes were all playing together when we picked up Clyde," Slim recalled. He said Emmet was old enough to be both his and Clyde's daddy and thought he was probably a friend of Clyde's dad. Slim continued, "Emmet played saxophone, I knew him when I was a teenager. I came to Chattanooga in 1956, when I was fourteen, and met Clyde in 1959. Their band wasn't very good, but we were doing well." And in a statement that reflected Clyde's future career he said, "Clyde always made the right move!"

We passed by the Soldiers and Sailors Memorial Auditorium, a historic performance hall dedicated on Veterans Day, 1922. The sturdy brick edifice had stood the test of time, hosting thousands of events over the years, including shows headlined by, among others, Cab Calloway, Count Basie, Muddy Waters, Howlin' Wolf, Ray Charles, James Brown, Nat King Cole, and Wilson Pickett. After their shows, they would "stroll the few blocks down to the clubs on the Big 9 to hear the local groups play."[3] This is how some Chattanooga musicians got their first big breaks. It's possible that the auditorium is where James Brown first heard Clyde following one of his shows.

We stopped by the river to listen to the *thump-thump* of the grain elevator, the pounding sound of industry that Clyde told me inspired his first drumbeats.

"Some weekends," said Slim, "we were in Knoxville or Nashville and were booked by multiple social clubs in the area, but mostly we played on Ninth Street. There were clubs in south and east Chattanooga, the west side, but mostly Ninth Street was what was happening. Clyde would move the equipment around for our gigs. He'd call me and say, 'I've got it all set up, whenever you guys get ready to come down, it's all ready.'"

What were some of the places like back then?

"Chattanooga was bursting with venues back in the day. In addition to the VFW Hall, there was the American Legion Hall, the Elks Lodge, the Brown Derby, the Stardust Lounge, the Wigwam, and Kelly's Place, which featured a large dance floor. There were many places along Ninth Street," Slim recalled. "The Silver Moon, Masonic Hall, and Grenadier Hall. For jazz, there were Crenshaws, Malibu, and so many more. I have forgotten all their names. Nightclubs lined eight to ten blocks with music pouring into the streets. Back then, there were big bands. They played for three or four hundred people. Sadly, today there are just beer joints and places like that.

"Many who got the chance to play had fellow musician Frazier Benefield to thank. Benefield was most active in town in the 1940s and '50s. Frazier had connections and booked us gigs around town. He helped a lot of jazz musicians get their start here. Willie 'Pop' Stubbs, a trombone player, started with him. One of them went with Count Basie. He gave us our learning field, so to speak."

In the 1950s and '60s, Eighth and Ninth streets were a hub for local musicians. "I worked with just about everyone who played here," Slim said. "We had a group called the Cascades long before the professional group. Clyde was one of the original members. We hadn't played together long before we picked him up as our drummer. We started as a five-piece group and played from Ninth Street to Knoxville."

But Slim said even that wasn't enough. "We decided we couldn't compete with '60s music, with all their horns, without making the band bigger. Clyde was still in the rhythm section, along with Rudy Foster. We added some horns, which caught on. That gave us the hottest new band in town. Our band was tight."

After our tour of the once thriving music district, we stopped at a downtown coffee house to continue talking.

"One time we were playing in Nashville, there was a good band playing jazz with guitar and bass. We were hanging out, no one else was bold enough to go up. But Clyde was and went up to jam with them. He made mistakes but had the right attitude. He just wasn't scared to give it a try."

Clyde and Slim started playing together in the late '50s. They stuck together until Clyde left town to play with James Brown in 1965.

"On my twentieth birthday, we played in Knoxville," Slim recalled. "Clyde left with an old guitar player who used to play with the Five Lawyers—his name was Lenell Pawling. He was somewhat of a clown. He and Clyde became friends and played gigs together. I talked Clyde into venturing out with him, and they ended up in Macon, Georgia, where Brown encountered him. From then on . . . well, the rest is history.

"Everybody else ventured off, took jobs, and made music on the side. I told my lady friend the other night that Clyde's the only one who made a living playing music. He had the right attitude and was free to move around. You couldn't hurt the guy's feelings, no matter what you would say to him. He wasn't the greatest drummer when we picked him up. We had guys considered 'bad drummers,' and they moved on. We got Clyde."

Slim said Clyde could get monotonous when he played. He hit the table. "Boom, boom, boom! He kept the time, and he had that drive. We used to criticize him. We'd say, 'Don't you hear what this number does, what that number does?' Clyde is the type of person that thrives on criticism and then plays better. So, the next time we played, he'd do something different. Eventually, he let the chips fly."

How did he became the funky drummer?

"That came about after he left with Brown," he said. "I give him a lot of credit—he had his own ways and was creative. All the Cascades were innovative, which allowed Clyde to go as far as he's gone. We were young and did things differently. We didn't like to stay with the basic old patterns. We would hear music and interpret it our way, add a little something to it or take something away.

"Clyde would give you whatever you needed—not that it was strictly by the rules in meters. But we would say, 'This is what we want it to sound like.' So that's what he would give us. I remember one time we arranged Buddy Rich's 'Bye Bye Blues.' It's a very slow old-time jazz piece. It would put you to sleep. We wanted it up-tempo. We would give the introduction 'ba, ba, ba, ba,' and Clyde would go 'Bump, ba, da, Bump, ba, da.'" Slim mouthed the rhythm while keeping time tapping his leg. "We'd say we want you to do something different, and he'd say OK, and we'd play *da, da, de, de, de, de, de, de, de, de, bump, ba, da, bump, ba da.* He would play it right afterward. You couldn't lose him. He was bold.

"There was a time in music when each instrument was outstanding," Slim continued. "The keyboard, the bass, the drums. There was a time when the drums were unique instruments, but then it passed—the music changed. Now, the guys keep time and do whatever drummers do."

Clyde and Slim played together in the Cascades from roughly 1960 to the middle of the decade. "During that time, the band would break up and get back together," Slim said. "The band eventually split up, and guys started going their own ways. Many went into the service. Clyde had something else he wanted to do."

But before Clyde left to join Brown, the band would play with just about anyone looking for a backup group. That included some big names.

In Chattanooga, Slim gazed down at the street corners that held so many memories. "We backed Otis Redding for three nights here in Chattanooga," Slim said. "We were packing them in." Years later, on *The Third Story* podcast—hosted by Leo Sidran, musician Ben Sidran's son—Clyde described his first encounter with Redding. "I met Otis out of Phil Walden's Artist and Promotion Company[4] in Macon, Georgia," he said. "We would hang around that office a lot. They needed a band, and I was playing with [Eddie] Kirkland [known as the Gypsy of the Blues; also played with John Lee Hooker and was Otis Redding's guitarist and band leader].[5] They called us up, and we went out with Otis. He was hot. He drank Ballantine Scotch—a bottle a show. It's strong stuff."[6]

Clyde spoke of Redding's greatness. "If [Redding] were living when I was with Brown, Brown wouldn't have been where he was. Because Otis had that soul. He had that character and that lead foundation that Brown didn't have. He was more soulful than Brown, but Brown had something different. When Otis passed, Brown came in. Brown was lucky in a sense because if they had a battle, Brown wouldn't have been as big as he is today because Otis would have always been over him."[7] Before Kirkland died in 2001, he said, "No blues in Macon when I came. . . . I was funky before James Brown was funky."[8]

Slim told me that, after the three nights backing up Otis in Chattanooga, "We didn't find out until later that Otis had called and asked if he would send the band out to Texas to be his backup. He couldn't believe anyone could play his music that well, except the guys in Nashville or

Memphis, but we were on top of all the tunes. It wasn't a problem even if we had to vary the key we played.

"Otis sent the message that if the whole band couldn't come, send any of the guys, but he really wanted Clyde. Clyde went and played with them for a while before Otis went on tour. We found this out later, and I told a friend that I hated to think that we could have gone on tour with him and would have been on the plane when it crashed." Had they become members of Redding's band, Clyde and Slim might well have also died in the Lake Monona crash that killed Redding in the heart of Madison, the city Clyde would, in a few years, choose as his home.

"Otis was a strange guy," Slim said. "He didn't converse with us much. He stayed to himself. He showed up when it was time to do the show and would make his presence known. One of the nights we played with him in Chattanooga, Otis was onstage playing some song and wanted to end it, but Clyde wouldn't let him out of the song. Clyde would get carried away, and Otis would have to turn around and sing another verse."

I picture Clyde grinning at Otis, drumsticks and arms flying from snare drum to hi-hat, the two cymbals hitting together with the beat of Clyde's foot.

He lost his drumsticks, so he played with two wooden clothes hangers.

I looked at Slim, amazed. "It was pretty outrageous," he said.

6

"That's the Way It Was Done"

Lenell Glass, an accomplished jazz bassist, was another influential musician in Stubblefield's early musical development. Clyde played in his first band, the Cascades, with Lenell. Born and raised in Chattanooga, Lenell bought his first stand-up bass upon returning to the States after serving in the military overseas. He brought the instrument with him when he moved to Cleveland and, in the late 1950s, Chicago. There, he joined the three-person house band at the Playboy Club, performing with Sammy Davis Jr., Miles Davis, Buddy Guy, the Temptations, the Platters, and many other prominent musicians who came through town. In 1981, he joined the Ink Spots, touring with the group for eight years.

It was a frigid day in Madison when I sat down at my kitchen table in 1999 to call Lenell in warm and sunny Georgia. He was eager to talk about his early musical days playing rhythm and blues. He painted a vivid portrait of Clyde's early days, which formed the foundation of his style.

"When I was a little boy," Lenell began, "I had an uncle—we called him Uncle Charlie. He taught me, my younger brother, and a few others guitar. I later took up the bass. Rhythm and blues was ready to jump on the scene. R&B was new to people in the South when I started playing with the Blue Shufflers, around 1959. Clyde joined the band the following year. At first, R&B wasn't popular with white people who were listening to country western and hillbilly. That started changing around 1952. R&B became more popular with both whites and Blacks. It was around that time when B. B. King[1] was becoming well known.

"When we first started playing in bars, only white people were in the audience. The bars had segregated rooms, and we had to leave through the back door. In the 1950s and early '60s, if you wanted to play, that's the way it was done. Naturally, nobody liked it, but it didn't last long. As the music caught on, we were eventually able to mingle with the audience.

"When Clyde was a young fellow, before I joined the Cascades, I played with Jim Dandy, the Clovers, and the Midnighters. Chubby Checker listened to what we were doing because we were on top of the business. Louis Jordan came to Chattanooga around 1954 or '55 with his electric bass. We were playing a lot of Bill Doggett's music." (A pianist and organist, Doggett played with Jordan and Ella Fitzgerald, among others, and composed the songs "Honky Tonk" and "Hippy Dippy.")[2]

Lenell played jazz on the electric bass during his early days in Chattanooga—something that was unheard of at the time, he said. "The electric bass was popular, but only in rock and roll and rhythm and blues. I was playing jazz on my stand-up bass. I had to play both types of music, and I thought the electric bass should take care of both.

"Joe Dorsett started after the Blue Shufflers—he's still here in Chattanooga," Lenell continued. "He played bass guitar and has about six to eight pieces in his band that played rock and roll."

The Blue Shufflers started in the late '50s, Dorsett started around four or five years later. Lenell explained there was no competition with the Shufflers because Dorsett was focusing on rock and roll.

By this point, big bands were already influencing others. "We played their music," Lenell said. "They used four or five instruments and got a big sound. We'd play their songs with the instruments we had. You didn't have to have sixteen instruments because a chord from a piano or guitar would create the sound of horns. We were playing big band music before we started the Blue Shufflers. We were still the same band, but we weren't playing blues all the time, we were mixing it up. We were the first band playing rhythm and blues in this area of the South."

Other Ninth Street bands jumped on the bandwagon. "Everyone wanted to learn what we were doing," Lenell said. "There was one singing group called the Impressions. They began by learning guitar from us. After my uncle taught us, their guitar player was influenced by us. We played it all—big band, jazz, rock, and down to the blues. Everyone around this area in Georgia, Alabama, Mississippi, and Atlanta started being aware of what we were doing and hired us. When bands left Chattanooga they developed their own sound.

"I played guitar a bit and stand-up bass before I left Chattanooga," he said. "You can imagine that it was a different sound—I was the first one to play electric bass in the Playboy Club, maybe the first one professionally at all. They were not popular then. I left my upright bass at home and took my stand-up bass, which was electric, to the club. I got a lot of use out of it. Everyone liked it because if you know how to get the sound you want, you can get the sound of an upright. I got the ball rolling with the electric bass. I was always into change.

"At the Playboy Club, it was never boring because we changed shows every three weeks. We got to know the musicians and played a variety of styles of music. Ruth Brown[3] [known as the Queen of R&B] was popular playing rhythm and blues then and recorded several records.[4]

"When you played at the Playboy Club, you were expected to be a competent musician in all styles of music. I went on the road with Johnny Mathis and toured the Midwest, mostly with pickup musicians in different areas. I was one of the musicians that made it on the roster. Every time Mathis came through, they would use the same musicians if they were available."

When Lenell started touring with Aretha Franklin, "There was a trio—just me, her, and a drummer, George Hobbs. She was playing her new songs and was new on the scene. She was scared and didn't know how she would be received in a place like the Playboy Club. At that time, a lot of people hadn't heard of her. If I had known then what I know now!

"When she left the club," Lenell continued, "her manager asked if we would like to join her band and tour with her. Everybody was trying to get into the Playboy Club to play, and since I had a bird in the hand, I figured I better hang on to it because I said to myself, 'She doesn't seem too stable.'" Lenell laughed at the memory. "At the time, I just thought she was just a fly-by-night. There were so many girls out there singing.

"She came through Chicago about 1960 or 1961. That's the same story with Stevie Wonder, Sammy Davis Jr., and anyone who came to the club. Everybody in the house band was qualified to play the music, but with Aretha, I had a chance to go on with her. I could've gone on with Johnny Mathis and a few others but chose to stay. My time there stretched out to sixteen years. I know most of the people who came along in the late 1950s up to the 1980s."

Over the years, Lenell would travel back and forth between Chicago and Chattanooga. Back home, he'd take part in the city's annual Ninth

Street Reunion. "It's almost like New Orleans," he said of the music festival, sounding proud of his hometown, the place where he helped Clyde, many decades before, get his start.

Sadly, this musical bond has since been lost. Another person who knew Clyde is no longer. Clyde told me he remembered Lenell fondly from his early days, someone who fostered his musical foundation on the streets and in the clubs of Chattanooga. Lenell died in 2002 in Chicago. He was sixty-nine years old.

7

"All I Could Say Was 'Wow'"

Stubblefield had another early influence during his musical development, the drummer Joe Burke. Or as Joe says, "When Clyde was a young fellow." Joe played with Lenell Glass in the Blue Shufflers, and they were, along with Slim, a crucial part of an unacknowledged Chattanooga musical heritage. In 1999, when I spoke by phone with Joe, he was living in Cohutta, Georgia, a small town with roughly seven hundred inhabitants. He began by speaking of the Chattanooga music scene of the 1950s.

"During my early days as a musician, I played with the Midnighters and Chubby Checker. We had a bass player in Chattanooga named Lucky [Joseph Scott], who played with Curtis Mayfield on all of Curtis's hits. Curtis listened to what we were doing because we were on top of the business. We played with the organist Bill Doggett. When the Fender electric bass entered the music world, the bass pattern changed.

"Louis Jordan came to Chattanooga around 1954. He was an alto bass singer. They had an electric bass player in his band; I don't think there were over two or three in America at that time. We were fascinated with its sound. We only had an upright bass with its 'thump, thump, thump.' We all chipped in and bought an electric bass for [Lenell] and our band.

"Bill Doggett played the Hammond organ with his foot. The electric bass was hooked to an amplifier, so it took the bassline farther. You could hear it throughout the auditorium. That was the beginning of electric bass instruments. It changed the business.

"We already had an electric guitar in our band," Joe continued. "Once we could hear the bass, the music changed completely. It was a humming sound, and you could turn it up loud in the auditoriums. It was beautiful.

"Clyde was a little guy who watched and followed us around on the street. I showed him what a cymbal was and gave him his first drumsticks. Clyde was very special. He had a tremendous sense of rhythm and hearing and caught on fast. He was intelligent and sharp. Soon after he started playing as a young teen, I heard him, and all I could say was, 'Wow!'"

Joe spoke of an old man in Chattanooga named Boxhead.

"Dewey Porter—his name was Boxy, and we called him Boxhead—he started Clyde on the drums, and that gave him his foundation, the beat he became. Clyde took that into the music world. When he joined James Brown, he changed the whole concept of music.

"Clyde was with Doc Covington and the Cascades," Joe added. "I believe Doc may be the genius of the whole thing. What Clyde was doing was correct; he played as if he had studied at a music conservatory. Miles Davis and other jazz musicians loved that rhythm but couldn't play it at the time; they play it now. When 'Cold Sweat' and 'I've Got the Feeling' came out, they didn't know what those rhythms were. Clyde and Chattanooga will never get the credit they deserve. They made the music industry a lot of money.

"I occasionally go to California and visit Doc, who shows me new sounds, new rhythms, and ways to play. I quit because I am a jazz drummer, and there is no market for that. There must be fifteen or twenty good artists playing jazz today. Everyone is now dance-oriented. James Brown and Clyde took all the other music away."

The foundation to develop funk rhythms had left Chattanooga with Stubblefield, and I felt Joe's sadness. I asked Joe how to describe Clyde's drumming.

"It's 1, 2, 3, 4; 2, 2, 3, 4—that's two measures to musicians, like a sentence is to you. I would play one measure: 1, 2, 3, 4; 1, 2, 3, 4. Doc Covington added to it: *ah, uh, ah, ah; ah, uh, ah, ah, AH; uh, ah, AH, ah; eh, ah, ah, uh.*

I had acquired a drum set and taken lessons a few years after first hearing and being inspired by Clyde and was able to try this on the drums. The first is a repeating pattern, and the second rhythm of Doc's adds different accents on the final notes.

"Rappers use the rhythm like a predicate in a sentence," Joe said. "It's two measures. The rappers love the beat. They say they got it from James Brown, but Brown got it from hearing Clyde play.

"Doc has a brother named James, and there was another musician, Lucky, both from Chattanooga. Lucky Scott joined the Impressions, eventually playing on Mayfield's 1972 *Super Fly* soundtrack."[1]

"They played with Curtis Mayfield. They are the ones who gave Curtis those patterns." Joe sings: *da, da, da; ba, da, da, da; ba diddly da.*

"Doc, Slim, Clyde, and the alto sax player were the architects of putting the musical punctuation into the rhythm, they are like the commas and periods in a sentence."

I thought about what Joe said, two measures becoming one sentence using a semicolon or colon, the music flowing together, not containing the sound inside the measure with music bars but bridging the rhythms together with ghost notes and accented beats.

"Curtis used to hang around in Chattanooga before he made it big. The Covingtons would be singing, and Curtis would sit and listen. They taught him how to tune his guitar," Joe said, laughing.

"When Curtis left Chattanooga, he went to play with Jerry Butler. Butler said Curtis was ready for the big time. The Covingtons were tremendously gifted but were in the wrong environment at the wrong time, unable to profit from their talent."

One of Joe's first bands included a collaboration with the International Sweethearts of Rhythm in 1947. The musicians were the country's first integrated all-women's band and played swing and jazz with saxophones in the 1940s.[2] "Later," Joe said, "I played with Frazier Benefield, the Blue Shufflers, then the Pacesetters."

"What was Clyde like back then?"

"He had a way with people," Joe said. "People in Chattanooga are huge critics, but the Cascades gained a large following, and the crowds grew. Everyone was talking about them. It was either in Chattanooga or Macon, Georgia, when James Brown first heard Clyde. People were crazy about him. He had a certain air about him.

"Clyde told me, 'Joe, someday I'm going to be better than you.' The next thing I knew, he was with Brown. We all flew to Atlanta to see him on the stage with James Brown." Joe laughed. "Clyde ran off a bunch of good drummers Brown had with him."

Joe spoke about the segregation in clubs in the 1950s.

"Sometimes we would play large clubs. We'd have to stay in the kitchen, or they would set aside special rooms for us. They gave us all the drinks we wanted but we couldn't interact with the customers. We played one club for two years and couldn't go out to mingle with the audience. I heard Lena Horne talking about that recently [on PBS's *American Masters* in 1996].[3] She had been living in California and came to Arkansas for a show. She had to stay in the kitchen.

"I wasn't offended by it," Joe continued. "We always got everything we wanted. After I left the band, I worked at a bank and as a computer operator."

This surprised me. "What do you mean you got everything you wanted?"

"I've been to many places and met people I would never have otherwise. We were at the best homes in Chattanooga on the mountain—the Lountins, the Frabascos—we played in all their homes."

"For private parties?"

"Yes. We could charge what we wanted but couldn't fraternize with the guests."

I asked Joe about Ed Lemon, a white musician with the Four Brothers, the first integrated band in Chattanooga.

"Ed always hung out on Ninth Street with us. He would come down to the clubs we played and bring his dates. He'd join us onstage. That was in the late '50s or early '60s, and it was taboo for white people to come to our clubs. He didn't care and started bringing ten or fifteen of his friends. But back then, it was against the law, and the police would come in and raid the place and say it was a disturbance. That's the way it was back in 1960–61."

William Price, a stand-up bass player for the Blue Shufflers, told Charles Moss how he couldn't play with white musicians or go to their clubs. "The music scene changed in Chattanooga," he said. "When the 1950s came to an end, the big band and R&B sounds gave way to jazz. As the 1960s continued, jazz turned into soul." He also talked about segregation: "You could deal with their most intimate details of family life—serve them, play music for them—but we couldn't socialize with them. We couldn't go to their clubs unless we played for them, but they could come to ours."[4]

"Can you talk about the musicians from your band the Inclines: Joe Bennett, Jackie Wilson, Jimmy Swan, and Lavone Jones?"

"Joe Bennett played the upright bass. The thumping instrument. Jimmy Swan was like Jackie Wilson; he was a singer. He used to jump onstage. Have you ever heard, 'Shout, shout, you make me want to shout'?

"Of course."

"He sang like them. Jimmy Swan was terrific, the kids loved him. They had a unique way of delivering songs. Jimmy was a good friend of Little Richard's, who was in his group. Lavone Jones had a young girl's voice, sort of like Brandie. We could never do anything with our talent because we were in the wrong place. We should have gone out to L.A. and paid our dues."

Joe said with regret, "Before that, and this was my mistake, Leah, I didn't realize how talented they were. After we broke up, all these big-time people came and got them. Then I realized—wow!

"I had taken them out to California but was worried about whether they would put up with washing dishes and doing what we needed to do to survive until we got a break. At the time, I was talking so far over their heads. I worked at the bank and told them about the payday in music and how big it could be. If you stayed in it maybe twenty years, you might make a million dollars. And you couldn't make that kind of money on a regular job.

"They could never see the benefit of wearing uniforms and maintaining the consistency of it. I wished I would have pushed to make more records until we got a hit. We made two records, and only one of them [*The Atlanta Boogaloo*][5] was a hit." He explained how they played with a B3 organ, horns, and a solid funk beat. You can clearly hear Joe's drum solo at the end of the single and the influence he had on Clyde.

"They didn't understand some people made thousands of records and never made a hit," Joe continued. "I talked to some of them about a year ago, and they said how sorry they were. They realized now what I was trying to tell them back then. I was trying to make records, keep a payroll, and get them a weekly paycheck, which became too much of a hassle. I couldn't get enough work to keep them happy."

Joe said they had many firsts that other bands copied. "We had a musician that played two trumpets. We had a trumpet and a bass. The Commodores borrowed our sound and our look. Lucky, the bass player, would play along with the only lead instrument, the trumpet. You could hear the bass playing with the trumpet in the song, which was unique. The bass would play the harmony of melodic lines, making a full sound.

The Commodores were going to college in Tuskegee, Alabama, and came to Chattanooga and heard us play. They bought a bass and trumpet and copied our sound. It was heartbreaking. We contributed a lot of ideas to the music business."

The Inclines recorded "The Atlanta Boogaloo" and "The Pressure Cooker" not long before James Brown released *Cold Sweat* in 1967. Joe said, "We had two drummers, one called Tyron McCullough—he was super-talented. He had a sound similar to Smokey Robinson. He and Lucky played with Curtis Mayfield. They made two or three albums with him. He has since passed away."

The Inclines had a following in Chattanooga, but their popularity began to fade by the mid-1960s, when Stubblefield joined Brown.

"We thought we were at the top of the business because of 'The Pressure Cooker,'" Joe told me.[6] "But we learned we were behind the times.

"I credit both Clyde and James Brown for the genius of advancing the music. Brown heard Clyde playing and kept a watch on him throughout the South for maybe eight or nine months before he brought him into his band. It wasn't like he accidentally picked up a drummer. He had the ear to hear Clyde's unique beat.

"That feel gave the drums a different kind of homework. Before that, the drummer had some freedom to create different rhythms, but the electric bass sounds had to be constant. What we call the two and four, he had to bump, bump, bump, continuously. You can hear the pop, two, pop, two on recordings. Soon after, we started using the electric bass and a constant drum rhythm. A tune called 'The Funky Broadway' around the same time James Brown came out with 'Cold Sweat.' It helped to transform the way that people danced."

"The beat to me feels grounding and freeing at the same time," I said.

"It was an amazing and different beat, a turn as large as night and day," Joe said. "We all said, 'That's Clyde on drums, I know him!' No one would believe we knew him."

"We were putting on our outfits and Indian uniforms when we first heard 'Cold Sweat.'" (I remember Slim mentioned the Wigwam club, which is where they might have been.)

I told Lenell about Ben Sidran, one of Clyde's jazz collaborators who wrote the music to the documentary film *Hoop Dreams*, and Joe said, "Well, I'll be. His ears and playing have always been sharp. Slim and the rest of them have never played with another band."

I thought, unlike Clyde who led a rich and varied musical career throughout his life.

"Maybe you could all get back together," I suggested.

"We got tired of playing up and down the streets in Chattanooga," he said. "Playing all night for thirty or forty bucks."

"You'd make a lot more today," I said.

"Most of the guys have just stopped."

I told Joe that I had seen Clyde play the night before in Madison, at the Chamber. "Tell Joe to call me," he had said.

"I drove up there in 1988 to see him," Joe told me. "I couldn't find him. I called one number, and they said he didn't live there anymore. It was November 15, and it was snowing and thirty degrees."

"It's snowing today."

"That's the coldest place on earth."

I smiled. "Not quite. International Falls, Minnesota, or Antarctica is worse."

Cold or not, Madison was the place Clyde now called home.

Set Break

"Clyde had something else he wanted to do."

—**ROBERT "SLIM" EPPINGER**

When I was in Macon, Georgia, I wasn't planning on being with no one. I was just planning on playing music. I never looked for anything special, never.

—**CLYDE STUBBLEFIELD**, "The Clyde Stubblefield Interview" (2020), *Jake Feinberg Show*

Set 2

The World

Clyde brought his style with him. James Brown immediately jumped on it. But that was Clyde's style, that James Brown took over. "Cold Sweat," "I Got the Feelin'," and a lot of tunes. That was all Clyde Stubblefield.

—**FRED WESLEY**

[Jabo] Starks was the Beatles to Clyde's Stones. A clean shuffle drummer to Clyde's free jazz left hand.

—**QUESTLOVE**

8

Bringing the Funk

> Funk is the absence of any and everything you can think of, but the very essence of all that is. And saying that, I'm saying funk is anything that we create in our minds that we want to do, what we want to be, but we don't have the resources.
> —**BOOTSY COLLINS**

Stubblefield embodied this idea; he had no access to worldly resources when he first began his rhythmic journey to achieve the sounds that were an intrinsic part of himself, and that he would share with the world. He even made do with coat hangers in a concert with Otis Redding when he forgot his drumsticks. Clyde came from extreme poverty but found his way to the world stage—a story that sounds like the American dream—but, unlike some, he maintained his true warm, giving, creative self in the process. He also paid the price for turning his back on his association with fame.

Stubblefield grew up in the segregated South but easily made friends with all he encountered in a predominately white northern world. He had the funk deep within him and had a vision of who he wanted to be and what he wanted to do. But what he played did not come from planning or practice. Stubblefield said, "I don't know how to read music. I don't know nothing about notes. All I know is 1-2-3-4, 1-2-3-4 or whatever goes after that, but I don't question how I play. I just sit down and if I think of something, I might think of—(*dud, pop, ba da duch-e-do pop, ba da, duch pop*[1])—and that's just what I do. I got to hear that on the drums. See, I gotta hit it, I know I can do it. If I can hum it, I can play it, so that's the way I think."[2]

Funk connects with a wide range of musical disciplines and is a descendant of blues, jazz, and R&B. Rickey Vincent writes in his book *Funk*, "New Orleans music opened the vast rhythmic chasm of African music for practitioners of the funk. It should come as no surprise, then, that across the Atlantic ocean, from South Africa to Morocco, African musicians with their ears to the West heard the funk and internalized it as their own. Multifaceted saxophonist Manu Dibango was one of the first Africans to incorporate the funk into his sound."[3]

The word "funk" has had an array of uses that have spanned many centuries and meanings, depending on its context and whether it was used as a noun or verb. Funk has been described as a type of music, a rhythm, a scent, food, a concept, a philosophy, a way of life, and the feel of a neighborhood. Anthropologist Robert Farris Thompson traced the origins of the word back to the Kongo language in Africa (present-day Congo and Gabon). The people of the Kongo believed that the smell of a hardworking elder in the Kongo culture was good luck. "Lu-fuki"[4] was associated with the positive energy and the physical exertion of a person, two qualities that were the essence of Clyde.

Both words "funky" and "lu-fuki" have been used for praising individuals and their artistic creations. If one has "worked out to achieve their goals" and exerted themselves to accomplish their aims, they are complimented by being called "funky." Thompson theorized that "lu-fuki" might have combined with the French Louisiana word "fumet," referring to "the aroma of food and wine.[5] In the fourteenth century, the German word "fonke" meant a spark. It took four hundred years for its meaning to have an emotional connotation, to mean "depression or ill-humor" as in being "in a funk."[6]

Funk has had racist connotations with a negative slant related to sweat and body odor (perhaps going back to the Kongo language). Its meaning later changed to the more enticing atmosphere and feel of being in smoky jazz clubs and was written about in a 1954 issue of *Time* magazine. Many African American musicians, including the Isley Brothers, developed "a rhythmic mix of soul, jazz, and rhythm and blues,"[7] and Wilson Pickett released "The Funky Broadway" in 1967.

Robbie Kowal, in talking about Vincent's book *Funk*, said that the "thesis is that funk was a cultural movement not just in music; it was a fashion, a film, a way of thinking, a way of life."

The Funk Brothers, the mostly unknown backup musicians who were highlighted in the film *Standing in the Shadows of Motown*, were on every Motown hit from 1959–72 and "are the musicians who collectively recorded more number one hit songs than the Beach Boys, the Rolling Stones, Elvis, and the Beatles combined."[8] Along with being incredibly creative musicians who should have been acknowledged decades before, The Funk Brothers were definitely funky, but their sound was essentially the soul music that came to define Motown.

In regard to what defined Brown's version of funk, I asked Fred Wesley, who was a trombonist with Brown while Clyde was in the band, "Was it the One, the polyrhythms, the ghost notes, or all three that were Clyde's contributions to James Brown?"

Wesley described it this way: "We never referred to it as the One, but when Bootsy was in the band, he made a strong accent on the One and James Brown called it the One. But looking back at what Clyde was doing [before Bootsy], he accented the One a lot. He played heavy accents on the One [mouths tune and rhythm]. It became a thing in that beat of the bar of music. Afterward, everyone jumped on it."

In the mid-1960s, funk music's defining association was forever changed when James Brown emphasized the rhythm not only in the danceable rhythmic drive of the drums but by making all the instruments in his band become the sounds that reflected that rhythm. He changed the focus of the beat to the emphasis on the first beat of the measure and made it all about the One. That was when Stubblefield's contribution to the band became dominant.

9

Getting Louder

> I was seeing the thread that was connecting everything together, which is pretty much the blues. And everything soul or funk kind of starts with that.
> —**D'ANGELO**

Funk music stands atop Lookout Mountain, which peers down on the city of Chattanooga, rich with a soul and blues history. It is a musical history stretching back to West Africa, the echoes of freedom ringing from Dr. King's spiritual heights when he said "I've been to the mountaintop." It was in the mountain's shadow where Clyde's childhood and early days of unique rhythm development took place. He listened to the sounds in his world—both natural and man-made—including the Tennessee River snaking its way through Chattanooga.

Clyde absorbed the rhythms of the pounding noise of the grain elevator that stands along the river. I imagine the lapping of the river and the pounding of the elevator mixing in his soul into an early version of a polyrhythmic groove. Unlike the blues, country music, and work songs in the field born of the agrarian age, funk is hard-driving and is the product of the industrial age. I believe the pounding of the grain elevator stayed in Clyde's psyche, creating the future rhythm of an entirely new musical genre.

In Clyde's own words, "I consider us to be human metronomes. When I was a kid, going downtown with my mom, I walked in time. You stumble over yourself if you don't. I'd hum a song while walking, and I think that's how I got into the rhythm of drums. Keeping it natural."

James Brown went searching for the roots of those rhythms when he decided to bring to the world—in his words—a brand-new bag, infused with an infectious sound and screams so loud that people listened. It forged a completely new direction from the previous version of funk and was played by musicians who wore neatly pressed clothes and toured relentlessly. Propelling that tenacious beat was a rhythm that was the essence of Clyde and his interpretation of his world, and it would change how people listened and danced to the music. It was the new sound of Black America, the backbeat of Brown's band, and it became the soundtrack of the increasing intensity in the streets and concert halls. It was the rhythm of the One, and thanks to Clyde's drumming, it was ready to be heard.

Remarkably, neither Clyde Stubblefield nor Jabo Starks, his drumming partner for the entirety of his time in James Brown's band, ever took drumming lessons. Jabo's knowledge and experience of drumming were steeped in the sounds and rhythms of the Gospel church and the traditions of African American religion and cultural struggle. Clyde's emanated from what he felt deep inside himself, and from the sounds that surrounded him in his world; the industrial hums and pounding of factories and the trains that powered through Chattanooga, which was becoming a hub for the entire South. The natural world, with the Tennessee River, gently meandering through the city, merged with his inner guidance and knowledge of what he wanted and how to get there. He followed his own syncopated footsteps and rhythmic road.

The contrasting origins of Clyde's and Jabo's rhythms and their interpretations of them, combined with the different influences on their musical backgrounds, influenced the ways they played their styles of drumming. "Jabo's style was more of a blues shuffle, mine was more funk and soul. We took it over," Clyde said in the documentary *Mr. Dynamite: The Rise of James Brown*.[1] In the same documentary Jabo said, "You have to understand this: We're two different drummers. I play like I play. We can play the same tune, but different ways. You never played together on James's shows, but when he wanted to hear something different from Clyde, he'd point to me."

Their rhythmic expressions and how they shared them with their fellow musicians and the world contrasted and complemented each other. Together they created an entire polyrhythmic world that James Brown used by alternating between them onstage. They embodied two worlds merging, a reflection of the American experience of the 1950s and '60s: the influences of the industrial age and the musical blossoming of R&B, soul, Motown, and funk. These influences would have a far-reaching effect on not only African American culture but the entire nation.

Amplifiers increased the volume, and radio, records, and concerts spread the message to larger audiences. Later in Stubblefield's career, along with other musicians who brought funk to the world, he utilized highly engineered drum kits (Pearl, Yamaha, Ludwig), electric guitars and basses, and amplified vocals. These instruments drove the beat that propelled the vocals.[2]

Funk music became more intense, the voices louder, and as they grew, they echoed the world of civil rights. Likewise, the voices in the streets were both increasing in numbers and intensifying in volume and demands, in civil rights and antiwar protests during the long hot summer. From the Edmund Pettus Bridge where Martin Luther King Jr. stood defiant and was bloodied with hundreds in Selma, Alabama, to the streets and cities across America. The message of Martin Luther King Jr.'s eloquent dream, expressed from the steps of the Lincoln Memorial, to the silent symbol of Black Power on the Olympic podium in 1968 in Mexico City, was heard around the world.

Many of Brown's views were in line with the Black Panthers' demands to keep kids off the streets and to develop community centers, but he did not support the extreme faction of the Panthers that promoted violence. The Panthers call to action was as urgent as Brown's music. The emphasis on the musical measure and beat was on the One—ONE, two, three, four. The time was now for voices being heard in the streets and in song, for equality, to be not second or third, but first—driven by the ONE.

10

A Buck Dancer's Choice

James Brown made history, attained massive wealth, and won several awards in his lifetime, including being inducted into the Rock and Roll Hall of Fame in 1986 and being awarded a lifetime achievement Grammy in 1992. But Stubblefield and many of those closest to Brown's musical success during the late 1960s to the early '70s would not have given him an award for being a caring, philanthropic, or benevolent bandleader.

James Joe Brown Jr. was born in Barnwell, South Carolina, on May 3, 1933. He spent the first years of his life in abject poverty, wearing rags for clothes and walking barefoot. As an only child, he spent most of his time alone. "It gave me my own mind," he said of his upbringing. The family's wooden shack stood in a pine forest and was windowless, without running water or electricity. Their nearest neighbor was ten miles away. After her husband tried to kill her, James's mother fled her home and abusive husband and moved to New York. James was four at the time. A short time later, his father left James at a brothel on Twiggs Street in Augusta, Georgia, that was run by the boy's aunt Honey.

While living at the brothel as a boy, James worked odd jobs, shining shoes, singing, and dancing for pennies for soldiers on leave. At age twelve, he was permanently expelled from school for wearing "insufficient clothing." He spent much of his time alone on the streets, where he learned to buck dance, sometimes called "buck and wing." The folk dance originated with African Americans during slavery. James used this style of dancing to entertain troops and entice them into brothels. Native people[1] also used to dance a form of this. Buck dancers used a weighted foot rhythm, developing unique styles in a rhythmic and percussive way that was later associated with the blues.[2]

James not only learned to dance at Honey's brothel, but he also took up the piano, guitar, and harmonica. As a child, he attended different churches, learning a call-and-response singing style, led by preachers, that had been common among enslaved people. As an adult, James took his buck dancing on the road, making it a key ingredient in his performances. I believe the roots of that percussive rhythm were on his mind one day in Augusta when he first heard Stubblefield play his singular rhythms. Maybe he pictured himself dancing to Stubblefield's beat, buck dancing his style on the road to fame.

But before he had a chance to embark on a musical career, James was imprisoned. Sentenced to eight to sixteen years in prison, he was released after three. A musician named Bobby Byrd had started a choir at the Georgia Youth Prison, and when he heard Brown sing, he asked his family to sponsor James for early release. Brown joined Byrd's band, the Gospel Starlighters, and in 1954, they opened for Little Richard, who helped promote them. In 1956, they renamed the band the Flames—a name that showed just how much they wanted to energize their audiences with fiery performances. They launched their career with their first single, "Please, Please, Please." With Live at the Apollo, in 1963, they initiated groundbreaking live recordings that stayed on the charts for sixty-six weeks.

Blues music, in plunging into the downside of life, conveys an aura of resignation. Soul, on the other hand, incorporates both rhythm and blues and gospel music. James Brown, for his part, grew up with jazz. He kept looking ahead, sharing messages of positivity and hope for Black people.

"Brown's uncanny ability to 'scream' on key, to sing slow soulful ballads, as well as electrifying up-tempo tunes, to plumb the rhythmic possibilities of the human voice and instrumental accompaniment, and to blend blues, gospel, jazz, and country vocal styles together made him one of the most influential vocalists of the 20th century," writes Jeff Wallenfeldt.[3] Cecil Taylor talked about Brown in A. B. Spellman's *Four Lives in the Bebop Business*, saying, "But when James Brown goes into his thing, he goes; it's like a complete catharsis. He goes. Everything goes and there ain't no holding back. And it's beautiful. That's the technique of rhythm-and-blues singing, man, and no academy but the genuine tradition of a people can give it to you."[4]

Preacher/Abuser

The skills Brown learned at his aunt's brothel and at churches laid the foundation for his career onstage. Brown claimed he was a kind of preacher. Vierkant states, "What was the pulpit for the preacher was the stage for the performer. What he communicated to the audience he owes to the church."[5] Brown's skills as a musician and arranger, and his ability to communicate with his audience, accounted for his self-proclaimed titles "Soul Brother No. 1" and later, in the 1970s, "the Godfather of Soul."

The image that James Brown cultivated of himself was that of a man who had created his own path, pulled himself up out of poverty, and became a success in the America he believed in. He knew the sound and rhythms he was looking for, and how to find, develop, and promote those qualities in others. Fred Wesley knew there was more behind the persona. He knew Brown well, joining him as his trombone player in 1967 and later becoming his band leader until he quit in 1975. In Wesley's words, "Brown's fear of a return to poverty was the demon that drove him."[6]

Brown's music influenced Elvis, the Beatles, the Rolling Stones, and others. So, too, did his dancing and performing style. "The black press proudly pointed out the critical influence of black blues, rhythm-and-blues and gospel music on Presley's style."[7] Though Elvis's music had its roots in Black music, Brown and Elvis became friends and regarded each other highly. "Presley took cues from Brown's physicality on-stage, and Brown paid attention right back. 'I wasn't just a fan,' Brown later wrote. 'I was his brother.'" Brown attended Elvis's funeral and was distraught at losing his fellow musician and friend.[8] Brown later collaborated with white musicians, but most of his band members throughout his fifty-three-year career were African American. He did not, however, extend to those in his band or family the support or opportunities for upward mobility and equality that he promoted in his public persona and politics.

Brown supported the African American community in many ways, musically and politically, yet he did not escape his past. He followed the path of the abused child who grows up to be an abuser. Brown's failings, I believe, mirrored those of the United States itself in the mid-twentieth century. These problems expressed themselves as individualism at the cost of a caring community—they elevated the dollar to the status of religion. Brown hoarded his wealth without acknowledging or compensating those who helped him get to the top. He was still essentially solo buck dancing, redefining it as he went—no longer enticing soldiers to a brothel, but enticing the world to his shows. Not paying his band members what they were worth, or at all, then verbally abusing them. And in the case of the women in his life, physically abusing them. He knew what brought in audiences and what kept them coming back. His motto was "Kill 'em and leave."

Brown was no stranger to abrupt, and sometimes violent, departures. His mother left after his father had tried to kill her, and his father left him alone at his aunt's brothel. They did essentially kill his childhood and leave him on his own. Throughout his career, Brown always planned for band members to leave, which is why he had a half dozen drummers waiting in tow. His motto may have been "kill 'em and leave," but most everyone in his life got fed up and left him instead.

If growing up poor and alone gave him "his own mind," Brown later went searching for his soul, the part that was missing in his life, to become "Soul Brother Number 1." But before he could manage that, he had to search out a new rhythm that emphasized the beginning of the measure, the beat that landed on the One, the beat that made him number one. Those rhythms he found through Clyde Stubblefield.

Clyde Joins The Famous Flames

Clyde spoke about his first encounters with James Brown.

"I was in a band called the Cascades, and we would back up Otis Redding when he would come through town. Otis was from Macon, Georgia, and eventually I moved down there. I wasn't regular with Otis. I could have been but didn't. I was just having fun playing my music around town. I went to a club one night. A friend of James Brown's owned it. I went there and I was jamming, and James was around somewhere. Someone came up to me in between tunes and said, 'At set break, Mr. Brown would like to talk with you.' I didn't know him. I just knew one of his songs. I wasn't expecting anything from him.

"When I got through, I went over to a table where he was sitting. He said, 'I want you to come and check out my band, see if you can play with them.' I told him, 'Cool, no problem.' He was playing in Augusta, Georgia, the next week. James's friend who owned the club came and picked me up where I was living. We drove down to Augusta. He took me onstage and the place was packed with people. I was shaking and scared as could be. He had five drum sets onstage. I was thinking, 'Damn, what is he doing with five drummers?' He said, 'Sit down and jam with me.' I sat down at one of the sets and he said, 'No, get closer to the organ.' I got closer to the organ, and we jammed. He liked it and was smiling. It wasn't his whole band, just a few members. We got through, and I went to his dressing room, and he gave me $100. I was like, 'Whoa, the man's got money!'

"We talked a while, and he said, 'I'll be calling you.' I got in the car and went back to Macon. For a week or two I was thinking, 'This guy's not going to call me.' His friend who owned the club came and found me and said, 'Mr. Brown wants you and he wants you in North Carolina.' They put me on a flight and sent me to North Carolina. I went to the auditorium where he was performing. That was the only night I watched from the side of the stage. The rest of the nights I was onstage to perform. That's where I met John Jabo Starks—the other drummer who used to work with B. B. King and Bobby Bland.

"We [Clyde and Jabo] said, 'We got to narrow this down, so we can play more!' It got knocked down to three drummers. The other guy didn't play that much, but Jabo and I played a lot. Eventually James got rid of the other drummer. Jabo had a set of songs and I had a set of songs."

11

Clyde and Mr. Brown

> Nobody follows James Brown!
> —**JAMES BROWN**

In 1964, one year before Stubblefield joined Brown's band, white and Black musicians collided in spectacular fanfare at the Teenage Awards Music International at the Santa Monica Civic Auditorium. Along with James Brown and The Famous Flames, the show featured Chuck Berry, Marvin Gaye, the Rolling Stones, Smokey Robinson and the Miracles, Gerry and the Pacemakers, Lesley Gore, Jan and Dean, and the Supremes.

The Rolling Stones were set to be the headliners, but Brown told Steve Binder, who was directing his first rock concert film, "Nobody follows James Brown."[1] Brown made sure the Stones learned the lesson: "Kill 'em and leave." Brown's intense singing and dancing buried the Stones in funk. He made sure that the world knew who truly had soul—and who only mimicked it for rock and roll audiences. As he did over his fifty-year career, Brown dropped to his knees to convey complete collapse then was helped up with a cape draped over his shoulders, only to begin singing and dancing again. He was telling white America, as well as anyone in his band—if not the whole world—that anyone could try and knock him down, but he (Brown) would always rise again, just as he always had.

Keith Richards said that following James Brown and The Famous Flames was the worst mistake the Rolling Stones had ever made in their career.[2] In the movie *Get On Up*, which Mick Jagger produced, Brown is pictured watching the Stones exit the stage after a disappointing set. "Welcome to America," he tells them dismissively. Only members of the Stones knew exactly what James Brown said that day, but the message was clear.

A year later, Stubblefield auditioned for Brown at a live gig in Augusta. That day, his rhythms left Chattanooga and were taken onto the world stage. It was the first time he and Jabo Starks met. As a young teenager in the 1950s, Clyde heard Jabo and Bobby "Blue" Bland play "Turn on Your Love Light" on a neighborhood jukebox. Clyde was now on the verge of becoming Jabo's drumming partner—a collaboration that would come to define modern funk music.

Even though Starks had been hired only two weeks before and was one of a handful of drummers on the band's roster, Brown wanted to add one more. Starks said the overstuffed lineup of drummers was a strategy Brown had adopted after an earlier conflict with his band had led to a standoff. Maceo Parker, Brown's saxophone player, said, "James liked having a variety of drummers, including Nat Kendrick and Clayton Fillyau [who James called 'Biggun'], for the different types of songs in the show, because he didn't feel one drummer could do everything equally well."[3] But Joe Burke told me that, a year or so after Clyde and Jabo joined the band, "Clyde ran everyone else off." Clyde echoed this sentiment when he said, with a laugh, "Until we got down to Jabo and I."[4]

"Chattanooga's musicians had that unique Louisiana sound," Burke said about the music that covers zydeco, jazz, blues, Cajun, Creole, swamp pop, early African, Caribbean. "Clyde picked it up. He could hear any sound and play it. I loved to listen to him play." Burke added that Clyde was one of four or five drummers that Brown had. "One of them was named Foot," he said. "I know him personally. He was an excellent army drummer, and he was ragging on Clyde, and the next thing I knew Foot was gone."

Joe continued, "I'm talking about drummers like Clayton Fillyau, John 'Jabo' Starks, Clyde Stubblefield, Melvin Parker; the drummers who took Brown's rhythmical grunts and turned them into living drum parts with pretty much zero recognition. If you worked for Brown, by just being on the payroll, any claims to recognition for musical contribution were waivered in favor of silent anonymity and a regular paycheck. [From what I heard; the paycheck was not always there either.]

It would take at least two decades in the wilderness before the drum world woke up to what these unsung heroes contributed to the history of funk music."

Starks said, "The saying was, when Fillyau was the drummer with James, he had just one drummer, one guitar player, one bass player. . . . They were about to not play; they were rebelling against James for something . . . so he had to agree with them. And they said he made a statement after then: 'I'll never be caught without two of everything.' So I guess that's where it started. But when Clyde and I joined the group, we jelled together. And then he started letting the other drummers go." Essentially competitors for the same seat, Stubblefield and Starks could easily have ended up as rivals. Starks said one reason they didn't was that their skills weren't redundant: Each brought something unique to the group. As a matter of fact, Clyde's admiration for Jabo was there from the beginning; at his audition for The Famous Flames he said to Jabo, "You played with Bobby Bland? He was my favorite."

"There was a lot of music and rhythms that were Chattanooga homegrown," Joe said. "The seed was planted here in Chattanooga, and Brown reaped the harvest—the whole music industry did. They all used the concept, even the rappers. They phrase with their mouths according to that unique beat. I was amazed when I first heard it."

But Stubblefield wasn't immediately allowed to join the first night as a working member of the band. He was made to wait and watch from the sidelines, but not for long. Brown used the same waiting-and-watching tactic on others, but sometimes longer than one night. Maceo Parker had to watch while his brother Melvin played in the band the first day. Brown told Maceo, "Just because you say you can do something doesn't make it so. . . . You just sit in the audience and watch awhile."[5]

The band never knew what Brown was going to do onstage; all of them had to have their eyes glued to him to watch for cues. During rehearsals and shows, Brown would signal a musician in the middle of a song that he wanted them to take the lead or solo, and they had to "come in without messing up the groove," said Parker.[6] "You had to be on it to be in James's band."[7]

Stubblefield's audition made musical history. In little time, he found himself in a band with the potential for fame, fortune, and world travel. From the mid-1960s through the early '70s, Stubblefield and Starks created the grooves on many of Brown's biggest hits. In the process, they laid the foundation for modern funk drumming. "James Brown was, of course, a dynamic music creator," said Fred Wesley. "But his music was formed by the style of John 'Jabo' Starks and Clyde Stubblefield." Ben Sidran agreed: "Clyde invented it, and J. B. gave it context. Together, that was what was so strong."

Clyde said, "James Brown never told me what to play. I didn't know what he wanted me to play. We didn't communicate like that. We'd go into King Studios as a band and start jamming. He would walk in and put some lyrics to it. He put lyrics on the things we were jamming on. He told us to 'keep playing it.'"

"As soon as we set up, it happened," Clyde said with a laugh. "We'd just start jamming. And everything came from those jams." Stubblefield said that Brown directed the band as if it were a vehicle. "Once we got going, he'd put his hand up as if to 'brake here,' as if he was driving a car. He gave the direction, but it was our rhythm." The *everything* that Stubblefield is talking about is Brown's compositional groove, which many believe the drummer should have received publishing credits for. Clyde said, "James wrote there, in those jams. We'd get on it and keep jamming until Brown would walk in—he traveled in separate planes from us—but when he'd get there, hear it, and dig it, he'd say, 'Let me put some words to it.' It was always like that. We knew what we were doing, and it felt good, so it was all very easy, natural, and came together quickly."[8]

Once he was onboard, though, Stubblefield discovered that day-to-day life on tour with Brown was anything but glamorous. As Brown flew from gig to gig on his private Learjet—he was the first Black person to own one—Clyde and the rest of the band would have to settle for riding a bus around the country. Wally Ingram, a friend and collaborator of Clyde's in Madison, told me that Clyde was the one person Brown couldn't do without so occasionally Clyde flew with James—but only "if there was a gig of utmost importance and they couldn't make it on the bus in time."

The bus, Parker said, was an old Continental Trailways workhorse whose vintage red stripe lined its side. There was no place to eat or sleep, and a pecking order determined the seating arrangement. But, as Parker said, "Melvin [his brother] was assigned a seat right up in the front, and I was way in the back. I didn't really take it as an insult, though. If you were on the bus, then you were part of the band, and that was all that mattered."[9] With hundreds of shows a year, the road was long, grueling, and seemingly never-ending.

Fred Wesley told another story of life on the bus. "Brown had a hostess. She used to make sandwiches and keep order on the bus. Clyde and I were sitting in the back making a lot of noise—we were talking and laughing, and we both had big laughs. The lady said, 'I'm going to tell James Brown on you, making all this noise and everything.' We said, 'we don't care if you tell James.' She told on us." Then Brown told the hostess, "You want me to fire my drummer and my band leader?" The hostess backed off, Wesley said. "But Clyde and I used to keep that stuff going on. We were young, and we were like that."

In the late '60s and early '70s, Brown's entourage also included James Palmer, a federal marshal forever clad in a suit, tie, and trench coat. No one seemed to know what he did or who hired him. Martha High, a singer with the band, suspected Palmer was sent to oversee Brown's payments to the IRS. "He was a big cat,"[10] Wesley recalled. Whatever his role was, the marshal was instrumental in keeping five people in Brown's circle—including Clyde—out of the army. How he did it was another mystery.

"While the band traveled in the bus," Parker said, "James would swoop in at the last minute, fresh and rested from his private plane, just before showtime. And since he could come and go as he pleased, he didn't think twice about conducting pointless rehearsals all night if he wasn't happy about something."[11] Brown would spend hours making sure every hair on his head was in place, his clothes were perfectly pressed, and his shoes were polished to a shine. He expected everyone else to arrive the same way, even if they didn't have the resources to live up to his demands.

Under Brown's rules, everyone had to be called "mister": Mr. Brown, Mr. Parker, Mr. Stubblefield, Mr. Ellis. Brown did not allow drugs or drinking onstage or backstage. Uniforms had to be ready for the night and shoes had to be impeccably shined (some with Vaseline). Brown enforced the rules to make the band appear dignified. Clyde was used to playing on the streets of Chattanooga, living on his own terms. I believe he saw right away what it would take to stay in the band: keep quiet and make the best of it.

Clyde said that while on tour, band members would be subjected to surprise "inspections." And there were fines—lots of them. There were fines for everything from being late, to missing a note, nonpolished shoes, or a crease in one's suit. Each "infraction" of not having one's clothes in perfect order led to a dock in pay of five to ten dollars. Missing a note or losing a step meant a deduction of fifteen to twenty dollars. During a practice session or a live show, he would show how much each musician owed with a flash of his hand—five fingers meant five dollars. Parker said Brown kept track of them in his head and tallied them at the end of the day. At one point, Clyde joked that, after all the fines, there would be nothing left of his paycheck.

Brown was paranoid that others would steal his lyrics. And so he wrote them on napkins and pieces of paper that only he could decipher. Recording sessions were considered a loose affair. Brown would have an idea for a song then hash it out with the bandleader, who worked out the parts on the spot. When Stubblefield was with the band, Pee Wee Ellis was the man with whom Brown hashed it out. In the studio, the musicians rarely knew what they were going to perform. The emphasis was on the bass and drums, but Clyde said that "nobody in the studio knew what was going on except the horn players."[12] No one knew who was to play the sax solo; they had to watch James for the cue.

One time, one of the band members complained about having to walk a long distance to the hotel from the bus, with luggage and instruments in tow. A few days later, there was an unannounced stop at the city limits. Brown told the tired musicians they had to find their own ride to the hotel—and they had better be at rehearsal on time. This punishment went on for a few days at different stops until the offender apologized. Peer pressure and group punishment were common. Parker said Brown had eyes and ears wherever they went to spy on them. Parker once mimicked Brown on the bus, and the next day Brown called him in and said, "Next time you want to talk about me, you better have your guns ready."[13] For Clyde and the rest of Brown's band, life on the road was no easy ride. Both drummers said working with Brown could be tough. Musicians were pretty much at his beck and call. "Sometimes you don't have to make a mistake," said Stubblefield, who said he had to pay Brown more than once. "You just do a little something different and he'd call that a fine, if you didn't follow him musically, thirty dollars out of your paycheck. Actually, we didn't get nothing from anything, just a salary. The most money I made with Brown was $300 and I don't remember getting any check from recordings. It was just my regular salary."[14]

Joey Banks and Cris Plata were friends and musical collaborators of Clyde's in Madison. "I think there was always a rift between [Clyde] and James Brown," Joey told me. "There is one scene in the movie *Get on Up*, where Maceo approaches Brown about getting paid. Brown says, 'I'm not paying you guys right now.' [The actor playing] Clyde throws down the sticks and says, 'Fuck you,' and storms out. I think that was an indicator of their relationship." Joey continued, "If [Clyde] was the same person that he always was, he would not have wanted to be treated unfairly and probably would have been vocal about it. He told me he quit three times but was not specific about the reasons, but probably money related." Clyde was not there for the firing of the band, but Clyde's comment in the movie reflected what John Medeski said, that when Clyde was done with something, he'd say "fuck it" and move on.

Plata said that Clyde told him he'd "had a bellyful of Mr. Brown. At the end of the night, you'd be playing for ten dollars a show. Then we would be at a restaurant, and he would tip a waiter one hundred dollars." Although I am sure the waiter appreciated it, that kind of behavior was a sore that kept getting deeper, not only for Clyde but a lot of the band members. Plata said, "Brown would do things like that instead of compensating those who contributed to his musical success."

Since Brown's views aligned with the nonviolent philosophy espoused by Martin Luther King Jr., it made his abusive behavior toward his band and women seem at odds. Like many who grew up severely abused, Brown seemed to need control. He demanded respect, but only for himself; it did not radiate outward. His band and family would always be in his shadow—"under my thumb," as Mick Jagger put it.

Clyde, Pee Wee Ellis, and other former band members told me how Brown could be overly controlling. In addition to the fines Brown levied, he also charged band members. Clyde told Cris Plata that Brown "issued their uniforms, which they also had to pay to clean." Pee Wee Ellis echoed similar stories. "I was a conduit [between Brown and the band]. Yeah, I took a lot of flak. Until it got to be too much."[15] He laughed. When I asked what made it too much, Pee Wee didn't answer.

There were, of course, opportunities and experiences Clyde would never have had to play his music and travel if he had stayed in Chattanooga. Clyde said, "I did most of the overseas traveling with Brown. I went to Europe, China, Japan; I did some Vietnam shows. It was a great time and I didn't expect all this stuff to happen. I started playing these rhythms with Brown on tunes like 'Cold Sweat' and 'I Got the Feelin'.' People would ask me, 'How'd you do that?' I'd say, 'I don't know,' 'cause I don't know what I'm doing actually. It just comes out of my soul. I loved it. One day I was on the bus with Maceo Parker. One of James's hit songs came on. Maceo exclaimed, 'That's us!' I said, 'Wow!'"

James Brown was a complex figure. He was a champion of education for Black people, and he would not allow Maceo Parker's brother Melvin into his band until he had gone back to college to finish his education. But Brown also supported Richard Nixon—not someone known to be a friend of the Black community. Nixon and Brown both thought that Black people should pull themselves up by their bootstraps with hard work. Though Brown achieved his goals as the self-proclaimed Hardest-Working Man in Show Business, it appears that the only way he could maintain that sense of importance was if he used his power to keep others from expressing themselves or gaining recognition. Brown never acknowledged that backing him was the hardest-working band in show business, a band that was soon to abandon ship.

12

How He Did What He Did

> Clyde brought his style with him. James Brown immediately jumped on it. But that was Clyde's style that James Brown took over. "Cold Sweat," "I Got the Feelin'," and a lot of tunes. That was all Clyde Stubblefield.
> —**FRED WESLEY**

The inimitable rhythms and syncopations at the heart of James Brown's music came from Clyde Stubblefield and Jabo Starks's polyrhythmic fusion that merged both the solid backbeat of their sound and the deep respect they had for each other. The two drummers created an original sound by infusing "ghost notes" inside the parameters of the main rhythm: essentially the art of pulling notes from the silent spaces surrounding the main beat. When Clyde and Jabo played together, they created an interwoven pattern with the strong bass drum on the One (Clyde) and the softer beats on the snare and cymbals (Jabo).[1] They developed a sound and rhythm that went beyond what had been done before in American music. The heart of that rhythm redefined the future of funk music.

A. A Grace Note Regarding Ghost Notes

Ghost notes, the almost silent beats heard on the drums, were one of the secret ingredients that made Clyde's music so enticing and difficult to replicate. "'Yeah, that's all me,' said Stubblefield. 'I came up with those beats for my soul, what I wanted and needed to hear. I played what I felt . . . and what felt good and right.' When Stubblefield felt good, the Godfather of Soul felt good."[2] Clyde played these almost inaudible notes immediately preceding the accent note on the snare drum. "While [the drummer's] left hand plays a variety of taps," Joey Banks explained, "the accents in between those taps are called grace notes or ghost notes. They're actual notes that are there, but they're quieter. The combination of the grace notes and the accents creates the dynamic that is [the drummer's] left hand." Banks says that the technique was the "magic of Clyde's feel." He continued, "There are also many double beats, and multiple beats going on with Clyde's left hand, but that's more of a shuffle [a series of triplet notes, with the middle note missing, often heard in blues music]. If you look at the shuffle, it's one of the more famous beats that utilize ghost notes."

"We've never quite been able to figure out how it gets done," producer Harry Weinger said in the documentary *Soul of the Funky Drummers*, filmed in upstate New York.

Clyde explained the detailed breakdown of the rhythm that Brown said had never been duplicated. "I play on my foot [a loud booming on the bass drum] along with playing the snare and the hi-hat. I put them together, it's all rhythms and syncopation. They call them ghost notes. I'm not sure if I understand what they mean by ghost notes. They're the notes that aren't there, but I put them there. It's just the way I do it. I came up with that out of the blue—it's my idea. It is how I feel the funk should be."[3]

Clyde went on to explain the improvised groove that became the rhythms of "Cold Sweat" and "Funky Drummer." He explained how he broke down the parts, separating the bass, snare, and ghost notes, and then he put it all back together. Clyde played the rhythms to "I Got the Feelin'" and "Cold Sweat" and showed the slight differences in syncopation and patterns between them, then he demonstrated the rhythm that defined modern funk, the sound that set Brown's music apart from all others—the beat that emphasized the One.

"The bass drum is the focal point of the drumbeat," Clyde continued. "When I play a beat, I think the overall dynamic level that I'm playing is where the bass drum needs to be because everybody needs to hear it and feel it comfortably. The snare is at that same level, but with an accent so there's not a very large gap, but without that gap, that emphasis won't work; it doesn't feel as good. The hi-hat and the ghost notes—all the chattery popcorn type of notes—are under the drums. I can play accents on the hi-hat, and things can ebb and flow. There is variation allowed in terms of where the different accents and volume levels can go, but generally, the high to low volume in the mix is like this: the loudest thing is the snare drum backbeats, then it's the bass drum, then it's the hi-hat, then it's the ghost notes on the snare. The snare is playing both the loudest and softest notes."

B. A Simple Beat

"Clyde had a funky beat that James Brown had never heard before. Jabo had a funky beat," John Medeski explained, "but James had heard it before. They were doing it to death. James added to Jabo's style and made it into a song. [They kept going, and they created more] beats James liked, and he made 'I Got the Feelin'' and 'Cold Sweat.' But 'I Got the Feelin',' that's the one that sticks out in my mind. It was a dynamic interpretation of what James Brown did on Clyde's beat."

Clyde said it was a "simple beat," but not many would agree it was simple, the rhythm that's been sampled hundreds of times. In *Soul of the Funky Drummers*, Weinger asked Clyde if he is "improvising within a certain framework." Clyde responded, "Correct. It is the feeling I have for that type of turn. I put it all together." Clyde then demonstrated on the drum and said, matter-of-factly, "So that's the 'Funky Drummer.' It's a simple beat on the bass drum." "That's it," he nonchalantly added with a smile.

In response to the question about a similar syncopation between "I Got the Feelin'" (1968) and "Cold Sweat," Clyde said, as he demonstrated the Funky Drummer, "On the tune ['I Got the Feelin''] the syncopation is the same. The bridge and my rhythm patterns are different, but just one small beat makes it stand out from the 'Cold Sweat' beat. It's the same beat drum pattern but with a different lick . . . and the bass popping on different licks, so it turns around into a whole new thing."

Clyde demonstrated the rhythm; to attempt to describe it grants no justice to how he uses the bass drum, snare drum, and hi-hat.

And that was James Brown's brand-new bag.

C. Dynamic Control

Few know more about Clyde's rhythmic style than his longtime friend David Stanoch, an expert drum teacher who collaborated with Clyde. Stanoch, who teaches at McNally Smith College of Music in Minneapolis, explained Clyde's music to me while sitting at his drum set as I watched and listened over the internet.

He explained that dynamic control of a musician's instruments involves regulating and dominating the volume; the soft and quiet, and the strong and loud delivery of each drum and cymbal played. Stanoch described in detail Clyde's dynamics. "Clyde had a big, authoritative sound with lots of inter-dynamics dancing within. On 'Mother Popcorn,' he doesn't play loudly, he plays dynamically." Stanoch described the elements, such as Clyde's extended play, which he calls "his forte" that made Clyde's rhythms one of a kind.

"On an instrument like this, for a beat to feel good—and this is a theory I teach and subscribe to—when it comes to how to make something feel good on the drums, it's 50 percent tempo and being able to play well in time, and the other 50 percent is your accent or dynamic control.

"One year at UW-Madison, I studied with Max Roach, the great jazz drummer who percussion professor Jim Latimer brought in as an artist in residence. Max taught there's an inter-dynamic balance and sense of lead and accompaniment necessary in the volume. So, if Clyde's playing a beat like 'Cold Sweat,' you want the snare drum accents at the top of the mix because those are the backbeats [typically on beats 2 and 4], and that's the essence of what syncopation is—stressing the weak beat is the thing that makes people want to dance, as opposed to march, which is what happens if you stress the strong beats [on 1 and 3].

"Clyde's playing on 'Mother Popcorn,' and many other songs with James Brown, is an excellent example of how microphones sound better if the drums aren't played very loud. You can get a good, recorded sound if you've got a solid sense of the inter-dynamic balance. Clyde's recorded sound on those James Brown songs is exceptional; they are perfect drum tracks. It's remarkable because nowadays they'll say the way to get good at that is to record yourself and listen back, and that's true. Nevertheless, Clyde had that ability before he'd even been in the studio. It was all right there [inside him]. Natural.

"The drums are a percussion instrument, but what does that mean?" David continued. "It means you make a sound when you hit it [he hits the bass drum, cymbal, the snare]. To create a sound, I have to go this way [aiming downward, hitting the drum with his stick], but dynamically on percussion, space—in terms of stick height and distance to the playing surface—is a relative thing. If you want to play softly, you stay close to the surface you're playing. The odds are you will start in a lighter dynamic range than if I have my hand up here [holds his hand up high]. If I raise my arm, then drop it like cutting a limb on a tree, because of the dropping weight, [bangs it hard] that's the volume you get [loud]. Clyde had backbeats that sounded like gunshots. I learned from him how to use velocity. Velocity is helpful, for example, when you're playing a fast beat and don't have time to go 'up here' to get that loud sound [raises his arm high off the drum]. That's how the velocity works: if I'm low to the surface, I can make a fast full stroke and get the same loud volume by snapping up and whipping the stick back down quickly.

"Because of years of watching him in clubs, I saw how he played in what I call a 'strike zone.' Not every drummer does what Buddy Rich and Dennis Chambers did. Everything is happening in this small area over the snare and next to the hi-hat. Everything is perfectly balanced and under control. When we made Katy's [Katy Tessman, the mother of David Stanoch's children] record in the studio, David explained how Clyde used to get the full dynamic contrast going by playing a 'cool' section, and then it gets 'hot.'"

"Can you elaborate on that?"

"The hot section is the full range of dynamics, getting louder by lifting higher and snapping down from the surfaces, and the soft/cool approach is the same beat with everything staying low. That's how he did it in the studio.

"Clyde was gifted in how he could hear those sounds; it was melodic to him. He said, 'If I can sing it, I can play it.' He didn't read music but could hear the rhythm, hear other people playing it, and imitate it. Like Buddy Rich, he could play many styles well because he had a good ear and instincts. Buddy and Clyde could both play what they heard, and both played with perfect intonation on the drums.

"When I mention intonation, most musicians go, 'Huh? Intonation is for brass and woodwind players, in orchestras.'[4] Well, of course, but that also applies to drum set orchestration. Maybe we're not playing exact notes, but it's a pitch, melodic, and the combinations, ideally, have a harmonic and dynamic balance. I tell my students that this is the sound they want to get. I'm not saying take a ruler and measure it; what you want to listen for is the tone. Clyde told me how James Brown always wanted the bass drum heavy on the One, so it would be different from the other beats in the bar; not much, but if it was 'Cold Sweat,' for example, say you read it from transcription in a drum book, it's usually mostly correct, but what they don't have is that accent on the downbeat—it's a simple thing but subtle and very effective for optimizing the feel.

"That's one of the main things that makes his feel so remarkable—his dynamic control. Max showed me an exercise where you could hear four limbs playing each on a different voice of the kit, like a chord of indeterminate pitch. He said, 'Now play me a quarter note pulse vamp and play everything as soft as you can but being able to hear each voice' [bangs in straight time]. I can listen equally to the bass, hi-hat, snare, and ride cymbal. I can hear all four voices in tempo and then, one limb at a time, crescendo and decrescendo. He showed me that but didn't explain why right away. It was much harder to play than he made it look.

"Max described the drum set as a collection of instruments we want to project as one voice when we play. I've got a bass and snare drum, tom-toms, and here's a cowbell; they are a collection of different instruments, just as an orchestra is a collection of many instruments. Still, you don't say I went to Orchestra Hall, and these people with all these assorted instruments came into the room and sat down, and they all started playing at the same time, and then they all got up and left. No, you say, I listened to the concert, the music, the program.

"Clyde played in this way. I understood it better after Max showed me the exercise. To play one limb louder than the other, it must rise off the surface and come back down. To play soft and be able to hear everything equally, you need to stay super low and close to the surface of the drum without coming up. To add volume, the stroke is getting bigger going this way [points up]. So that's what Clyde had naturally.

"Clyde had a beautiful accent control on his left hand—drummers often refer to it as legendary. He used what is sometimes called the 'pullout stroke,' where if you're playing a double stroke roll [that's two notes in each hand, alternating right to left], you accent the second bounce with a quick snap or squeeze of the fingers. Drummers often don't use their back fingers, so the roll is very top-heavy. If it's a clean double stroke roll, there's a wrist drop, the stick bounces, the fingers snap closed, and the wrist pulls back up, so the wrist and the fingers work equally to create an even-sounding execution of two notes. If you want it to be sloppy, you take the back fingers away; that's how people play a press roll, which is multiple bounces, not a double bounce. You can try to play doubles without any back fingers, but it will not sound clean or even.

"There's also a version of a double stroke called a 'control stroke,' which is the opposite of the pullout stroke. I'm still using the back fingers but purposefully accenting the first note and closing the fingers around the second bounce, keeping low to the head without a snap. Bernard Purdie is a master of this stroke. Clyde's pullout stroke is one thing about his playing that throws many people off. They work hard to figure it out; it's a very funky sound."

"Did he bring that sound with him to James Brown?"

"Yes, he did."

"When I spoke to the musicians in Chattanooga, they seemed to be playing in that style. I'm unsure what the influences are. Is some of that New Orleans, some of that blues, kind of African roots?"

"I can help you tie that together," Stanoch said. "My theory is, theirs is an African influence—it's a rhythm that's in the DNA. Yes, you hear that in the music of New Orleans, but Clyde was from Chattanooga. I believe he learned his rhythmic concept walking home from school and imitating those sounds he heard the machines making. He had no lessons, formal technique, or study, but he worked it out because he could hear it. I think he found the sound he heard in his head and realized it in his way. He had the tenacity to figure it out himself."

A lot of bands, many from New Orleans, came through Chattanooga when Ninth Street was bustling with music. I believe that Clyde heard and absorbed these rhythms just as he took in the sounds of the city that surrounded him.

D. Extended Play

Rickey Vincent, author of *Funk: The Music, the People, and the Rhythm of the One*, explained extended play and how Brown gave permission for the groove to be the center of the sound. Extended play is longer than a song but shorter than an album. "Cold Sweat" was seven minutes, much longer than a typical 45 record of the mid-1960s. Vincent described the depth one feels when they are in Clyde's presence, describing it as meditation that "holds you there with echoes, and at the same time something else is present."

The sounds and rhythms Clyde brought to James Brown's funk was further clarified by Rickey when I asked, "It seems that Clyde's rhythm created a paradigm shift that caused a musical change with the infusion of his rhythms. Do you agree?"

"The extended play was Clyde's forte," Rickey said. "He inhabited those rhythms. He was part of the reason James Brown gave us extended play. James Brown Africanized rhythm and blues; he did away with the chord structure, the expectation of a chord, a refrain, two verses, and a chorus. He emphasized the One holding the pocket [the groove] together and not wavering. It's all about the groove becoming its own thing, not just groove for four bars before the arranging takes over. The groove is the center. Clyde gave us that groove, so, in that sense, I agree with you. Everything changed when he showed up because he established the extended play.

"The pocket Clyde brought with him to Brown is R&B, its echoes of Africa, Chattanooga, New Orleans, all these concurrent rhythms that manifested when they were needed the most. I think Clyde Stubblefield was the focal point of what James Brown did at that time: giving extended play primacy and permission to be the center of the sound. Not everybody understood how that connects to all the other awakenings, like 'Say It Loud— I'm Black, and I'm Proud.' The awakening was happening as extended play as the groove was taking shape as the indomitable groove, the unbreakable groove. When you somehow inhabit Clyde Stubblefield's rhythm, it's simultaneously soft and pliable yet impenetrable."

"Can you explain that?"

"When you're around Clyde, there's a surface-level and another-level presence. You feel it hold you there. That's what I mean by his impenetrable groove. Many of these musicians play subtle improvisations between the bars as they go, so it's always in motion, even if the beat is steady. Clyde knows how to hold you; if you meditate on that, he's holding you there with echoes, and something else is present. When I break it down, Jabo is sometimes more aggressive on those top hits. While Clyde is known for being on some of the meanest funk songs ever, when you unpack his pocket, he has a tender touch. That's how I feel his rhythm. I feel a soft touch, even with some of the meanest funk pockets you can get. The sweetness about his sound and the person overlaps."

"His soft touch being the ghost notes in his rhythm?"

"Yes! He knows how, all the masters know how to make noise with silence. I don't think they were taking direction from Mr. Brown about that kind of thing. I believe Brown would listen and then take whatever he wanted from them."

13

Cold Sweat

"Cold Sweat" broke one genre and helped create another.[1]
—**NATALIE WEINER**, music journalist

On May 1, 1966, James Brown and The Famous Flames grew even more famous with their first appearance on *The Ed Sullivan Show*, one of the most influential variety shows in American history. Powered by Brown's quick dance moves and Clyde and Jabo's drumming, the band's rousing appearance—during which they played an eight-and-a-half-minute medley of "Papa's Got a Brand New Bag," "I Feel Good," "Prisoner of Love," and "It's a Man's World"—helped the group cross over, reaching both Black and white audiences on a wide scale. The band returned to *The Ed Sullivan Show* on October 30, 1966, playing "Please, Please, Please" and "Night Train." Clyde said about that night, "The audience didn't look at the band, but they felt the grooves. Brown was the attraction. He'd do the dances, the splits and all that. But I always knew the band was the hottest thing."[2]

Even though Stubblefield appeared on Sullivan's iconic show—and had been playing with Brown's band for two years—it wasn't until May 1967 that he was included in a recording with the Godfather of Soul. One day that month, Brown walked into the King Studios in Cincinnati, where Stubblefield was laying down some rhythms with the band. James liked what he heard and added some lyrics about a cold sweat.

In doing so, they created a new direction in the world of music. While playing his two-bar rhythm, Clyde slipped in a ghost note, barely heard, becoming part of the electrical sparks and patterns in the brain waves of those listening. After the 16th and 32nd notes, as more almost-silent notes made their way across a measure, there was a pause, leaving space for the listener to crawl through and find their own private world.

Then the bang—Clyde hit it hard. Brown uttered his now-famous phrase—"Let's give the drummer some"—and the rest is history.[3] RJ Smith writes in *The One* that "Stubblefield didn't know Brown was going to say it, and his response was to keep on doing what he had been doing, as the band dropped out and Stubblefield takes his indelible, unshow-offy solo—a progression of hummingbird dips and sips."[4]

Smith continues, "He isn't giving you the time, he doesn't whomp the backbeat. It's there in negative relief as he plays around it, hanging a big wreath around it so you know where it is and can shoot a cannonball clear through it. The two-bar pattern he plays is a constant throughout the song, and when Stubblefield gets to the last beat of the second measure, that final four, he holds off on it . . . hold it . . . hold it . . . When he hits it, it's like a cannonball has landed."[5] Peter Guralnick, in his book *Sweet Soul Music*, writes that James Brown "hit his stride" starting in 1965, the year Clyde joined the band. Brown was, he writes, "exploding in the process not only the easy assumptions of pop but some of the cherished tradition of soul music itself."[6]

Natalie Weiner writes that, "with one raw, irresistible song, James Brown found the sound of the racial unrest of 1967."[7] Rickey Vincent, in *Funk*, writes that James Brown's 'Cold Sweat' is "often acknowledged as the closest thing to the first funk groove. . . . No one could get a handle on what to do next."[8]

James Brown and The Famous Flames released "Cold Sweat" during the first week of July 1967, and it spent much of the summer on the top 40 charts. In Weiner's words, the single, cowritten by then-bandleader Alfred "Pee Wee" Ellis, was the "Ground Zero of funk [and] rejected R&B's highly composed aesthetic in favor of something simple, raw, and spontaneous. Instead of being rooted in blues or Tin Pan Alley like the vast majority of R&B at the time, it was based on jazz, according to . . . Ellis." "I've been told," Ellis said in *Mr. Dynamite*, "'Cold Sweat' was the first really funk composition. I didn't write it to be so monumental, but my jazz influence was creeping into [Brown's] R&B so the combination of the two is where funk came from."[9]

As Ellis said, "I wrote it on the bus between New York and Cincinnati. . . . The band set up in a semicircle in the studio with one microphone. One take. Like the similarly revolutionary 'Kind of Blue' tune by Miles Davis it references, 'Cold Sweat' has just two chords, providing ample room for the kinds of extended vamps that Brown had long favored in his live shows. But when combined with the complex, African-inspired polyrhythms Brown had been experimenting with, the outcome was something transcendent."[10] It also lasted for seven minutes, a feature Clyde excelled at; extended play.

Brown wrote that "Cold Sweat" was an up-tempo remake of a 1962 song called "I Don't Care," which Brown said was "a slow, bluesy tune then. It was good that way, but I was really getting into my funk bag now and it became an almost completely different tune, except for the lyrics. It had the scratch guitar, the fast-hitting sound from the bass, and the funky, funky rhythms played by Clyde Stubblefield. 'Cold Sweat' has a pattern that hasn't been duplicated yet."[11]

In the documentary *Soul of the Funky Drummers*, Harry Weinger says to Clyde, "What's unique about it is that it made you famous and made you the envy of every drummer."

With a guarded laugh, Clyde responds, "Well, I didn't get too much [recognition/compensation], after that. With the tune, I had just gotten to the studio; I was in the booth and started playing this riff. . . . I was sitting in the booth playing that type of rhythm and everybody folded in with me. That's how 'Cold Sweat' started."

Maceo Parker, the funk and soul-jazz saxophonist in Brown's band (1964–70; 1973–75; 1984–88), referred to "Cold Sweat" as the first truly recognized funk composition. Jazz bassist Christian McBride said, "There was the juxtaposition of something being extremely tight and very loose at the same time—that's what jazz is really all about."[12]

While in Chattanooga, I asked Joe Burke how he saw that music as different from the kind of music he played before Clyde recorded "Cold Sweat." "If you listen to 'The Funky Broadway' and then play 'Cold Sweat,' you can hear the difference," he said. "Both were unique."

Following Joe's suggestion, I listened to both songs many times. In "The Funky Broadway," I heard a steady beat with a predictable rhythm, the music staying within the rhythm contained within the measure. In "Cold Sweat,"[13] I hear the insertion of the ghost notes, the off-beat rhythm, and the music seems to follow the rhythm. Instead of being the backbone of the music, the drums are an integral part of the music.

It sounds to me like it blurs the bridge that transverses the measure. A musician friend described the beat for the "The Funky Broadway" as being on the downbeat—the two and four, whereas "Cold Sweat" emphasizes the upbeat, the last beat of the measure.

Clyde's funk beat completely changed the way people heard and danced to music. That rhythm also dictated how people experienced Brown's music. It was the structure that held it all together in an entirely new way, all punctuated by Clyde's ghost notes, "heard under the main sound of the groove."[14] The music was then amplified, reaching larger audiences in concerts and on the radio. "Cold Sweat," Weiner writes, "perfectly crystallizes what would become canonical traits of funk: extended polyrhythmic grooves, instrumental breaks, guttural ad libs." Weiner continues, "Brown stepped outside the box that had defined R&B and never looked back."[15]

Weiner adds, "The song is built on a groove stripped bare, with drummer Clyde Stubblefield, Nolen, and bassist Bernard Odum creating layers of rhythmic push and pull that would soon become funk's signature. Every instrument, including Brown's voice, becomes percussion serving the beat's tireless push forward. . . . It's catharsis and endurance in one, as the beat loops and loops and loops."[16] Which may have paved the way for the looping of "Funky Drummer" that later became the basis for hip-hop.

"Cold Sweat" was powerful in another way—it spoke to the unrest of the times. As Weiner writes, the song "captured the growing fury of America's cities and catalyzed an uprising. In other words, it was the beginning of funk."[17]

Integration exposed more white people to funk. In 1968, while I watched the Chicago riots on TV, twenty-five miles south from my suburban home, "Cold Sweat" was becoming the soundtrack of the rising tensions. To me, the song's notes represented the underlying rhythms of what segregated America was not hearing. The ghost notes were getting louder as segregation was failing. They became the backbeat to the uprisings of the era of the untold millions.

Clyde Stubblefield and James Brown played their music in the middle of a civil rights struggle that swept across the nation. Their music reached the public through radio, records, and touring, and helped empower and give voice to the African American community both inside and outside the military. During this same time, African American musicians mounted their own fight—against the established music industry of white America. At the heart of this battle was James Brown and his band. Through fast thinking and collaboration, they were about to help mitigate some of the effects of that struggle.

14

Aftermath of an Assassination, Boston Garden

One of James Brown's most important contributions to the Black community occurred on April 5, 1968, the day after Martin Luther King Jr. was assassinated in Memphis. Brown was scheduled to play in Boston that night, and there was concern that the unrest overtaking a dozen cities across the country would also engulf Boston.

Tom Atkins, an African American Boston city councilor, proposed that Brown's concert at the cavernous Boston Garden be broadcast on public TV. Mayor Kevin White, the police, the promoter, and Brown collaborated to make this happen. Due to a fear of potential riots, Mayor White and community leaders encouraged people to line up for refunds and watch the broadcast at home. Ultimately, only two thousand people attended the sold out show in an arena that could hold more than fifteen thousand people.

Fred Wesley had joined the band only a few months before. He described the night in Boston to me. "We were all apprehensive," he said. "We didn't know if there would be a war between the races if we went on, if we would continue to tour, or what was going to happen. We followed Brown. He decided to go ahead with the show, but we were all tense. We didn't have a plan, but we did the show, and it came out all right. James talked, and the people listened. [He told them] we are men, and we are proud. We are going to hold up Dr. King's legacy and make it work, and he did that. There was a strong movement from the band to make it happen. It was James Brown, but everybody in the band followed him. I was new in the band, but it was something that I knew had to happen. We were ready in case things went badly, but we did the show as usual.

The prevailing attitude [among] the band was let's get it done, let's do this show."

Outside, the atmosphere was tense. Everyone wondered if Boston would spark, too, like other cities burning across the country. Inside the Boston Garden, Clyde and his bandmates were impeccably dressed: bow ties straight and securely clasped under their collars, jackets pressed, shirts starched, with cufflinks holding their white shirts just below their wrists. Maceo Parker, the show's MC, said there was no anger coming from the audience, and he complimented the crowd. "We've got a nice-looking audience tonight," he told them. When he started telling a joke, "Clyde on cue started playing a shuffle on the snare."[1] They started appropriately with "Get it Together." They played the standards, "There Was a Time," "I Feel Good," "Cold Sweat," and "I Got the Feelin'." Marva Whitney sang Etta James's "Tell Mama," and "Check Yourself." Mayor White called on Blacks and whites to honor King's memory and follow his principles of nonviolence. Brown called White a "swinging cat" and asked for a round of applause for the mayor.

As a young boy, Brown had shined shoes for pennies with a rag outside a radio station that he would one day own. That night on the Boston Garden's stage, all the musicians' shoes were spit and polished, reflective of the past Brown left behind. James wore Italian black-and-white patent leather loafers made by Rossi. His dancing shoes that night stepped in rapid, syncopated time, in a cold sweat—bump, bump, bump—and he and Clyde were bound in a symbiotic union.

Clyde began his one-minute solo sitting on his drum throne, never taking his eyes off Brown. The Godfather of Soul stood a few feet away, glaring at him, sending messages through his intense stare. Brown's precise movements, side to side, bouncing up and down in his finely crafted performance, was honed to simultaneously convey a sense of control and freedom. Serious, intense, and intent on getting every nuance the way Brown demanded, Clyde made every upstroke and downbeat that transferred into Brown's precise and rhythmic dance steps. With the drum solo over, the TV camera remained on Clyde, relief visible on his face. He was onstage with James Brown, the Godfather of Soul, solidifying the rhythm that helped keep a city from going up in flames. Brown buck danced away from the drums and back to his microphone and spun around three times as skillfully as a ballerina on pointe. At that moment, as James turned away from Clyde and toward the audience, Clyde was able to breathe.

As the songs continued, the ground beneath the stage pounded with Clyde's rhythmic mixture of strength and dexterity while Brown screamed out his lyrics proclaiming to the entire world that he would never return to that shack in South Carolina. Broadcasting the show that night likely saved lives throughout the Boston area. There was less violence than even on a typical night because so many stayed home and watched the King of Soul on TV. The show was rebroadcast multiple times throughout the weekend. The city, and the band, felt enormously relieved. Parker said he realized that night the healing power of music. After the show, Brown sent messages to many cities to help regain calm. The next day, the band was off to Rochester, New York, as violence continued to explode in cities across the United States.[2]

"Even though I was going to take a financial bath, I knew I had to go on and keep the peace. There are some things more important than money,"[3] Brown said with an air of altruism. Even so, Brown demanded payment from the city of $60,000, for loss of ticket sales.[4] I am sure Clyde and the rest of the band saw a pittance of that and knew better than Brown how there are some things more important than money. President Lyndon B. Johnson had declared a national state of emergency, but in Boston, Brown and his band had kept the peace.

There was one instance that I heard of Clyde praising Brown. It was after this Boston Garden concert, arguably the most important show of Brown's life. Clyde said Brown "was the king and [the crowd] respected him. There was no more fighting. He was damn good." After the crowd rushed the stage and the band stopped playing the police and guards pushed everyone off the stage. Brown calmed everyone, Clyde said. "I didn't know what to say about that myself. I'm sitting there on the drums, still just waiting. You know, like wow, what's going on?" Brown spoke to everyone there and said, "Hold it, hold it, hold it, wait a minute. That's all right, it's all right, it's all right." The concert went on smoothly and Clyde and the rest of the band were relieved and thankful for how Brown had handled it.

Despite that, the rebellion and struggle for acknowledgment and equality were not only rising on the streets, but they were also growing in Clyde. Brown's fragile ego stood on a foundation of poverty and abuse that could crack with any perceived slight from his band. And soon, the bubble of goodwill and peace would again burst, and Brown would fine Clyde and the rest of his band for any reason he chose.

Perhaps the dream of playing to Clyde's inner drummer began to build inside him that night in Boston. I can imagine Clyde's thoughts turning to Slim and the Cascades and the sounds of the Tennessee River peacefully rolling along, lapping against the shores of his hometown of Chattanooga. He may have peered into the future and dreamed of seeing his brother Frank, in Madison, with the waters gently rolling onto the shores of Lake Monona.

FIGURE 1. The Cascades, Clyde's first band in Chattanooga, circa 1958. Clyde is in the back row on the left, and Robert "Slim" Eppinger is in the first row, far right. Courtesy of Robert "Slim" Eppinger.

FIGURE 2. Grain elevator along the Tennessee River, Chattanooga, the birthplace of Clyde's funk and the pounding, thumping sounds Clyde heard as a boy. Photo credit D. Leah Steinberg.

FIGURE 3. Mad City Pop and Jazz Festival, 1979. James "Pie" Cowan on hand drums with Clyde on drums behind. Photo credit James "Pie" Cowan.

FIGURE 4. Cris Plata and Extra Hot band photo, 1987. Courtesy of Cris Plata.

FIGURE 5. Tina and the Tigers band photo, 1982. Photo credit St. John. Courtesy of Christine (Tina) Vitale.

FIGURE 6. Clyde fixing his drum. Vilas Park, Madison, 1996. Photo credit D. Leah Steinberg.

FIGURE 7. Clyde, right front; producer Jack LeTourneau (1951–2017), left front; and Michael Stone of Stone Foundation (RIP 2023) in back. Photo credit James "Pie" Cowan.

FIGURE 8. 2004 Madison Area Music Awards (MAMA) lifetime achievement award presentation to Clyde Stubblefield with Pauli Ryan, left, and James "Pie" Cowan, right. Photo credit James "Pie" Cowan.

FIGURE 9. Clyde and his wife, Jody Hannon, at home with their two dogs, October 10, 2015. Courtesy of Jody Hannon.

FIGURE 10. Cris Plata and Extra Hot with Clyde. Yahara Place Park, around 1998. Photo credit D. Leah Steinberg.

FIGURE 11. Clyde Stubblefield band poster, early 2000s. Photo credit David Loeb. Courtesy of Brian Kell, BKintermedia, formerly Beat King Entertainment.

FIGURE 12. Cover of *Madison Magazine*, August 2003. Courtesy of Tim Burton, *Madison Magazine*.

FIGURE 13. Clyde and Joey Banks at the King Club, Madison, 2004. Courtesy of Joey Banks.

FIGURE 14. Clyde doing what he enjoys best. Madison Park, June 2002. Photo credit Brent Nicastro.

FIGURE 15. Fred Thomas, bass player; Jabo Starks, drummer; and Clyde, drummer, of the James Brown band. Photo credit Robbie Kowal.

FIGURE 16. Rickey Vincent, Clyde, and Robbie Kowal at the Mezzanine, San Francisco, November 3, 2012. Photo credit Rickey Vincent.

FIGURE 17. Clyde and Jabo Starks. Photo credit Robbie Kowal.

FIGURE 18. Clyde's signature on drum head for Robert Bowler, owner of Drummer's Tradition, San Rafael, California. Inset: Clyde and Jabo signatures to David Stanoch. Photo credit David Stanoch for the two signatures of Clyde and Jabo. Inset photo credit D. Leah Steinberg.

THE CAPITAL CITY HUES
The News for ALL of Madison!
Vol. 10 No. 20 • October 1, 2015 • Free • www.capitalcityhues.com

The Beats of a Generation

Clyde Stubblefield Is the Most Sampled Drummer in History

FIGURE 19. *The Capital City Hues* 10, no. 20 (October 1, 2015). Courtesy of Jonathan Gramling, *Capital City Hues*, Madison.

FIGURE 20. Clyde and the author, 2014. Photo credit D. Leah Steinberg.

FIGURE 21. Clyde at his drum set. High Noon Saloon, 2014. Photo credit D. Leah Steinberg.

FIGURE 22. Clyde on the photographer's porch, Madison, October 1983. Photo credit Brent Nicastro.

FIGURE 23. Bench honoring Clyde with close-up of plaque. Brittingham Park, Madison. Photo credit Brent Nicastro.

15

Surrounding the Groove

In *The Racial Mountain*, Langston Hughes called the struggle of the Black man (to say nothing of the Black woman) an "almost insuperable obstacle to his attempt to define himself as a Black artist, practicing a Black-based art, in a country that is deathly afraid of both its artists and its Blacks."[1]

Music bridged the river between the church and politics. Soul was gospel brought out of the church into the streets, it was the light shining on a brighter day, not only in the afterlife but for this life; integration in the schools, jobs, or, as Aretha Franklin sang, R-E-S-P-E-C-T.[2] She had come a long way from the days Lenell Glass backed her up. In "Black Music and Black Possibility," Craig Werner writes, "Responding to the calls of ordinary people and charismatic leaders, the music articulated the ongoing drive for freedom that remains the beating heart of African American history."[3] He further states, "Soul provided the soundtrack for the freedom movement as it gathered energy from the sit-ins, the freedom rides, and the hard fought campaigns in the streets of Birmingham and the halls of Congress."[4]

Music and politics were intricately and symbiotically joined in the late 1960s. The two strands were woven into personal and political collaborations, sometimes aiding each other's agenda and sometimes binding them in complicated ways. Some of these relationships formed around the music of James Brown and The Famous Flames. Even though the Black Panthers criticized Brown for his capitalism, they later used "I'm Black and I'm Proud," Brown's main message, as their anthem. While the phrase was forever linked to Brown, he undermined his own musicians' pride when he fined his band members for minor infractions, shoes not being spit and polished, a note not played on time, a shirt not perfectly pressed. Brown was kicked out of elementary school for being dressed in rags and went to jail as a teenager for theft, and this must have led to his pride in the progress he had made in life. It also led to him being a perfectionist, for if he was perfect no one could kick him out of school or send him to jail. He expected similar perfection from everyone around him, punishing them when it was not achieved to his standards.

The music world that Clyde entered in the mid-1960s was embroiled in a political and racial upheaval centered on a struggle for rights and respect. The environment touched every aspect of Black American life, from education and the economy to the war in Vietnam. Clyde had experienced severe poverty and struggle growing up in a segregated Chattanooga. He was also apolitical. "He hated politics, period," Joey Banks, a friend and drummer in Madison said. Nevertheless, Clyde sat high on his drum throne behind a politically influential band. He laid down his grooves during years of social and political upheaval, and they provided the backbeat that defined the integration of funk music and the Black Power movements.

The civil rights and freedom movement had many facets and moving parts. James Brown did not fit neatly into any one paradigm, and he had a complicated relationship with the civil rights movement. RJ Smith wrote, in his biography of James Brown, *The One*, "His beliefs were built on ego, a concern for civil rights, and his Southern-steeped Americanism. Nothing could untangle all the strands."[5] He fought hard to raise himself up out of poverty and embraced American individualism, crawling his way up and expecting those around him to do the same. Though in the case of his band, he purposely blocked them from achieving that goal. As Wesley said, Brown's fear of returning to poverty was never far from his mind.[6] The African American population had divergent ways of rising up. Brown was a father figure and mentor to Reverend Al Sharpton, who was steeped in political activism from a young age. Unlike Sharpton, Brown continued his updated version of solo buck dancing, making himself the One, though he had a band of the most talented musicians of the day to help him dance and sing his way to the top.

As Brown was gaining fame and riches on his self-made path upward, many African Americans, men, women, and children and were rising up together, incurring physical and sexual violence along the way. The freedom riders, African Americans along with some white civil rights activists, rode buses together through the South in 1961 to challenge segregation. A ruling in 1946 made segregation illegal in interstate transportation, and "in 1960 the U.S. Supreme Court ruled in *Boynton v. Virginia* that segregation in the facilities provided for interstate travelers, such as bus terminals, restaurants, and restrooms, was also unconstitutional."[7]

Black women played an equally important role in the struggle. Being on the bottom of the racial and gender ladder, women had to fight twice as hard to overcome racism in addition to sexism. Danielle McGuire writes that "African-American women were the backbone of the Montgomery bus boycott."[8] Domestic workers, maids and cooks, formed the majority of those who rode the buses and had the power to stop the wheels from rolling.[9] Fannie Lou Hamer, a sharecropper and organizer for the Student Nonviolent Coordinating Committee (SNCC),[10] whose mother and grandmother taught her the painful truth of the history of Black women in the South, went on to work on voter registration and grassroots organizing. She challenged segregation, lost her job, and in the process suffered several beatings. Rosa Parks refused to give up her bus seat, sparking a one-year boycott of riding buses in Montgomery after her arrest. Later, Angela Davis continued the struggle, making headlines with her feminist, political activism and career as author and professor.[11] Meanwhile tens of thousands of Black women struggled, on a personal and more global basis, from familial and political violence.

On June 9, 1963, women from the SNCC, including Hamer, were returning from a citizenship training. Predominately run by women, the trainings taught reading and writing along with how to pass voter registration tests. In South Carolina, they stopped to eat at a white lunch counter in a bus station, and they were arrested. "Once in custody, each activist received a savage and sexually abusive beating by the Winona [Mississippi] police," writes McGuire.[12] June Johnson was only sixteen, and as the police assaulted her they yelled, "We're going to teach you how to say 'yes, sir' to a Mississippi white man." Hamer told her story of horrible physical and sexual abuse from that day in prison at the 1964 Democratic National Convention.[13] Peniel Joseph writes, "On the cusp of the women's movement, the Panther's rhetoric on gender politics became more progressive yet remained conflicted internally, rife with contradictions that reflected the wider Black Power and New Left's own vertigo."[14]

Anne Danielsen writes that Brown's "golden age" began in 1965, with the release of "Papa's Got a Brand New Bag."[15] This was the year Clyde joined the band. "The music of James Brown from this period was important to the struggle for a Black cultural identity and history as a means of demonstrating an African influence of African American music and culture."[16] Werner writes that the song was the backbeat to the new politics rising and "served notice that a new breed of brothers and sisters was ready to take control."[17] Brown's new kind of music was powered by Clyde's funky polyrhythmic beat, its ghost notes propelling the movement forward with the rhythm of the One.

Brown's politics embraced some of the values of the Black nationalists, who advocated for self-determination and a separate Black nation. He did not believe, as some musicians did, that music was colorblind. He worried about the appropriation of Black culture.[18] Even though Brown contributed significantly to the Black community, his relationship with the Black community was complicated. He had a lifetime membership to the National Association for the Advancement of Colored People, organized voter registration drives for the SNCC, and financially supported the Congress of Racial Equality.

Brown also sponsored thousands of free Christmas meals to people in New York ghettos and helped with scholarships to help keep Black children in school. He said he believed in God, America, and the American dream. Brown "always marched to the beat of his own drum,"[19] as the critic Aisha Harris writes. He went his own way in both music and politics. Over the years, he achieved his personal goal of Black ownership and was a role model for Black America, selling millions of records and acquiring five radio stations in Knoxville, Tennessee, that appealed to both Black and white audiences.

The Black Panthers criticized Brown for his patriotism, which they viewed as driven by his embrace of capitalism. However, Brown's lyrics played an important part in the Black Power movement. When "Say It Loud—I'm Black and I'm Proud" came out in 1968, with Clyde holding down the rhythm, Black people began referring to themselves as Black rather than Negro. Billy X Jennings, a former Black Panther historian, said Brown couldn't have made that proclamation if there had not been "a group like the Black Panther Party that had set up a foundation of knowledge already."[20] The civil rights leader Andrew Young, former mayor of Atlanta, stated that "James Brown's 'I'm Black and I'm Proud' was an affirmation of self-respect, and it was a challenge to others to respect themselves and for them to respect him."[21] Brown brought together an array of children to sing on the recording, allowing them to feel that pride. Meanwhile, the members of his band and the people close to him were feeling less of that pride in Brown, becoming more divided and less appreciated.

16

Deep into the Jungle

In 1968, Stubblefield traveled with James Brown to Vietnam. "Say It Loud—I'm Black and I'm Proud" was recorded just before the tour in Asia and was released in August 1968, soon after the band returned. Stubblefield was one of seven musicians, who became known as the Saigon Seven, whom Brown picked from his large entourage. Several times while traveling they experienced a small sampling of what the soldiers faced. They flew only once on a plane; the rest of the time they were either in converted buses or helicopters. On one flight, the plane they traveled in was fired upon and oil dripped out and the cabin filled with black smoke. The smoke got the attention of the Viet Cong and the band soon heard explosions. Another time, during a mortar attack, the band members lay on the floor as soldiers stood over them, protecting the musicians from the bullets that pinged against the helicopter and whistled past their ears. The buses they traveled in had wires on the windows so grenades couldn't be thrown inside. There were always snipers at the door when traveling by helicopter, and once the band had to jump five feet out of a Chinook into the marshes. Another time, while traveling at night, they heard pings of metal bouncing off the helicopter, and during the last show of the tour, the band heard nearby Viet Cong fire.[1]

As the Vietnam War raged on, year after year, many Black Americans grew to sympathize with the plight of the Vietnamese. Muhammad Ali famously refused to report for military duty on religious grounds and was sentenced, as a result, to five years in prison for draft evasion. Although he never served time, he lost his world heavyweight championship title.

"My conscience," he said, "won't let me go shoot my brother, or some darker people, or some poor, hungry people in the mud for big powerful America."

After two years of lobbying the Johnson administration, James Brown became the first Black entertainer to play for U.S. troops in Vietnam. Race relations were tense at home and among soldiers, and the government feared the trip would inflame the situation. But Brown wanted to support the troops. Vice President Hubert Humphrey approved Brown's request in 1968. Many Blacks criticized the musician for going, saying it lent legitimacy to the war.

Traveling in a few helicopters, the Saigon Seven also made stops in Japan, South Korea, and Okinawa. The two-week tour began on June 5, 1968, just months after the Tet Offensive. Brown took only one drummer; he knew he couldn't bring the funk to the soldiers without Clyde. Also with him were Maceo Parker, Waylon Reed, Jimmy Nolen, Alfonzo Kellum, and Tim Drummond—the first white member of the Brown band. Having Drummond along showed that the band supported peaceful integration. The opening acts were singer Marva Whitney and saxophonist St. Clair Pinckney. When deciding who would go to Vietnam, Whitney recalled, "Everybody was looking at everybody, and the ones that didn't go, I think they were happy."[2]

Although there was a world of difference between performing on a USO tour and being drafted to the front lines, during their two weeks in Asia, Stubblefield and the band glimpsed what it was like to be in a war zone. Parker, the road manager, was given the title of military liaison since he had been in the service. The rest of the band were given honorary commissions as colonels and officers; if captured, they were told, officers were treated better. They were given fake ID cards and had to wear military fatigues for safety.

Many years later, Clyde sat down with Ben Sidran and his son Leo in Ben's attic in Madison and recorded some of his memories of being in Vietnam with The Famous Flames. "We flew to someplace and got in a big army truck," Clyde recalled. "We drove and drove. There was nothing but green, mountains, and jungle. We'd go to checkpoints, and we'd stop. [The soldiers said,] 'We'd better stop because they will bomb or shoot us if we don't.' I said, 'We better stop.'"

Clyde continued, "At one place, South Vietnamese were surrounding the camp trying to get the band to give them things." Inside the compound, everything was available: bars, bowling alleys, even theaters. Clyde mentioned how easily bombs could have landed in the middle of the compound.

They performed at only one place Bob Hope had played. All the other places were more out of the way and deep into the jungle.[3] "We came in with tuxedos on and patent leather shoes," Clyde said. I can imagine how ridiculous Clyde must have thought it was to wear those clothes in a war zone, but Brown never changed his outward presentation to the world, even in a war.

"The brothers [American soldiers] in the jungle are about ten feet away," Clyde added. "They called out, 'Hey, anyone over there smoke?' A few of us, me and two others, raised our hands. . . . They had a joint and poured red liquid on a nice-size doobie. They said Mama-san sent this; it was liquid opium. We smoked that joint, and I didn't want to come out of the woods. I was paranoid and scared, but the show was getting ready to start, and they called us onstage. They said, 'Get onstage,' and I went. But that show was out of sight, it was fabulous."[4]

Clyde talked about another time when he was extremely dehydrated, and a field nurse couldn't get a needle in his arm. Clyde said, "I perspired so much my skin was grayish, and they put me on this saline water drip. Water was running off me like a faucet while I was playing. Afterward, they said, 'We're going to have to lay you down and give you saline water.' My whole body started cooling down. I said I feel like an air conditioner on the inside."[5] Brown, for his part, was routinely replenished with IV fluids between sets.

While the band was staying at the Continental Hotel in Saigon, they heard gunfire outside. Signs were posted in the rooms saying not to open drapes or turn on lights after dark. The Presidential Palace across the street from the hotel had received mortar fire damage, and guards had orders that if they saw lights on at the hotel to act like there were snipers inside and open fire. One night, Brown knocked on the door of a dark hotel room where his band was eating, drinking, and enjoying themselves, and for a short time, he stepped out of his guarded persona and rigid no-socializing-with-the-band policy and opened up to them, sharing his thoughts and feelings on the war and the letters he had received from soldiers who were fans.[6]

During the last show, a soldier named Theodore Lovett sought out Parker, who was from his hometown. Lovett told him the army often used Black soldiers more than whites for dangerous combat missions and asked for Parker's help. A year later, Parker found out Lovett had been killed soon after their encounter in Vietnam. Charles Whitfield, a trumpet player with Parker's uncle in the Blue Notes, was also killed in the war. Black soldiers were killed in disproportionate numbers, despite TV journalist Frank McGee reporting that "there's no racial barrier of any sort here."[7]

During the tour's last show, the band heard nearby Viet Cong fire. Brown took the mic and continued the show, yelling, "Hit me!"[8] I wonder: Was Brown daring the Viet Cong, or summoning a younger self who was daring his father, or just calling out to Clyde to hit the One? Maybe all three.

I picture Clyde hearing a rhythm in the gunfire, like in Shostakovich's Symphony No. 7, beating the rhythm of war but instead trying to create a rhythm of peace in the middle of battle. I can also imagine him glaring at Brown as he yelled out, "Hit me!" I believe Clyde didn't want to hit it hard at that moment. He may have thought it was an infinitely better time to play his barely heard but powerful ghost notes.

Nevertheless, one of the things Clyde told Ben and Leo in their attic was, "The soldiers were glad to see us, they treated us well. Somewhere in Vietnam, they gave us a big bag of coffee. It looked like coffee. It was a mother," meaning some good pot. "It was our last two nights in Vietnam," Clyde continued. "We were getting ready to return to this army camp. We sat in this room, five or six of us, and smoked until our eyes were cherry red. We said nobody's going to take nothing back with us."[9]

Despite the disparity between being on tour and being a soldier, Brown wore an army hat and camouflage jacket when the band touched back down in New York. Brown's only complaint with the military was that they hadn't let him bring his full band to Vietnam—along with the guns he owned.

Clyde kept the tour in perspective and focused on the music when he told Ben Sidran, "We gave the soldiers a whole new charge. We came over with the funk and soul."[10]

17

"I Hate That Song"

On November 20, 1969, at King Studios in Cincinnati, Stubblefield and the band recorded "Funky Drummer." Brown walked with authority into the studio while Clyde was laying down some drum breaks, and the song was written that day. By March 1970 Stubblefield's legacy as the funky drummer was secured, recorded on a 45 vinyl record and written into the history books of music. Although "Funky Drummer" defined Stubblefield and became the name that radio hosts and DJs began calling him by, it was a song he grew to hate. Clyde wanted to be seen as more; he wanted to be remembered as someone who bridged genres in jazz, blues, country, and Tex-Mex.

One year after this historic event in music, Clyde would leave James Brown for good. "Funky Drummer" would eventually be copied and repeated thousands of times by hip-hop, R&B, and rock musicians. It became one of the most sampled drum rhythms in history. Yet Clyde never received credit or compensation for the backbeat that powered the engine of hip-hop's success.

Ben Sisario, a music writer for the *New York Times*, asked Questlove, "Does that mean that Clyde's whole influence through the 'Funky Drummer' sample distorts who he was as a musician? Since people weren't hearing the whole picture of whom he was, just hearing a five-second break?"

Questlove responded, "He's like the ghost in the machine. When you talk about the perfect beat, it's not even that 'Funky Drummer' wins in a technical aspect. But in an artistic aspect, it's hands down the most perfect beat you can loop—it's very lyrical, melodic, and rhythmic. It's perfect. It's magical. Everyone I know as a producer, that's gotten their start in hip-hop production, they all have their story about the first time they heard 'Funky Drummer.'"[1] In the movie *Mr. Dynamite: The Rise of James Brown*, Questlove said, "They only had one failed single, and that single's name was Funky Drummer. Go figure. The song that birthed my whole movement."

Clyde described the conditions under which the band recorded "Funky Drummer" in *Mr. Dynamite*: "We had been playing somewhere the night before. Just as we got to Cincinnati and we're going to check into the hotel to go to bed, Brown says, 'Take them to the studio.' We all were tired, but Brown wanted to record right then. I started laying down a drum pattern. Brown liked it, and we recorded it on the spot."

In 2014 the *LA Weekly* labeled Clyde no. 2 in the "Top 20 Drummers of All Time," stating, "Watching Clyde Stubblefield break down the drum pattern from 'Funky Drummer' is akin to watching Leonardo da Vinci give a Bob Ross–style lesson on how to paint Mona Lisa."[2]

Years later, in an interview with Tom Alesia at Clyde's apartment in Madison, Clyde pulled out an old CD of the song. He said he hadn't listened to it in years. He recalled thinking it was "boring, really boring. That beat doesn't excite me. So simple, so blah."[3] They listened to other tracks and Clyde said that "I Got the Feelin'" and "Give It Up or Turnit a Loose" "have some hot drum patterns. I love those songs. But this . . . I don't know."[4]

"'Funky Drummer' is built upon a challenging single-handed 16th-note hi-hat pattern. . . . Around that hi-hat part, Clyde adds syncopated bass drums and snares, open hi-hats and the use of ghost notes as well as accented snares. It creates a thick funky layered groove," *Total Drummer* wrote on their website.[5] Although "Funky Drummer" became the name that radio hosts and DJs used for him, it is not what defined Clyde. His musicianship spanned a wide range of musical styles.

What bothered Clyde most was not being recognized for his contributions. Years later, in the 2010 documentary *Copyright Criminals*, Clyde said, "[Brown] didn't tell me what to play. I played what I felt, but he owned it." Brown's strict control of the band—and the lack of acknowledgment from hip-hop artists—would keep Clyde from being given the credit he deserved. All of which fed into how Clyde felt about "Funky Drummer": "I hate that song," he said in *Mr. Dynamite*, and then stuck out his tongue.[6]

18

The Exodus

> The fact is, James Brown's band, the 1965–69 version, fronted by Pee Wee, was, I would argue, the greatest group of rhythm and blues musicians ever assembled.[1]
> —**JAMES MCBRIDE**

James Brown took advantage of his prominence in the music industry to keep his fellow African American musicians in line. He accomplished this through intimidation and control, assuring that they could not make it without him—a typical pattern of abuse that he learned during his childhood. As the years passed, Clyde and most of the band became increasingly fed up, tired of impossible expectations and little acknowledgment for their efforts. Onstage, the band came off as a tight unit, made up of Brown, Stubblefield, Jabo Starks, Pee Wee Ellis, Fred Wesley, and Maceo Parker. Together, they traveled the back roads of America. Offstage, it was different.

The beat that supported Brown's rhythm and his band and kept soul alive became constrained by Brown's tight hold on every aspect of his band. "Tighten up, Clyde," Brown would call out in the middle of a concert. But the tightening eventually cut off the air supply to the band's creativity. Clyde said Brown would change the rhythm in the middle of a song to throw them off. When that happened, Parker said that if it weren't for Pee Wee Ellis, the band director, they wouldn't have known what to do, where to go musically, or where to put the timing of the beats and accents. Ellis read and interpreted Brown's movements, grunts, and stomps, turning them into music the band could play.

"Onstage, Brown was the front man that channeled the energy coming from the band in a totally unique way, but it's very easy to fall into the illusion that it's all coming from you. There's no way that the JB sound could have come together without the Maceos, the Freds, the Pee Wees, Clydes, and on down the line," said drummer Michael Veal in *Mr. Dynamite*.[2]

Rickey Vincent, a scholar and host of the KPFA radio show *The History of Funk*, said that the complicated dynamic was about more than just Brown's controlling personality. "Brown's idea of a respectable show, which gives the audience something to take pride in, shows military efficiency in what they produced and projected," he said. "That efficiency established them, so they kept going with it. Brown's way included demotions and getting fined. He established this in this old-school approach, and I think most musicians accepted that going in. That alone wasn't offensive to many, but Brown took it too far. When he saw the band getting a bit too comfortable, joking, and clowning around on the bus, with any slight offense, he would lay down the law even tighter.

"The music industry sets artists up to not be mentors, but territorial in what they do and how they do it," Vincent added. "James Brown came from a different generation and grew up during the Depression. Growing up during the war years, there were people always traveling. Military people and musicians were staying at his aunt's brothel. He saw ambition and uniforms and understood the respect that a band in uniform garnered. It was a generational thing.

"I think unless you still have the scars from him, many folks forget the rest, the monster that he was. They accept the accomplishments he made. To come from absolutely nothing and become a household name and have a worldwide impact, all these things were in play, but the ones that took the brunt of it were his band and his wives and girlfriends. I see James Brown as a product of his times with the World War II ethic of preaching military discipline in the band's presentation, structure, and control. He didn't want to let that go. Especially when his band members had matured to where they were prepared to do their [own] projects. He clumsily gave a little space for Fred Wesley when he was still in the JBs, but Fred was quite bittersweet about it."

"It sounds like bootcamp," I said.

"They felt they were ready to lead their platoons, and they were being treated like privates and grunts. He didn't have another way. Another example was Ike Turner, writing songs and bringing Tina along [as an appendage] wasn't working. He couldn't change his ways with music or with Tina."

James McBride, speaking to Pee Wee Ellis in *Kill 'Em and Leave*, said, "After forty-five years of being the most unique voices in the music world, co-composer of at least twenty-six James Brown songs, including 'Say It Loud—I'm Black and I'm Proud,' 'Mother Popcorn,' 'Licking Stick,' and 'The Chicken' [all of which Clyde played on]. . . Let's talk about James Brown."

"Can't we talk about something else?" Ellis responded.[3]

The exodus from The Famous Flames began in July 1969, when Ellis left the band and never looked back. By March 1970, the best band Brown had ever assembled was in mutiny. Clyde, Jimmy Nolen, and Maceo Parker established their names in his band. "The guys in the band might grumble, but Brown knew how to handle their complaints. This time, though, something more serious was brewing."[4] It wasn't just the money; it was the not receiving any acknowledgment for their musical contributions, having to rehearse on days off, and living the regimented life of daily inspections. Brown employed basic union-busting tactics and divide and conquer. Parker said, "He opposed us trying to solve the problems as a group."[5] However, the group cornered him one night backstage before a show in Jacksonville, Florida.

Brown listened to the band's grievances, then immediately sent Bobby Byrd on Brown's private jet to retrieve the Pacesetters. This young band included Bootsy Collins and his brother Catfish. They had just finished their show at the Wine Bar in Columbus, Georgia, where they made fifteen dollars to divide between the band. Byrd swooped in and told them, "We are rolling," and Collins and the band eagerly followed.[6] It was Bootsy's first time on a jet.

In Jacksonville, the audience was excited for the show to begin, and Brown's band was waiting backstage to see what would happen after making their demands. When the Pacesetters arrived at the concert hall, Brown told them they were going on; they were given no explanation or time to practice. As the show was set to begin, Brown stomped down the hallway and announced to The Famous Flames, "I'm forfeiting my conversation with you all. You're all fired—everybody!"[7] Parker found out many years later that the Pacesetters thought they would play with Brown's band, not replace them.

Wesley spoke to me about what became known as "the Firing." "I wasn't there," he said. "I was already gone, I left before all of it went down, and when I returned [to Brown's band], Bootsy was the bandleader. I don't even know if Clyde was there when everything went down. [What] I know is what I've heard, and hearsay typically gets a lot of yeast thrown into what happened. The entire band of the Flames was upset about not being paid the money they were due, and they decided to rebel."

James had Bootsy's band on hold because he believed a mutiny was imminent. That night, Brown told the Pacesetters he'd pay $275 for the night. They were trying to figure out on napkins how much each would get, then he said to make it $350. They hurriedly scribbled down each of their shares. He said, "No, each of you." The next day Bootsy and the rest of the Pacesetters were on the Golden Eagle bus, and the heart and soul of James Brown's best band, the musicians who changed the course of music history, were gone. Brown's Famous Flames had turned quickly and irrevocably to ashes. But it wasn't the end of the former Flames' musical journeys or future collaborations.

Stubblefield, Parker, Wesley, and Ellis had cemented Brown's place in history. They were the music and the rhythm behind "Say it Loud—I'm Black, and I'm Proud," "Mother Popcorn," "Give It Up or Turnit a Loose," "Funky Drummer," "Ain't It Funky Now," "Santa Claus Go Straight to the Ghetto," and many other songs. But all that was over. Life was no better for those in Brown's personal life. The domestic abuse of his girlfriends, wives, and children was well known and reported and included several domestic abuse arrests over the years.

After Parker started his own band, Maceo and All the King's Men—with Jimmy Nolen, Bernard Odum, and his brother Melvin—the band was sabotaged at every turn. Brown paid radio stations not to play their music, had signs for their shows taken down, and booked shows on the same nights in the same towns—anything to break them. Brown made sure they all knew who had the power and control. A year later, all the Famous Flames had returned to Brown, including Clyde. They had been unable to make it on their own. When Ellis joined some sessions in 1985, Brown announced, "See, Pee Wee is the only one who never came back."[8]

Both Clyde and Pee Wee, and it seems anyone else who was ever in his band, wanted to get away and leave the past behind. It is in certain ways like having an abusive parent; they brought you into the world, and Brown was the one who gave these talented musicians just starting out their chance. But Brown held the reins and extracted the price.

"Soul is when a man has to struggle all his life to be equal to another man," Brown had once said.[9] Was there really soul between Brown and his band members then? When Brown brought Clyde into his band in 1965, he had followed Clyde's rhythms throughout the South and found his rhythms supported and furthered his music. But sharing the stage with his fellow musicians did not change Brown's desire to claim stardom and power exclusively for himself.

"Clyde did not like James Brown," Wesley told me. "He didn't like how he treated his band or how he treated people. When Clyde turns against you, you can't talk him out of it. You can't say anything that'll make him change his mind." After I mentioned Frank's story about Clyde's first days in Madison, Fred said, "I never met Frank, but I could see Clyde going and hiding out at his brother's house and never wanting to see James Brown or play anything for James Brown again."

Clyde had stuck with Brown for six years, longer than any of Brown's drummers, except Jabo Starks. It was the most important gig of his life. It made him famous and paid well—when they were paid. For Clyde, who grew up in the segregated South in the 1950s, performing with Brown was worth the trade-off.

Until it wasn't.

19

It's All About the One

> Pinpointing the moment funk was born (or even where it came from) is about as difficult as explaining what exactly it is.[1]
> —**NATALIE WEINER**

"James Brown had several drummers onstage, but there was only one playing at any one time. Because of their feeling for certain types of tunes, Brown would have Jabo play some and Clyde play others. They mostly played solo when they were with Brown," explained drummer David Stanoch, a friend of Clyde's. Later in their lives Clyde and Jabo began playing gigs together.

Long after their time with Brown, Clyde and Jabo got together to talk about their respective styles in *Soul of the Funky Drummers*; Stubblefield and Starks each demonstrated their unique and different styles.

"James wanted you to play it harder on the One?" Harry Weinger asked Clyde.

"That's right," Stubblefield said. He called out "One," and demonstrated by hitting the bass drum on the first beat. "You always hit the One, dominate the One. That's the One that turns you around and gets you ready to go again."

Clyde agreed that his rhythm only became famous with "Funky Drummer" and that it had been sampled hundreds of times.

"Just to be clear," Weinger said, "what people need to understand is, so much of that comes from you improvising within a certain framework."

"Correct. A feeling I have for that type of a turn, you know? I put it all together," Stubblefield said, adding, "So that's it, that's the 'Funky

Drummer.'" Clyde then put it all together and played the rhythm that gave him the name the "Funky Drummer." Clyde laughed. And with a nonchalant air and a smile, said, "That's it."

Clyde described how the syncopation is similar and different in "I Got the Feelin'" and "Cold Sweat." "The bridge and my rhythm patterns are different, but it's just one small beat that makes it stand out from the 'Cold Sweat' beat. It's like the same beat drum pattern, but with a different lick on it . . . and the bass popping on different licks, it all turns around into a whole new thing."

While Clyde demonstrated the syncopation of "Mother Popcorn," Fred Thomas, a bass player with Brown, joined in. Weinger called it "incredibly funky." Then Clyde followed up with "Give It Up or Turnit a Loose." The song, said Weinger, "was the remake that [Clyde] did originally with Catfish and the Original JBs, where Clyde did a slight variation on the original version." Clyde noted that "the slight variation was a lick on the backbeat."

Stubblefield talked about how he and Starks's styles balanced each other onstage. "Jabo is gospel. He's got a gospel feeling and playing drummer, bluesy, jazzy, and funky all this in one. I was the dominant funk person. Jabo was the swing shuffle funk, so we both had different funk grooves. We would take the band forward. All the band members would follow us. We had to show we were the leaders of the band. Brown did not have a band like that until Jabo and I got with him."

Stark described what he heard Clyde doing and how they played differently.

"Clyde's foot is dominant while he's playing. I'm on top, I'm playing my foot, but I'm not as dominant and forceful as Clyde. So that's the difference in the playing—you don't lose the groove, but it's not as forceful."

Clyde explained why his foot was so important.

"I kept looking at the person up front, and at that moment my foot was [hitting the] one—1-2-3-4 [he hit the bass drum on the 1, counted 1, then played the rest of the drums].

"Jabo plays more of moving drums on top, I play more of a sturdy drum on top with a sturdier foot drive. So, he's more of a swing funk-type player [he moved his arms in a circular motion], and I'm more of a sturdy funk-type player [he moved in a solid up-and-down motion]."

Weinger asked Starks about the "sanctified feel [he used] to get that kind of a happy thing you get on the snare."

"It's a holiness feel. You've got that oomph going. It's still on the One though. You had to make that known."

Clyde agreed: "Right."

Clyde was always keeping his eyes on Brown while they were onstage. "Any moves [Brown and the other musicians] made, we tried to make it with them or whatever they needed to make their show be right. We didn't have to watch the guitar player, the bass player, or nothing like that. We're going with our stuff," Clyde said with a laugh.

Starks played with Bobby "Blue" Bland's band[2] before joining Brown's band, which brought a lighter touch than Stubblefield to Brown's band. Weinger asked Starks, "[So] what you do is never purely technical?"

"No. I think I am very basic in my setup and I'm traditional in my stick holding [underhanded with the left hand and overhand the right]," Starks explained. How Clyde played traditionally from his hi-hat to his snare, and he sits high above the drums and, Starks said, "plays from the top." Regarding his own style, Starks said he "doesn't try to emulate somebody else. The same thing about practicing."

Stubblefield said that when he played the drums, the rhythms "are not technical, they are from within." He didn't do a lot of rudimentary practicing, he added. It was important to "focus your mind; this is what I want to do, and it's not complicated because once you get the basic beat, it's as simple as 1-2-3-4. It's what you do in between the one and four [that creates the rhythm]."

Clyde played "pencil stick" [both hands on top of the sticks] and talked about how he and Starks would set up their drums in the same way, and how they were comfortable playing on each other's sets. He considered the most important things to be simplicity and comfort. "It's like getting into a car, putting on your seat belt, and adjusting your seat and mirror. When I set up my drums . . . I have everything in range where I don't have to do a lot of stretching," Clyde explained. Clyde always set up his own drums to his feel. "I have four cymbals, and everything comes from the basic [2/4] beat. Everything else comes from that."

Clyde compared the setup of his drums to being a cook. "It's like being a chef in the kitchen. You don't want to go over here and start some cooking, then go to the stove over there, and do something else. Everything is burning. But you keep everything in the area where you can do anything you want."

Clyde said he was always practicing. "I practice mentally—walking, thinking. When I sit down, I'm practicing. I don't have to have drumsticks in my hand. I'm constantly practicing. Talking to you, I'm practicing now. I'm hitting rhythms. I could be talking to you and rocking and I'm in a rhythm all the time I'm talking to you. I practice constantly without drums or drumsticks, and that's good for a young person to know. You don't have to have the instrument to practice, but you do have to have discipline within your mind, in yourself, to be able to practice without those instruments. Then you sit down and perform what you have thought about. That's the idea of playing drums or any instrument."

How Clyde and Starks put it all together, how they played and complemented each other—and how they changed the future and redefined funk, is described in *Soul of the Funky Drummers*. Clyde and Starks needed each other to complete their rhythmic patterns. In *Black Talk*, Ben Sidran writes, "It should be stressed that James Brown's screams and the two drummers he employed to generate an enormous rhythmic dynamism were more revolutionary than were his somewhat controversial lyrics which include 'I'm Black and I'm Proud' and 'I Don't Want Nobody to Give Me Nothing (Open The Door, I'll Get It Myself),' *especially* because they were not *recognized* as being revolutionary."[3]

And perhaps the most revolutionary aspect of all was how Clyde and Jabo worked and played music together.

"We're brothers," Starks said [of Clyde]. "That's the way that I look at it. It's a brotherly love." Stubblefield concurred. "Actually," he said, "we've never had an argument." The film ends with Starks saying: "We would like to thank all the musicians that worked with us today." Then Clyde: "Peace, love, and happiness and good health to everyone." Together, they say "Thank you."

20

"Clyde Leaves a Mark on Your Soul"

Fred Wesley learned to play big band music in Huntsville, Alabama, while in the 55th Army Band. Fred's real passion, however, was jazz. He wanted to make it big as a trombone player in the jazz world, but he didn't accomplish that until later in life. His career took the path of the many musical tributaries of the Delta, with the time he spent with Clyde in funk and soul.

Ray Charles's bandleader, Raymond Reed, was a friend of Fred's, and whenever they needed a trombone player, he was called on to fill in. Fred performed five gigs with Charles, who covered everything from R&B, soul, blues, gospel, jazz, country, and rock and roll. "We played gigs in Chicago, Washington, DC," Fred said. "And one in Alaska."

Wesley had other extensive musical collaborations. "The Count Basie gig was a fun gig for me because I learned to play big band music in the Army," he said. "Around ten years later, I received the call from Raymond to play with James Brown, who had originally hired me to play with Count Basie." Fred was with Brown in the '60s and early '70s, leaving for good in 1975.

In 1968, Brown asked Wesley to join his band. After Pee Wee Ellis left, Fred became Brown's musical director. And after leaving the Famous Flames, Fred furthered his funk career, playing with Bootsy Collins and George Clinton in Parliament-Funkadelic on the band's famous Mother Ship tour. In 1978, Fred joined the Count Basie Orchestra, returning to his roots in jazz, which was his passion. In 1988 he released his first jazz album, *To Someone.*

Wesley's journey included a stint with Van Morrison. Eventually, he formed his own group, the Fred Wesley Band, which has been together for thirty years. When I spoke to him from his home in South Carolina in 2021, he had a few shows scheduled on the road.

"It all stems from James Brown," Fred said of his career, "but I didn't want to play with him. I was studying and playing jazz and wanted to go with someone like Art Blakey, Art Silver, or even Ray Charles—someone I could improve my jazz playing with, but the gig came around to play in Brown's band. I had played in jazz sessions with Raymond Reed, a fine jazz trumpet player, and he remembered me. He called me and asked me whether I wanted to play with Brown. I said, 'I don't know.' Going with Brown was more about meeting Pee Wee and Maceo and all those great jazz players playing in Brown's band. So, I said 'OK, I'll do it for a little while.' But I also did it to get out of Mobile, Alabama, into a larger city where I could be discovered as a great jazz trombone player."

Fred first met Clyde in February 1968, soon after the release of "Cold Sweat." Clyde was "a bit of a star at that time," Fred said. "I always wanted to meet him and see what drummer played that funky beat. Clyde was a wonderful drummer and a great guy.

"Playing in the band with Clyde was a pleasure. Anytime I played a solo, Clyde was kicking me in my butt, and I'd have to be playing along with him. Maceo, Pee Wee, and I enjoyed playing in the band. Jabo admired Clyde, but, of course, he had a different style. But Clyde had a new style that was very good for him. He was a star.

"We used to say Clyde would keep big James dancing his little legs off. He could hold James in a strong dance style; Clyde kept James going. Many drummers would get tired—that's why [James] had Clyde. At one point, he had five drummers onstage. When I arrived, it was just him and Jabo. But Clyde could keep James going all night long. And he did.

"I left the band in 1970 and moved to California. But in '71, when I had almost starved myself and my family to death, Brown came to Los Angeles and asked me, 'Would you like to have your job back?' I went back, but he lied to me. He said Pee Wee and the rest of the band were coming back. But nobody came back. I had to come in with a brand-new band and do everything James Brown told me. I was a yes man. But it was to my benefit. I learned a lot—how to record and write music and songs from Brown. I stayed with him for an additional four years. My contribution was that I was James's yes man. He would tell me to do things. But Clyde wasn't with the band when I was the bandleader. Clyde left sometime in 1970. We remained friends, and we talked often."

Fred didn't have many opportunities to work with Clyde after he left Brown, but he told me, "I ran into him once in Madison, Wisconsin, and played with him when I was there. His band was a real funky band, and he had some local guys. It was a pleasure to sit in with Clyde in that funky groove again. I did some albums with him and wrote a tune for him called 'The Chick'n Pick'n.'"[1] (Fred played at Blue Monday gigs I regularly attended. I had probably seen them play together but didn't realize it at the time.)

I asked, "When you left the band and moved more into your version of jazz music, did you incorporate Clyde's groove into your jazz?"

"Of course!" Fred said. "Clyde leaves a mark on your soul. You'll never forget how he played, and I never will. He influenced most of my music. As far as drummers are concerned, anything he didn't influence, Jabo did. I will always remember Clyde because he was a dynamic drummer. One of a kind. I'm sure that all the funky drummers and all the sampling that has been done attest to the fact that he was the funky drummer. He wasn't just famous because of 'Cold Sweat,' but because he had a style that was all his own. All drummers study him to be viable. You must study Clyde Stubblefield to be a good drummer. He was a teacher, he taught me how to do it, and I learned well."

21

"The Only Thing in Life"

I was grateful to be able to interview Pee Wee Ellis in September 2019, two years before he passed away on September 23, 2021, in Dorset, England.

Ellis was a highly regarded, successful, world-renowned jazz saxophone musician before and after his time with the James Brown Band. "Pee Wee Ellis was a composer, arranger, saxophonist and keyboard player, bandleader, musical director, writer and arranger, a musician whose repertoire encompasses all manner of music from jazz through soul and funk to rock,"[1] writes Richard Williams in an obituary for Ellis. He served as the musical director for Brown's band from 1965 to 1969, when Clyde was one of the band's drummers. He was onstage at the Boston Garden in 1968, and he collaborated with Clyde with the King All-Stars and Cal Green in 2013. When I spoke with Ellis, he was at his home in the town of Frome, in Somerset County, England.

I began by asking him what he remembered about his time playing with Clyde.

"We were just working stiffs when we played with the James Brown Band," he said. "Clyde and I sometimes would hang out after gigs."

"When did you first meet?"

"When I joined the band in 1965. We became good friends, but we were busy and occupied with the work."

"What do you remember most about Clyde?"

"I didn't need to give him much instruction [when Ellis was the bandleader]. He was an extremely good musician, naturally gifted, and was able to pick up any music I presented to him. I could really depend on him. He had a natural talent. It was raw, from the heart."

"I always thought that without Clyde's rhythm and background beat, there wouldn't have been the James Brown funk. Is that correct?"

"That goes for several members of the band, including Maceo [Parker], the tenor, alto, and baritone saxophonist, and Bernard Odum, the bass guitar player. We were a tight unit. We played off each other and supported each other. Clyde was the backbone. We all depended on him for that steady beat."

I asked Ellis about the origins of modern funk. "Did that coalesce when Clyde started with the band? Did he bring that rhythm with him to the band?"

"Yes, he did."

"How do you see yours and Clyde's contribution to African American music history?"

"We helped to provide a platform for Afro-American music. I came into the James Brown band from a jazz background and had a twist on the music, which turned out to be a good thing."

"You infused your jazz into the funk music? You brought the essence of jazz into that music?"

"That's correct."

"I know there were musicians that didn't read music when you were the musical director. How did you transcribe and describe that music to the other musicians?"

"I talked to the other musicians," he explained. "Mostly one on one. I didn't have a formula. I taught their parts to them individually, then I taught them each the other musicians' parts. Everyone then knew what everyone's parts were. That way, they could depend on each other when they played."

"You wrote and played 'I'm Black and I'm Proud,' which had a huge effect on the Afro-American community. How do you feel about that?"

"I am proud to have been the catalyst for that to happen. I am happy that Clyde was there. He contributed a lot to that recording."

"How was it when in 2011 you did the concert Still Black, Still Proud, the African Tribute to James Brown?[2] Did it bring up old memories?"

"Yes, it did," he said with a laugh. "We created all that music so long ago and didn't think anything of it except that it was what we did at work. I had no idea it would still be popular today. It was an initial shock."

We ended our talk on that note, but Ellis contacted me a few days later.

He wrote, "Clyde was a good man, a good friend, and I'll always be grateful to have been there with him doing the work we did. There was precious little time for exploring details and specifics in a working situation that involved traveling and hurrying to the next gig. We had to make sure our shoes were shined, uniforms were pressed, and were ready for the daily rehearsal routine at five o'clock. I needed to be sure I had the music prepared for the day.

"When we had time, we worked on new musical pieces on the bus [which we did a lot], but mostly involved the guitars and bass players that didn't read music but had great intuition for the style. It was good that Clyde was there to provide the essence and essential part of the puzzle that we all relied on. That made my job easy. Knowing Clyde was there to do what he did best, by instinct, was a big relief when we had to get something ready for Mr. Brown for when he showed up. That was the normal way it worked. Get it ready for Mr. Brown, and then he'd add something or take something away, and we'd be on our way to another recording. It may have turned out to be a hit or just another string on our bow for an addition to the show. Afterward, the routine was to get ready for the show, get back on the bus, then off to another town. Then do it all over again. It was a way of life, and we did it like it was the only thing in life that was important."

Clyde was scheduled to go to Zambia and Nigeria with James Brown in December 1970. Clyde had a ticket but changed his mind at the airport at the last minute and decided to go to Detroit, according to Kathie Bowman, Clyde's manager for the last twenty years of his career.

"Why didn't he go to Africa with them?" I asked.

"Who knows why Clyde did anything," Bowman said.

Maybe he wanted to check out the Motown scene. I remembered Slim in Chattanooga telling me Clyde couldn't go back there after they were busted for "some substance" at a hotel, and he split town and didn't return for decades. Perhaps he couldn't legally leave the country during the trip to Zambia, or he thought he might get arrested at the airport. He did, however, travel to Vietnam with James Brown, most likely arranged through military channels and flights that provided clearance ahead of time. Clyde did mention how he had been to several other countries, so that part of the story is a mystery.

The journey of the Funky Drummer, the song and the man, began in March 1970, and in just over a year, Clyde reached his turning point. He turned his back on Mr. Brown—the Godfather of Soul—and on the song that gave him the title of Funky Drummer. The song would also become the backbone of hip-hop, leading ultimately to Clyde becoming, without compensation, the most sampled drummer in history.

Set Break

Two thousand miles I roam,
just to make Madison my home.

—**CLYDE STUBBLEFIELD**, to the tune of Otis Redding's "(Sittin' on) The Dock of the Bay"

So many roads I tell you
New York to San Francisco
All I want is one
To take me home

From the high road to the low
So many roads I know
So many roads—So many roads

—**JERRY GARCIA AND ROBERT HUNTER**

Set 3

Madison, Wisconsin

The Rhythms of His Time

22

Beyond the One

The Last Show

Dane County Coliseum, Madison, Wisconsin

> You can go through the whole roster of people who've played with JB and see what that association left them. For the most part, the answer is nothing. To come out from James's shadow, you had to have the vision to see where you wanted to go and the work ethic to get there.[1]
> —**MACEO PARKER**

James Brown and His Soul Review, with his powerhouse polyrhythmic funk duo of Clyde and Jabo, arrived at the Dane County Coliseum in Madison, Wisconsin, on July 8, 1969.[2] The band was at its apex, and these elite musicians had put the Famous Flames at the top of the funk charts. While in town, Clyde visited with his older brother and his family, who had settled in Madison, and enjoyed a taste of Madison's alluring summers, with its four lakes, art fairs, farmer's market, and spectacular sunsets.

Clyde's time in town, though, was short, and the grueling pace of the tour continued, causing further dissent among Brown's most successful band. The following spring, on March 9, 1970, most of the band was fired after a mutiny that had been building for years. Except for Jabo Starks, the entire band that propelled Brown to stardom was gone. Brown made it nearly impossible for his former band members to make it independently, controlling from the shadows and pulling the strings like a puppeteer.

Brown needed them. Even though Motown was prominent in the late 1960s, folk and rock music developed a strong foundation and profited from adopting musical styles and songs from Black musicians.

Journalist Chris Jancelewicz writes, "It wasn't out of the ordinary for a Black musician to be selected by a record company to come in and write some songs, then be given some paltry payment as the agents turned around and gave the song to a white musician."[3] Not only did Black musicians struggle with the racism of the late 1960s and early '70s in the music industry, but the same powers also used their influence behind the scenes to make sure Brown was the main supply of Black funk and soul to the music world. From all accounts, Brown sabotaged his hitmakers in a typically abusive dynamic, making sure people knew that, almost exclusively, he was the One, the sole name of Funk. He molded his world as meticulously as the shoes he polished as a child to a buffed shine on the streets. What could have resulted in independent success for his band members became a reformed James Brown band, the JBs, months after the mass firing.

The JBs were back in Madison on July 26, 1970. Clyde had returned to the band for a time a few months after his twenty-seventh birthday, playing the show at the Dane County Coliseum. That year, he would step into his new life. On Friday, July 26, the band repeated its finely crafted performance under the Coliseum dome that resembled a spaceship in the middle of an expansive grassy field. As the sun went down at 8:40 p.m. on one of the longest days of the year, the distinctive style of a high-intensity JB show was underway, with Brown's leaping and elaborate dance routines replete with splits and falling to his knees with a cape draped over him, as he had hundreds of times before, and emotionally pleading "Please, Please, Please." The horn players danced to their finely choreographed routines, with the usual dress code, most likely wearing their freshly pressed suits and ties, possibly tuxedos. A reporter with the *Wisconsin State Journal* wrote that Brown had with him a "troupe of dancers, a 21-piece orchestra with four drummers, two working and two standing by." The "working" drummers were Clyde and Jabo.[4]

Clyde may have promised Brown he would rejoin the band, but after the show, he retreated to his brother Frank's house. Many people who knew Clyde before and after his time with Brown told me they were unsure of the time frame of his departures. A poster from the Coliseum (now the Alliant Energy Center) and a small notice in the *Capital Times* announcing Brown's shows in 1969 and 1970 are the only remaining records. Nothing acknowledges who was with Brown. Fred Wesley said Clyde left prior to when the rest of the band was fired, which contradicts what was portrayed in the movie *Get On Up*, which shows Clyde throwing down his sticks and walking out with the group. Many of Clyde's close friends and bandmates in Madison did not know the exact date. Clyde rarely discussed his time with Brown.

What Clyde did in the later part of 1970 and early 1971, before he became an integral part of the Madison music scene, is a mystery. I like to think he spent the time relaxing, recuperating, focusing, and planning for his new life. Clyde had finally put his plan into effect. It seems that day in the hot summer of 1970 was Clyde's final show, but it is possible he played a few more in the coming year. One more short stint with Brown in 1971 and another departure would coincide with what Clyde's future bandmate and friend Joey Banks told me: Clyde left the band three times. His brother Frank told me, "Clyde hid out at my house. James Brown was so mad at him that he never spoke to him again."

He brought one item with him when Brown fired him. Clyde and Jabo made their own snare drums that Clyde painted when they went to Japan. His wife, Jody, said, "He grabbed the snare and took it with him. Inside of that drum is probably the earliest autograph of Clyde's, written in pencil it is signed the 'Funky Drumer,' with one 'm.'" Jody said she was the only one he would allow to correct his spelling. Bandmates have differing memories of events leading to Clyde standing at his brother's door, but everyone agreed Clyde did not discuss his past. Tom Strader told me, "At his tribute ceremony, Michael Feldman mumbled under his breath as he flung the question cards [as he would on his NPR Whad'ya Know radio show], but said it loud enough to be heard, 'I've known Clyde over twenty-seven years and never had one meaningful conversation.'"

Ben Sidran said, "He lived in the moment." When asked about James Brown, Clyde would reply, "James Who?"

Clyde left the abusive world that defined Brown's band for good. Settling in Madison helped him realize his creative dreams and cultivate a quieter life. He turned away from fame but regained his dignity and the chance to live his true self. The long days on the road, paychecks withheld or not given, lack of recognition for his contributions, and strict conformity in dress and musical styles, or the risk of being fined fell away.

He began playing music when and with whom he wanted, branching out into new genres—jazz, country, rock—while maintaining his blues and funk roots. He was able to come full circle to the innovative freedom from his beginnings on the musical streets of Chattanooga. But he still struggled financially, sometimes playing small gigs for five dollars a show. Clyde's influence, which many musicians refused to acknowledge, before and after Brown and the record companies that did not compensate his innovations and contributions, unfortunately remained unchanged. James Brown owned everything Clyde and the other members of the band created. Hip-hop never recognized until much later that Stubblefield laid the foundation for its whole genre of music.

But he maintained a positive attitude and began anew in an extreme climate, a place where the years of struggle in Brown's band, like the thawing of the lakes surrounding Madison in the spring, had the chance to melt away. Clyde spent his first official night in the Madison area at his brother's house in DeForest, a small town fifteen miles north of the city. I can picture Frank bringing drinks to the porch as they toasted a new horizon in the sweltering heat of a Midwest night. They may have said few words, but I imagine his newly cultivated freedom commemorated with a click of beers or a joint and a shared farewell to Clyde's many years on the road. A hopeful nod to something new, shining from within, guiding, illuminating a path in the capital city, that would stretch out over forty-six years.

Madison's seasons come with extreme changes: the array of colors in autumn leaves, the freezing rain, blizzards, tornados, thunderstorms, budding flowers, humidity, snow, and ice, and, of course, the temperatures ranging from below zero to sweltering heat. All of these can be transformative. One's thoughts, feelings, hopes, and memories can change their hues and then fall away just as the leaves break down and nourish the earth. There is hope for a new beginning, a promise renews as the snow melts in spring when the air becomes lighter. A walk in a field of blooming lilac trees ranging from white, lavender, deep purple, and blue, and the changing autumn colors of browns, reds, oranges, and pink can transform perspective, forming almost silent sounds in the air like Clyde's barely heard ghost notes. Just as Clyde's music career and genres were changing, perhaps the seasons helped him move past his years with James Brown and his memories of growing up in poverty as a Black child in the 1940s South. But in some respects, the past is always present, and some things never change.

Madison is a small northern city, a capital with a state university in a state known for forests, rivers, radical politics, cheese, and football. Here, famous musicians lived inconspicuous, everyday lives. The city became a haven for musicians who wanted to get away from the big-city blues scene of Chicago. In Madison, you could have a less hectic life, play your music, and go on tour, but be anonymous if you wish. Clyde joined this exclusive group, which included jazz musician Ben Sidran; blues master Luther Allison, who had a club named for him after he died; and Roscoe Mitchell from the Art Ensemble of Chicago, who focused on avant-garde, free jazz, and atonal music. Roscoe was virtually unknown in Madison but famous around the world. He had moved from Chicago and lived outside Madison but frequently visited and played gigs there and was a friend of my next-door neighbor Primous Fountain, a world-class composer. They routinely played in local clubs around town.

Wisconsin's history is rich and complicated. Equidistant between Lake Mendota and Lake Monona, in the narrowest part of the isthmus, at the corner of Madison's Capitol Square, stands the statue of Lady Forward, symbolizing the Wisconsin state motto (one word: "Forward") and the progressive political movements of Wisconsin. Around a thousand years prior, Native Americans built earthen mounds in the shapes of animals, birds, reptiles, and water spirits. Across the lake from the Capitol is the largest effigy mound in the world, constructed by the Woodland Indians,[5] a bird with a wingspan of 624 feet whose body stretches 131 feet long. Three to four feet high, the bird rises from the ground of Mendota Mental Health Institute on the northeast side of Madison, just miles from where Clyde spent his early years in town. Clyde embraced the motto of moving forward and the freedom of flight and shelter of the giant bird's wings as he navigated into a new phase of his life.

In the early days of the 1970s, Clyde followed his own North Star to independence and freedom. His musical future, along with playing with Sidran and Allison, included Joey Banks, a blues player, and the Tex-Mex band Cris Plata and Extra Hot, which included Plata's wife, Ann, a bass player. Clyde was a staple with Blue Monday, a weekly residency he maintained for decades.

In that small dark club, a half block from the Capitol at the Chamber on King Street and across from the refurbished Majestic Theater, I first heard Clyde lay down his rhythms that captivated me as I sat on a barstool ten feet away. There were never many people there, but he played as if thousands were listening. He was a regular on Michael Feldman's nationally syndicated *Whad'ya Know?* show on NPR Wisconsin Public Radio from the early 1990s to 2015. The show's band featured Clyde on drums, John Thulin on piano, and bassists Jeffry Eckels (1987–2003) and Jeff Hamann (2003–16). He eventually reconnected with people from his past from the James Brown band and his days in Chattanooga. The seasons passed, and the years and decades circled around Clyde in Mad City, as it is jokingly and affectionately called.

Madison's art and music scenes thrived in the 1970s. The capital city did not know that their newest citizen, a humble, kind, friendly, and talented force of the music world, was quietly settling in their midst. He would bring new meaning to its predictable seasonal groove. Over the next four decades, Clyde would infuse his contributions to African American music into the backbeat of Madison. Many years later, Stubblefield told Sidran, "You and I brought R&B to southcentral Wisconsin. There was none there. We invented that."[6] Ben said Clyde felt it was the most important contribution he made, and that Clyde was prouder of bringing R&B there than his work with Brown. In the early '70s, Clyde had a more disciplined style of drumming, reflective of the rigid rules and performance style of Brown. As the seasons and years rolled on, his music became varied, free, jamming, and more . . . Clyde.

Stubblefield was in the vanguard, creating the revolution of funk music. As the seasons rolled on, his musical styles diverged, but the steady beats of his rhythms remained the same. During his years in Madison, he embraced his roots through the styles of music that sprang from the tributaries of the Delta—rhythm and blues, jazz, blues, Tex-Mex, folk, country, rock and roll, and, of course, funk. Funk's steady beat was held together by the ripples of American music, with branches woven from the waters and ghost notes of the past. Clyde's tapestry became a creative mix of his unique drumming styles.

His polyrhythms and those that "landed on the One" would become as recognizable to his listeners as the seasonal changes were to everyone who lived in those climates. Like the stretched-out wings of the giant bird constructed of rich Wisconsin soil, Clyde's new home state reached out to the Funky Drummer over the next forty-eight years. The cyclical groove that settles in the bones of an upper Midwesterner is as quickly felt as a heartbeat and as steady as those landing on Clyde's drumheads in syncopated time.

Madison: Early Days

Along the shore of Lake Monona in the capital city stands a plaque dedicated to Otis Redding. On December 10, 1967, Redding's plane crashed into an icy Lake Monona, not a mile from where I first heard Clyde play. Clyde had the opportunity to continue playing with Otis before he joined Brown's band. If he had he may well have been on that plane. Years later, Clyde would sing "(Sittin' on) The Dock of the Bay," and change the line to, "Two thousand miles I roam, just to make Madison my home."

During Clyde's tenure at the Chamber, later renamed the King Club, he played on Blue Mondays with Luther Allison, an internationally renowned guitarist. They played blues, electric blues, Chicago blues, and blues-funk. Clyde and Luther were friends and collaborators, and both lived in and around Madison for many years.

During the years after the Chamber closed in 1996 and before the King Club opened in the same space in 2000, Clyde played Mondays at O'Cayz Corral and at the Crystal Corner Bar on Williamson Street. Ironically, a hip-hop nightclub called Mass Appeal was in the same location at 114 King Street and was open from 1996 to 2000, sandwiched between when the Chamber closed and the King Club opened, promoting the very music Clyde's unacknowledged rhythms were sampled from.

Clyde and Jabo Starks reunited in Madison in 2000, forming a new group called The FunkMasters. On Friday, March 10, 2000, they appeared together at the Club Tavern in Middleton. Tickets were only seven dollars at the door. Later that month they recorded together at Smart Studios, with Ben Sidran helping with production.[7]

Clyde mainly played his music in Madison, but he occasionally traveled around the country and abroad. Madison, a predominately white city, the capital of the Dairy State, wasn't a place to make a great living as an African American drummer. Despite that, Clyde was happy living in his adopted home and developed an appreciative and dedicated following.

Like everyone living in the northern Midwest climate, Clyde struggled with long and freezing Wisconsin winters, trying to stay warm, shoveling snow, and keeping his car from breaking down. He left behind the craziness of the road and Brown's band, but survival was hard. He settled into domestic life. He had been married twice before he met Jody Hannon, with whom he spent his final twenty-five years. He was surrounded in town by his brother, nieces, and nephews. An adult son whom Clyde did not know about, James "Dewney" Stubblefield," showed up at his door one day. James sadly passed away before Clyde.

23

Madison Music

Ben Sidran, Joey Banks, Cris Plata

Clyde's musical journey branched out to include the music genres of jazz, blues, rock, Tex-Mex, and country during the time he lived in Madison. In doing so he brought the tributaries of Delta music North. In the coming decades, he would play music with just about every musician who resided in and around Madison.

Funk Meets Jazz: Clyde and Ben

Clyde met Ben Sidran at the Jazz Workshop in downtown Madison on State Street, the mile-long street that connects the Capitol to the university. Ben said the Workshop was a place that alternated between being a strip club and a jazz club. When it was a jazz club, the strippers worked as waitresses.[1] Approximately a year after Clyde arrived in Madison in 1971, Ben fondly remembers a night when a man walked into the Workshop; his first impression of Clyde was seeing his warm smile. That night, jazz met funk, and it didn't take long before Clyde and Ben were playing music together. They forged a musical collaboration and friendship that lasted for the next forty-six years. Every Monday night at the Nitty Gritty, between 1972 and 1976, the two men, along with Curly Cooke (guitar) and Gary Zappa (bass), jammed for entire sets and laid down grooves laced with jazz. When Ben and Clyde played, the dance floor was inevitably crowded. Looking back, Ben said "it wasn't about money or record gigs but the feeling in the room."[2] The Gritty, as it is still called, is a bar popular with locals and university students. It has a rich history,[3] and among those who have performed there are Muddy

Waters, B. B. King, Bonnie Raitt, Charlie Musselwhite, and Buddy Guy. In 1970, Jefferson Airplane played a four-hour jam at the club with the Luther Allison Blues Band. Many years later, I heard Luther's soulful blues mix with Clyde's funky rhythms at the Chamber.

Between 1977 and 1979, with a slight variation of band members from the Gritty, Ben Sidran and Clyde held a weekly gig at La Creperie, a small French bistro on State Street. On the street below, the students, politicians, and seasons passed by. Wherever they played around town, the crowds were small and no one made much money. Luckily, Madison was an easy place to live in the 1970s. There were plenty of co-ops of all kinds—housing, food, health, and even mechanics' co-ops, the result of the city's radical/progressive atmosphere. Rents were low, and people didn't care much about fame, fortune, or putting on airs. Many people dropped out of college, worked at low-paying jobs, and got by, later returning to finish school.

During those years, in 1997, for example, after the Chamber closed and before the King Club opened, Clyde played on Mondays at O'Cayz Corral, on Thursdays at the Club Tavern, and on Sundays at the Crystal Corner Bar on Williamson Street.

Joey Banks

Clyde settled in a primarily white Wisconsin community where Joey Banks, an African American musician, was raised. Joey began attending music jams where he filled in and drummed with various bands in town from the time he was a teenager. "Clyde didn't have a problem establishing himself as a musician," Joey said. "I only know my relationship with him, and I can speak about his relationship with the community of Madison because I grew up here—I'm part of that community."

Joey was fifteen when he first met Clyde at a jam at Morgan's nightclub, which he frequented, along with the Club de Wash. Joey told me, "When I went to Paul Black's Monday jam at the Club de Wash, people knew me not as a musician but as a young kid that could play, and they let me. Those were the two places where I started integrating into the Madison community. I met Clyde around three years after he settled in Madison," around 1973.

Joey continued, "Clyde never got the money he deserved for his talent and reputation. If somebody asked him to play a gig or get his band together, he would do it and then negotiate the money later. He wasn't a good businessman. Clyde would play for a joint and a chicken sandwich. He would be at a party, hang out, and play. If he received one hundred dollars, he would be OK with that. In the long term, that ended up hurting him." That reminded me of Slim saying that, in Clyde's early days in Chattanooga, money was not their primary goal, that they just enjoyed playing. I believe Clyde carried those memories with him. Mostly in Madison, it was true that you could get by and live a good life without much money. But as the years went on, it was not as easy.

Joey elaborated, "It is the story of his life that he would always say yes. He was in party mode—sometimes, the party was more important than the money. That's the kind of person he was." Kathie Williams became his manager in December 1999 and took over securing gigs and proper payment for his musicianship.

"Fast-forward," Joey continued, "to 2014 to when Clyde had health issues. People offered ridiculous amounts of money, not in a good way. They would offer him five hundred dollars for a show, which was low. I think it's because his reputation was he would work for nothing. He was nationally and internationally known, living in this small music community [that was in] some ways oversaturated. Playing every Monday didn't help him locally because who would come to see you on a Saturday and pay more if they can see you for five dollars on Monday at the King Club?"

Clyde enjoyed working with Joey's drum students in the Black Star Drum Line Joey formed in 2008. "Clyde supported my drum students," Joey said, "and put together refurbished drum kits for kids that didn't have them so they could take drum lessons." Their website states their goal: "To give kids (ages 9–18) in the Madison community an opportunity for creative expression through the 'Percussive Arts,' Director Joey B. Banks incorporates diversity, respect for self and others, unity, and mastery as the core elements of the youth development model."[4] Joey and Clyde began that together and Joey continued the tradition. "He enjoyed being around the kids. I wrote the funky drum line piece based on the 'Funky Drummer' that's, of course, his influence." Joey brought his drum students together yearly to perform with Clyde and the Madison Blues All-Stars. He also brought his students down to Funky Mondays. "I teach my kids Clyde's funk segment, so he is going to live on forever. I'm teaching my students how to play Clyde's beats."

Clyde and Cris Plata: Extra Hot

Several avenues of music flourished from the funk Stubblefield brought with him to the northern capital city, infusing funk into the backbeat of genres that one wouldn't associate together. Country shows and talent competitions are not places one would imagine seeing the world-renowned funk drummer who played behind the King of Soul, but that was part of Clyde's world when Clyde met Cris Plata in the late fall of 1988. Clyde was playing music around town with whoever he could. He played with an R&B group called Blume and for seven years was a member of Marcy and the Highlights, a "variety dance band."[5] He also had an R&B band, Clyde Stubblefield and the Motown Players.

But that wasn't all. Clyde became a longtime member of Cris Plata's Tex-Mex country music band and was an intricate part of all Plata's albums. Early in the band's career, while on a trip to Texas, the band was reading aloud road signs, trying to come up with a name for the band. One of the musicians yelled out, "Flash flood, turn around, don't drown." But Clyde said, "I'm not going to play with you if you call yourself Flash Flood. It sounds like you should be Johnny Rodriguez and the Flash Flood." Plata then said, "OK, smarty-pants, what should I call my group?" Clyde took a dramatic pause and replied, "Extra Hot." Plata said, "OK, like hot sauce, I'm good with that." So, the band became Cris Plata and Extra Hot.

"Clyde played with Tina and the Tigers, a pop revue, in his early days in Madison. Clyde hit the drum with tremendous power, playing syncopated beats with his right foot.[6] It was extraordinary.[7] His right side on the kick drum was phenomenal. I've never seen anybody that could keep time and play those syncopated beats simultaneously," Plata said.

As the years passed, Clyde's shift from funk to folk and country Tex-Mex music was as seamless as his drum grooves. Plata told me, "I heard Clyde playing when I was a teenager listening to James Brown's recordings but didn't realize who he was. Nobody gave credit on the album jackets to the band members, just James Brown. I knew his rhythms from listening to the radio, almost through osmosis. Many years later, I read an article in the Madison paper that Clyde was playing in a country band. My music tends to be folk and country folk and has a lot of different influences. I needed a drummer for my work and someone with experience in the studio."

Cris went to see Clyde play at McGovern's bar in 1987, in Sun Prairie (fifteen miles northeast of Madison), and was completely knocked out. "It was some of the finest country drumming I ever heard. After the show, I introduced myself. Being from the South, I was taught to introduce myself with a proper greeting of 'Sir,' and treat a person with respect. That always impressed Clyde. I told him, 'I have a project I am working on, and if you would be interested, I'd like to hire you as a studio drummer.'

"Clyde was gregarious. 'Yeah,' he said to me, 'you got it.' I asked him, do you want to talk about money? 'No,' he said, 'we'll talk about it when we get together.' I said, 'There are different styles of music that I'm playing. It's all country; there's no funk in it.' I didn't know anything about funk music and asked him, 'Would you be willing to run through the songs as a rehearsal at your house? I can come over, and my wife will bring her bass. I want you to have an idea of the material and what you think needs to happen.' He said, 'Great, come on over on Sunday.' That was two days after I saw him at the club Friday night."

Clyde gave Plata his address and showed up Sunday morning as arranged. He went to the door and knocked several times with no answer. He told me, "I rang the doorbell many times, and I was getting frustrated. My wife Ann was with me and said, 'Maybe he's still asleep.' I heard some rustling, and the door opened a crack. A white guy with long hair and a beard said, 'What do you want?' 'Is Clyde Stubblefield here?' I asked. He said, 'No, he lives here but isn't here now. He's playing up North somewhere.' I said, 'OK, is he going to be back today?' 'No, he won't be back until the middle of the week.' I told him to tell Clyde that Cris Plata was here for the rehearsal we had agreed on. He said, 'OK.' So, we're walking away, and I'm furious."

Plata had told Clyde he would compensate him for rehearsal time, and on the way home he told Ann, "I'm just going to call another drummer if he can't keep the appointment we agreed on." Ann said, "Give him a chance. Maybe he forgot about it." Cris said, "No, no." And she said, "Just give him a chance."

"So, in the middle of the week, [Clyde] called very apologetically and said, 'I forgot all about it, buddy. I'll meet you at the studio, and we can play.' I thought, 'You have never heard the song, and will you meet me there?' But I said, 'OK, that's fine.' That was my first encounter with him. I always kidded him and said I should have gone with my instincts, not listened to my wife, and not played with him. We always kidded each other like that." Clyde played on every album Cris made. His final album was 2015's *Migration Road.* By that time, he already had his thumb and pointing finger amputated. Clyde was only able to play tambourines and sticks. "I had him on every recording of mine, [*Spreading the Rumor, Fresh Horses, Ziggy Dreams in Color, Life is Hard*], and on every project except the last one [*Migration Road*], Clyde played drums," Plata said.

Plata spoke about how they became like brothers. He said there were similarities between his growing up in South Texas and Clyde in Chattanooga, and both of them being nonwhite musicians in Madison in the Dairy State. He said they would warn each other about certain people to watch out for. He said, "We would broach the subject when we would play gigs and could tell someone had something against you strictly due to your skin color. As a minority, you always had your radar on, and if we got a vibe from someone, nine times out of ten times, it was accurate; a person looking for some way to either put you down, argue, or start a fight. We also talked about our backgrounds causing us problems."

Even so, Plata said, "Clyde would put everybody at ease. After a while, even my mother-in-law, who tended not to like Black people, was charmed by Clyde. She eventually referred to him as 'my black son.' He could win over almost anyone, even if they did not usually associate with a person of color."

Smart Studios

Clyde's integration into the Madison music scene continued when Butch Vig of Garbage needed some new rhythms for some of the albums he was producing at his Smart Studios in Madison. Butch Vig and Steve Marker met in an electronic music class at the University of Wisconsin during the 1980s. "When I first met Steve, he had a four-track," Vig said in the documentary *The Smart Studios Story.* "Before we would start recording, we'd go downtown to the Plaza Bar [affectionately called the Za by locals] and buy these dirt-cheap pitchers of beer and drink until bar time"—last call for drinks, fifteen minutes before closing. "We'd look at each other and say, 'Let's get smart.' We'd go back to Dave's apartment, plug in guitars and drums, and start rocking on [his] four-track until the sun came up. Neither Steve nor I were very proud of the fact that that is where we got our name."[8]

And that's how Smart Studios came to be. Back then, in 1983, the studio's original goal was to produce local bands, and as it grew, it amassed a wealth of musical history. It survived and prospered for over three decades. Vig said they were "trying to figure things out initially by the seat of [their] pants. We just wanted to have a place to hang out. We were working twelve to thirteen hours, then going to the Crystal Corner [a local bar], have a few beers, and say, 'Let's go back to the studio.'"[9]

The first home of Smart Studios was the Gisholdt Building, a giant warehouse built in the early 1900s. Vig and Marker rented a 900-square-foot studio, leaving a thousand egg crates superglued to the wall when they vacated after a thirty-day notice. The Gisholdt was an early manufacturing building kitty-corner from Smart's eventual home at 1254 E. Washington, on the corner of N. Baldwin Street, thirteen blocks east of the Capitol dome. Vig called it "one damn ugly-looking building."[10]

The studio became legendary in Madison, eventually developing an international reputation in 1991 when it recorded one of the all-time best-selling records,[11] Nirvana's *Nevermind*. Vig and Marker soon formed the band Garbage, and their first album came out in 1995.

Vig was filling his studio nonstop during the 1990s with punk musicians. Inside, the building was "just another Midwestern factory or warehouse left behind by the economic decline of the 1980s."[12] Meanwhile, outside the red brick walls, the Madison music scene was rolling along as if Kurt Cobain had never stepped foot in town. Blues, jazz, R&B, and R&R continued along their low-keyed path with quality-filled musicians having fun and creating music with each other.

Stubblefield worked with several Madison musicians recording at Smart Studios throughout the years, including Vig on Garbage's first album, *Garbage*. David Stanoch said, "Wally [Ingram] and I did session work at Smart Studios with Butch Vig on Garbage in Madison. There were a couple of tunes Clyde played on [cuts 2 and 5, "Queer" and "Not My Idea"]. Butch realized those tunes would work well with a groove like the Funky Drummer sample, but Butch said, 'You don't use the sample when the genius who played the sample lives down the street from you.'"[13] Stanoch said, "That's Butch for you, so Clyde got paid, and that's not a sample; that's Clyde tracking for Butch."

Along with Vig, Clyde collaborated at Smart with Ben Sidran and his son Leo. They produced *Clyde Stubblefield: The Original*, released in 2003, with Clyde's original R&B, jazz, funk, and hip-hop rhythms and with Nardis, Ben's band (a Miles Davis song and record label—and Sidran spelled backward), playing grooves and tunes.

Clyde played on *Fresh Horses*, Cris and Ann Plata's first album for their band, Cris Plata and Extra Hot. That was his first recording session with Clyde inside that "ugly" brick building. "One of the lucky breaks I caught," Plata said, "was in my first-ever recording session working with Bryan David and Butch Vig, owners of Smart. I was producing my album the day I recorded with Clyde, but Butch might as well have been. He had the drums set up for Clyde." Cris didn't know anything about Clyde's playing style other than the night he offered him work in Sun Prairie. "The winter before, I hired a bass player. Ann played a little guitar before we dated, and at a recording session in late 1988, Butch isolated the bass to work on the tone, and Ann asked him about the sound. She liked it and said, 'I'm going to buy a bass guitar and learn to play it.' I taught her a few Mexican guitar runs, and she went to a local music store, Ward-Brodt, to take a few lessons." Ann took a half-dozen music lessons with John Tubbs and wrote a chart for one of Cris's compositions, "El Pueblo De Mi Corazon" ("The City of My Heart").

When Plata was ready to record his first album, he went to the UW Music School to hire a bass player he had heard of. But Plata couldn't afford his rates, so when he got home, he told Ann, "You're my bass player." She said, "What?" "Yes," he told her, "You're going to play in the session with me." "I don't know anything," she said. He told her she'd be fine.

"When we showed up at the studio, Clyde was already there." They recorded for five days in July 1989. On the first day, July 17, the temperatures outside were what is referred to as a typical "if you don't like the weather, wait ten minutes" type of day, ranging from 56 to 88 degrees on a rainless summer day. "We walked in, and Clyde nonchalantly walked over to Ann and said, 'This first song we're doing, is it a shuffle?' Ann looked at him and said, 'What's a shuffle?' She wasn't kidding. Clyde looked at her with this puzzled look. He turned around, looked at me, and said, 'Oh, OK.' It didn't faze him. We ran through the song once, and he looked at me and said, 'I got it.' I said, 'OK, let's roll the tape,' and he came up with this amazing drum pattern after hearing the song once. I was so inspired by that and thought, *this is easy*. That was my first collaboration with Clyde—it was memorable. He could hear the progression once and know what the song needed. He had never played Mexican folk music before and nailed it the first time.

"Clyde's beat was phenomenal. After our session, he said to Ann, 'You're a pretty good bass player.' Ann responded, 'I just started playing.' He said, 'Really?' The one thing that Ann laments about is that he ruined her for other drummers. When your first experience playing in a rhythm section is with a world-class drummer. . . ."

I finished the sentence: "It's hard to work with anyone else."

"Yes, it is! Ann grew up in the '60s when many people were into the Beatles and other rock and roll. Ann was a farm girl from Columbus, Wisconsin, but a big Motown fan. Motown had a world-class bass player—James Jamerson. He played with the famed Funk Brothers[14] Motown recording house band. She liked his groove. That was what Clyde was all about. Ann and Clyde were groove players, and they hit it off. Ann kept the groove going, and Clyde could be creative in finding more intricate and creative drum patterns.

"Clyde liked to give people nicknames. We were in the studio, and Ann was moving things around. He said, 'Just relax, Ann. I'm going to call you Aunt Bee from Mayberry.' From that time on, he always called her Aunt Bee. He'd tell her, 'That's what I like about you, Aunt Bee, I can go off into outer space, and then when I need to come back on the One, there you are.'

"Those two were like peas in a pod. When you're playing in a rhythm section as a bass player just starting, and the first person you play a session with is Clyde Stubblefield, it sets the stage. Every time she played in gigs with him was a learning experience. She said she got her musical education playing gigs in real-time with Clyde." Cris played a gig with Clyde at the Wisconsin State Fair in 1993 in West Allis, Wisconsin. "We were on the line-up before Lee Roy Parnell, a big country act.[15] He was backstage after the end of the last set we did and said to me, 'Is that Clyde Stubblefield?' I said, 'Yes, that's him.' He said, 'Wow, can I meet him?' I said, 'Come on over.'" His whole band surrounded Clyde. They said, "We were just listening to you on our stereo system on these James Brown songs." He was immensely tickled about that. After that encounter, Lee Roy and Clyde stayed in touch.

"Clyde could take any group or musician and elevate them by his musicianship. He'd inspire you to play the music you didn't believe you could play. You'd play something, reverse it, and practice it repeatedly, but you wanted to do better with him lifting you up. That was the special quality he had. I've never played with another drummer that could do that. I'd play something, and he'd say, 'Try doing this.'

"After we stopped playing together, I'd rehearse with other drummers, and they'd want to rehearse dynamics. And I'd say, with a puzzled look, 'Rehearse dynamics?' And they would say, 'You know, if we get to this section and want to slow it down.' With Clyde, I'd look at him and nod my head and play softer, and he would play softer. We would never have to rehearse dynamics."

Cris would rehearse, but Clyde would just show up at a gig. "He taught me you don't need to rehearse if you are a world-class player. The thing with Clyde was he hated to rehearse. [I remember him telling me he always kept his drums in his car, so he would have them ready for a gig, and that he didn't rehearse.] I'd ask him if he wanted to, and he'd say, 'No, I don't have time for that. When you play music, it's like having a conversation with somebody. Do you rehearse your conversations with people before you talk to them? When we're playing music, we're talking to each other, but with instruments. If you say something, then I say something, you say something, and I say something. With my foot, I got the bass player; with my hi-hat, I got the guitar player; with my tom, I got the keyboard player. And that's how I do it. I can play with everyone.'"

Cris continued, "Clyde said the newness wears off if you rehearse too much. It might be polished and tight, but it sounds rehearsed. It's like having a jazz background and having a rough outline of a song, then it goes wherever you take it, and Clyde would follow you. If I wanted to go in a different direction, you could call each other back by listening to each other. I learned from him to listen closely to the other band members.

"As a folk musician, I was mostly by myself. I didn't have much rhythmic training, so it wasn't easy to learn to play with a drummer, but not with Clyde. I didn't have to pay attention to what the drummer was doing with Clyde because he listened and complimented what I was playing. He inspired and taught me about funk musicianship, and after a while, I enjoyed playing funk. If I played a [funk] lick on a guitar, he would hear and add to it, egging me on to do it again, and then he would do something else. It was fun. Sometimes he would go out in outer space, and you would get lost and just be hanging on by the skin of your teeth.

"In all the years I played with Clyde, he never actually played my songs the same way. He told me he liked playing with me. He told me, 'You're not afraid to play original material. A lot of the bands I play with only play copy tunes.' He called covers copy tunes. He said, 'That's all they do. They are afraid even to play one of their original songs.' I told Clyde I'm a songwriter; if I don't do my songs, nobody else will play them. He wanted to play the music that he or anyone hadn't played before.

"One time, I told him what he was playing at a show was such a cool drum pattern. He said, 'Yeah, just stop talking about it.' Clyde didn't like me to say, 'Wow, you are great,' or go on about his playing. He wanted me to lead the band and be myself because he always told me, 'You are the show. We're here to make you sound good and groove!'

"He didn't like people fawning over him. That struck me as funny. Many musicians I know are egotistical and love it when you go on and on about how great they are. But he wasn't that way; it was all about the groove to him. That's all he wanted was the groove."

Drum Fill: The Kitchen

The one song Clyde Stubblefield wrote in his career, "Party's in the Kitchen," was recorded on the album *Revenge of the Funky Drummer*,[16] released seven years after the "Funky Drummer" loop hit its height as the foundation for hip-hop. In writing it, Clyde may have had in mind his analogy comparing how he set up his drums to being a cook.

The kitchen is a recurring theme in African American music history. Robert Johnson recorded "Come on in My Kitchen" on the *King of the Delta Blues Singers* in 1937 on Vocalion Records. Johnson sings the lyrics, "You better come on in my kitchen. It's goin' to be rainin' outdoors."[17] Dr. Kelley Fanto Deetz, director of education at Stratford Hall Plantation in Virginia, explained the importance of the kitchen to me: "The plantation kitchens were absolutely spaces for gossip and the transmission of news from around the country. The kitchens were the crossroads between the enslaved and free communities, and *everyone* passed through those spaces." She continued, "Evidence is seen in so many casual references to folks hanging out in kitchens. I can't think of a smoking gun source, or quote, but after reading hundreds of slave narratives and diaries of white plantation owners, the kitchens were absolutely ground zero for information."

In fact, Clyde, who famously never gave drum lessons, gave me my only "lesson" as I sat in his kitchen on the far east side of Madison. He taught me the two against three rhythm demonstrating, "You hit two in one hand to every three that you make with the other hand, that's what forms the rhythm."

24

"A Life Lesson"

John Medeski learned some life lessons from Clyde when, in mid-September 1998, Clyde joined John Scofield and the band Medeski, Martin, & Wood on a two-week, ten-show tour of the East Coast, traveling to New York, Vermont, Maine, Massachusetts, Connecticut, and New Jersey. Billy Martin, their drummer, was on family leave having his first child and they asked Clyde to join the tour. Wally Ingram had introduced John and Clyde at Alpine Valley, in East Troy, Wisconsin, during the Horizons of Rock Developing Everywhere (HORDE) tour the previous summer, and John asked Clyde to join the Medeski, Martin, & Wood (MMW) tour.

But Clyde made MMW wait an extra day. David Stanoch was producing a record in Madison, and Clyde was scheduled to play on it the day he was to join the tour. Stanoch said, "We were scheduled to record Katy's album. Clyde said he told MMW, 'Nope, I can't come until the day after because I told Davey I was going to play on Katy's record.' He honored the date and then took off. I adored him for that, he was that kind of a guy.

"Everything about working with Clyde was amazing. First of all, he's Clyde. Playing with an original was great; he played who he was," Stanoch said. This echoed Ben Sidran: "He lived in his skin." Medeski said, "Clyde had a powerful impact on the people he played with. To be onstage with him every night was the same as studying with a teacher." Which echoed Ann Plata's saying playing bass with Clyde onstage was an education in playing and performing.

John continued, "One of Clyde's main attributes is that he was one of the sweetest, light-filled people I've ever been on the road with. I saw him in the morning and late at night, checking into hotels and various life situations. The road can bring out the worst in people, but he was always a beam of sunshine. It didn't matter what time it was or what was going on. The way he treated people was unbelievable.

"More than the music, what I learned from him was a life lesson. I loved the music, of course, but seeing and playing with a musician who was also a great person was amazing. He was a very evolved human being. I think that's why he had feuds with James Brown, who was not the nicest person. Clyde was beautiful; he had a beautiful heart, soul, and spirit. He made everyone feel good, and his drumming made you feel good. He was solid. He taught me that you could treat people well and make others feel good, that there is no reason not to be nice to people."

John didn't remember when he hadn't listened to Brown's music. "I wasn't aware of Clyde living in Madison and doing his Monday night gig until a short time before we played together. John Scofield, Billy Martin, and I recorded an album just before the 1998 tour. It was right after our record *A Go Go* came out that same year. We did one gig with Billy, went to Europe, then toured in the United States with Clyde. It was an incredible opportunity, and I was excited to be playing with Clyde Stubblefield."

John thought there was probably some bootleg live recordings from the tour, but he doesn't keep up with his recordings because, he told me, he doesn't like to listen to himself. "The tour was short but amazing and memorable, and afterward, Clyde would sit in with MMW when we were in Madison." One of those times, a few months after the tour, in November 1998, I was at their show at the Barrymore Theater, a refurbished movie theater on the east side, built in 1929, with an old black ceiling full of holes of shining lights simulating stars in the night sky.

John talked about Clyde's ability to let things go and move on. He taught John acceptance. "The expression Clyde shared with us was when stuff gets bad, if it's not working: 'Fuck it.' He'd portray this concept in a deep, profound way, that it's just not worth it, saying, let go. If you read Buddhist or more ancient spiritual versions of that concept, that is what they would be saying."

"Don't hold on, let go, be in the moment."

"Yes! All those catchphrases of humility, acceptance, openness, and receptivity. Clyde's way of saying that was 'Fuck it.' He was that way. I loved him, he was very deep. It was one of my greatest experiences to know and play music with him. Sure, he's the funky drummer, but just being around him was an inspiration for how to be and live. You can see other people and love their music, but you can tell they're not like that."

"Very true. His personality and kindness came through on an individual level and through his music. It was extraordinary," I said.

When MMW played a song "out of Clyde's box," as John explained, and Clyde made mistakes with the timing, he "would crack up every time. He was a great example. It's Clyde's groove and feel for the totality. It's impossible not to be influenced by Clyde Stubblefield."

"How does the funk-jazz tradition influence your music?"

"It's hard for me to describe my music. I don't think about it; I do it. I believe any musician who looks at themselves from a historical perspective is not continuing to make music. The fact that Prince cared about him so much is a testament to Clyde's contributions. If you're playing music with the minutest bit of funk or dance groove, it's impossible not to have Clyde's influence. He's part of the fabric of everything. He's one of the foundations of the style of music and is inseparable from it."

John had another chance to play with Clyde soon after their 1998 tour. John was part of the making of the documentary *Soul of the Funky Drummers*. John said, "Clyde asked us to do it. That was an epic day, everything fell into place. Hanging out with Clyde and Jabo was wild. They traded stories, and I learned how to hear who was playing what on those recordings. I found out how they're listed wrong on the recordings. When you listen to it with them, their drumming style is obvious. Jabo on the bridge, Clyde on the bridge, Jabo on the main set, then they trade off. They told road stories. It was amazing to be a fly on the wall and be there and play with them."

"Did you know about the movement to get Clyde into the Rock and Roll Hall of Fame? His drumsticks were displayed in a permanent collection with many others in 2000, but he still hasn't been inducted."

John responded, "To show you what a crock all that is, the Grammys, the R&R Hall of Fame, it's all a crock of Disneyland crap. That he's not in the Hall of Fame already and that it didn't happen in his lifetime is enough reason for me to hate that place. Clyde was an icon. It's an epic sign of how screwed up the music business is. By being himself and playing the way he played, he gave so much to the music world and was given so little back. He couldn't even afford health insurance. Yet to be such a beam of sunshine, it's incredible.

"For Clyde, it was difficult having been sampled, and he knew that large sums of money were made from using his beats and not getting a penny. It's brutal. I think it ate at him, but he didn't have any sustained bitterness, I don't think. At least not that he took out on anybody."

In a different realm, John described another skill Clyde taught him—how to sleep wherever and whenever he needed rest. John said, "It was extremely valuable. I was beginning to go through what many people do, thinking I couldn't sleep on the plane or somewhere on the road that I needed sleep. He taught me that it's not something that happens that you can or can't do it. You must put your mind to it. He was right; sleeping is a learned skill. It's an essential skill for a traveling musician. It's about putting your mind to something you want to do. I learned that from Clyde, and I've been able to do it ever since. It came at a good time for me."

I thought about how Clyde could make anything he wanted happen: overcoming sleep issues, leaving Chattanooga, becoming a world-class drummer, or later when he left James Brown, beginning a new life, very different from his previous one.

John continued, "Another note on his sleeping that happened many times, he would be sound asleep on the bus, with his headphones on and listening to music loud enough that I could hear it. He snored in time to what he was listening to. It wasn't accidental, like windshield wipers syncing up with the radio. I remember three separate occasions when he was in the groove, snoring in time to the music. It was not a fluke; he was that in the groove. It blew my mind."

"I know a lot about sleep cycles, sleep disorders, and physiological and psychological effects on sleep due to my twenty-seven years in sleep medicine."

John asked how I would interpret Clyde's "snoring in sync." I smiled and responded, "I have not heard of something like that. Many internal sleep rhythms and brain rhythms are associated with various sleep stages, heart rhythms, and breathing patterns. They all work together or against each other, creating various levels of sleep disorders. Perhaps Clyde's snoring with the music was another level of synchronization that translated to him on a deep level, to the groove, as you said, that was completely him."

John said, "Honestly, I have to say, Clyde is one of those people I have remorse about not having the time and space to spend more time with after the tour. I mean, life is like that. He's one of those guys I think about a lot. It was his spirit, how he was."

Upbeat: Clyde's Childlike Nature

John Medeski shared an amusing anecdote that showed Clyde's childlike nature and his love of fun. When Clyde was on tour with Medeski, Martin, & Wood in 1998, "he was really into the Teletubbies," John said.

"The Teletubbies?"

"He loved the Teletubbies. We were hanging out up in his room, listening to music late after a gig one night. The next morning, I got a call, it must have been seven in the morning. I had never seen them, and he said, 'The Teletubbies are on, watch them.' He really liked them."

Cris Plata told me a memorable story of a time they played a show in 1993 at Boerner Botanical Gardens southwest of Milwaukee. The band arrived at a building Cris described as a "beautiful little palatial place with columns in the front of it with a portico." They were brought a John Deere Gator to transport their instruments to the gardens where there was a stage set up for them to play.

"Clyde said 'I'll go first.' The assistant brought out the Gator, and he pointed, 'Here's the gas, and there's the brake, you pull this lever you go forward, and you pull this lever, and you go backward.'" Clyde loaded his drums and took off. "He's waving like he's in a parade, and he drove out and set up his drums. When he came back, he was still waving. He drove up, and then turned it around in the other direction, but as he was going to back up, he started going up the stairs of the place. I think he's driving well, but he keeps going and then hit one of the pillars. He knocked it down and got really close to one of the bay windows. He thought he was stepping on the brakes, but he stepped on the gas.

"He's riding the engine and it's shrieking, and we're laughing and staring at him, and he finally stopped. He had sheetrock dust all over his head. He turned and looked at Ann and she went over and pulled the pillar and the Gator off him. We ran and hid him in our trailer and knew we were going to get blamed. We eventually came back out but nobody from the gardens came outside. So, Clyde said, 'I guess I better go in and tell on myself.' He walked into the place and told the lady, 'I've had a little accident.' And the lady said, 'What's the matter?' He said, 'I accidentally hit one of the pillars.' She came outside and was beside herself. Ann went to where they were and said, 'Well actually, he's not at fault because he didn't know how to operate the vehicle and somebody from your staff should have been the one that was driving it.' So, we are trying to get out of this, we had a six-hundred-dollar gig, and it will probably cost us a thousand to pay for the damage. At that time there had been a TV show called 'Buffy the Vampire Killer.'

"Clyde was always giving people nicknames, so we started calling him Buffy the Pillar Killer. From that time on he was always Buffy. He kind of liked that name." Clyde's wife, Jody, told me they had a large trophy engraved Buffy the Pillar Killer. She said Clyde and Cris were like brothers from another mother. Cris said, "He would even call himself Buffy. We laughed all the way home."

25

"You Remind Me of Me"

Wally Ingram was another drummer and percussionist whom Clyde casually mentored and latter collaborated with. Wally played with Timbuk 3 when he lived in Madison, and later with Sheryl Crow, members of the Grateful Dead, and dozens of others. When he was a nineteen-year-old student at the University of Wisconsin, he played drums in a trio called Sometimes Y, an "indie-alternative band. They played at a small music club called Merlyn's,[1] and at many gigs around town."

"We were cheap," Wally told me. "And we'd open for everyone. REM was just one of the big bands. Butch Vig produced us. We played at Rick's Havana Club on Wednesday nights, where I met Michael Stone, who had a band called Stone Foundation.

"Michael said, 'You must meet Clyde,' then brought him to the Havana Club to see me play with Sometimes Y. If you looked to your left from the bar, the stage was right there, and you could see the drummer. Clyde was camped out on a barstool about ten feet away from me. I thought, oh my God, there's Clyde. I could tell he was checking me out. He had a stoic look on his face, but after the set, he was all smiles and said something I'll never forget: 'Man, you remind me of me.' I thought, oh really. That was a stretch of a compliment. I don't know what he saw in me that reminded him of himself, but I think he appreciated my groove, and we hit it off right away.

"I studied with Richard Davis [a famous jazz bass musician and professor at UW]. You can go to a great jazz gig and meet your heroes, and sometimes they have a 'jazz attitude' that is not always warm and fuzzy, but Clyde was different from most jazz musicians. I asked my green drummer questions I'm sure he had been asked a million times—Do you teach lessons? He emphatically said, 'No!' [I asked him that once and got the same response.] But he said, 'Come down here on Monday nights when my band plays.' So, I came down a couple of times to watch him.

"One night, Clyde realized I was in the audience and said, 'You're the drummer, kid. Would you like to go up? I'm going to take a break, [and then without waiting for an answer he said] you're going to sit in, you're up next.' So, I went up onstage. I thought, 'Oh my God, I'm going to play with Clyde's band.' He would hang out at the bar, talk to women, and have a drink. He did this with many other drummers, too, not just me. It was a chance for him to extend his break and, at the same time, put you in the hot seat with his band, who were probably thinking, 'Clyde's putting another drummer up here again for us to play with.' So they look you over, and they'd say, 'OK, we're going to do 'Mustang Sally.' You learn what it is to be in Clyde's seat, and that's your lesson. Being around him and listening was powerful. That was about as much mentoring as you could ever ask to get from somebody doing anything.

"The other silly question I asked him was, 'What do you think about when you're playing?' And then I thought to myself, 'Why would I even say that? I don't know what anybody thinks about when they're doing anything,' but anyway, I said it. He responded, 'Nothing! If you're thinking you're fucking up!' I think he was trying to say, clear your mind, get on the track, and go for a ride, and if you're thinking about your problems or what's going on, you might fall off the track. That was good advice I've taken with me. That's how we met, and we became good friends."

Clyde had also played with Pat MacDonald and the Essentials. Wally said, "My turn eventually came when I was a senior in college. I was asked to play with Pat, and Barbara Kooyman and Clyde would sit in. Clyde had played on one of their albums, so we had that common thread, and I went on to be in Timbuk 3.[2]

Clyde and Wally played together, double drumming in Madison at the old G. S. Vig's. They also performed double drumming with the Bandallamas,[3] formed by Wally and Chris Aaron (1970–2014), a prolific folk and blues guitarist. They produced the album *Eye to Eye*.[4] Wally said those shared times brought him and Clyde closer. "We teamed up in the '90s when I came back through town. I would go back to Madison for The O'Bros and Christmas parties. I'm currently in the Know-It-All Boyfriends, a project with Butch Vig. I would reach out to Clyde when I was on tour and invite him to my shows. He wouldn't always come, but we'd go to dinner at Red Lobster close to his home. It was his favorite place."

Clyde accompanied Wally and his band to Colorado in 2012 to play at the Belly Up in Aspen, where he played a few shows with them, including a post–Widespread Panic show. Clyde hadn't been to Colorado since his James Brown days and was thrilled to be in the mountains, even though the altitude and his diabetes and dialysis treatments were challenging.

"We'd be playing," Wally said, "and he would cramp up, call out 'Take it,' and stop and massage his legs. I feel fortunate that we spent some time there toward the end."

"Did Clyde change his musical styles when playing jazz, blues, Tex-Mex, or country?"

Wally said, "Clyde could swing and play jazz, and I believe it was in Clyde's wheelhouse to groove with backbeat style drumming across the board. He's not going to be your Tony Williams's[5] finesse approach to jazz, although I'm sure he could. Every time I saw Clyde play, a freight train of a motor was happening. Clyde could play ballads and used a cross-stick on the snare drum. He would adapt accordingly to every style. Country music is totally in his realm. He wouldn't play super funkified, breaking up the groove syncopation inappropriately, but would play what was right for the music. Clyde had an undeniable placement of the backbeat that lent itself perfectly to country, but I never heard Clyde play a polka. But I'm sure he also played weddings and regular country gigs."

I joked that he had lived in Wisconsin long enough that he should have played polka, although I couldn't imagine it.

"It's undeniably Clyde," Wally continued. "He adapted to all music styles and still maintained his personality. He didn't subscribe to traditional one-drop reggae drumming [1-2-3, kick the bass drum, cross sticks hitting simultaneously, then play a rim shot on the side of a drum]. Reggae wasn't Clyde; he didn't go there because he didn't feel it. If he ever played reggae, he played it his way.

"When he played with Brown, it was his way. You can't tell somebody that invented something how to do it any better than he is doing it himself. I believe confidence was never a problem after going through those hoops."

After that time, he was free from those rules and from Brown. On August 14, 2003, Brown performed at the Oneida Casino in Green Bay. That same week, as every week, Stubblefield played on Wednesday with the Chris Aaron Band in Green Bay and said, "If Brown knew it was me playing, he would say no."[6] I think the feeling was mutual.

I said, "When I finished my master's thesis, I decided I would get a drum set. Clyde was, of course, the inspiration. I took lessons at Ward-Brodt Music where I had worked when I first went to Madison, I wasn't too bad. One time, I went out to see him play at a country bar just east of town. He took a break and had me go up and play two or three songs."

"See, I told you, it wasn't unique to me," Wally said. "He'd size up almost any drummer he met and then leave the stage. It wasn't to embarrass you, his band, or himself, but he would always throw people in the fire. What did he do while you were playing? Do you remember?"

"I remember him walking around, talking to people, and maybe going to smoke a joint. He was out of sight for a bit, and I panicked."

"That was Clyde."

"I felt honored to be playing at his drum set."

Wally shook his head in agreement, "Join the club. You realize Clyde sits high up when you're up there."

"I couldn't believe people weren't looking at me thinking, what is she doing up there? Get her off the stage."

"There was probably a handful of them that might have been thinking that. It was usually the guys in his band; that's what I felt. That's part of learning the craft. You work your way up the line, and it can be a school of hard knocks."

"He didn't talk much about his time with Brown," Wally said. This echoed what others had said. "You could ask him, but I think it was more that he was happy not to be doing that anymore. I was in the presence of James several times at the Rock and Roll Hall of Fame and some festivals. After gigs, I hung out with him in his hotel room and listened to stories. I got insights into what it's like to be in the James Brown camp. There was an immaculate wardrobe hanging nearby, and his ironing board was being used as a makeshift bar as he pulled out various airplane bottles and offered me a drink! One by one, band members came in and collected the day's per diem in cash as Danny would count out on the ironing board, now desk. I met several musicians and mentioned Clyde to the veterans. They all responded with enthusiasm in their eyes and smiles. Clyde was held in the highest respect.

"I met several musicians who played with him from the late '90s into the early 2000s. Everyone had huge respect for Clyde. I believe he had a good relationship with Bootsy Collins. But he'd had enough."

Wally had played with Bob Weir and Phil Lesh of the Grateful Dead and I asked if he saw parallels between the Dead and Clyde's jamming styles.

"When I toured with Bobby and Phil [the only duo shows they played together in March 2018 were for six shows in New York, Chicago, and Boston], we didn't rehearse, mainly because they were trying to figure out what they wanted to do. Bobby and Phil, I believe, had rehearsed; they had a large master list of possible songs but didn't know whether they wanted to play as a duo or if they would add musicians, and if so, whom. It was almost an afterthought. I thought they were thinking they could use a rhythm element but not a straight-up drummer, and they didn't necessarily need a regular band; they could have guests come in at these different gigs. I had done a few things with Bobby, mainly benefits. There was a show in Aspen where I played an African djembe using brushes. That's my signature, a complete drum kit sound using just those. He loved it, and I think it was tucked in his memory. I received a text from Bobby, 'What are you doing? How are you doing? What are you doing tomorrow?' I wrote back that I was in my studio. 'Want to do a session with Phil and me?' It was a week or two before the tour. I asked what I should bring, and he said, 'Bring the drum you had in Aspen,' but I didn't know they were going on tour.

"I got there, and they're set up in his studio like they're onstage. I had my djembe, a pair of bongos, my throne, and a kick pedal. They said, 'We don't want a full drum kit. We're kicking things around to see what might work.' I didn't hear anything for a week and received another text where Bobby said, 'We'd like to have you come back up again but don't bring a standard drum kit—we don't want a bass drum.'

"I set up a stand-up hybrid drumming rig and was directed, I think, by Phil, to play as if another drummer is playing. I thought, well, which drummer? Maybe if it's Mickey, I play more Billy, or if it's Billy, should

I play more Mickey? So, who's the invisible drummer, and what's he playing?"

"Clyde!"

"Exactly! But they said, 'We don't necessarily want a big backbeat,' so there were things to think about, and not in a classic Clyde world of 'don't think when you're playing.' I was battling between what they were directing me and not thinking.

"I went once more to a rehearsal, but they didn't say, 'You've got the gig.' The guitar tech finally said, 'Well, what's the deal? We have to pack and get everything on a truck for New York. Is Wally doing the gig or not?' So, they said, 'Yeah, yeah.' I wouldn't get the song list till half an hour before the set, and I rarely got to soundcheck. Bobby would soundcheck, Phil would soundcheck, and I'd come in and do one or two songs. I had to put on my Clyde Stubblefield radar and antennas, listen, and play, trying to do the right thing, and it was very Clyde-like but without being alpha. I had to be a sympathetic element. Dave Schools, the bass player from Widespread Panic, texted me about how terrifying it is to get in that seat and try to play with Bob and Phil. He described being in a river rapid, getting thrown out of your raft, and trying to negotiate your way through the water, not get your leg broken, and make it down the river without drowning."

"How did your memory of Clyde help?"

"The most crucial idea was," he responded, "don't think—if you're thinking, you're fucking up."

Wally continued, "Here's a good Clyde connection. I think Billy [Kreutzmann, drummer for the Dead] and Clyde are similar-style drummers. Billy has an internal freight train going and a motor happening; he's groove-oriented. His mother was from New Orleans, and he has that background. He can swing and play shuffles and is not afraid to move the backbeat from 1-2-3-4-2-2-3-4 to playing on the One. He'll take liberties; nobody in that band will tell Bill what to do. Likewise, nobody would tell Clyde Stubblefield what to do, except perhaps James Brown. But I'd like to have seen that moment. I'm sure it must have happened, and Clyde had to suck it up, but I can't imagine the moment.

"I played at [O'Cayz Corral][7] every Wednesday with Pat MacDonald and the Essentials for the last year before the band broke up. I was the previous drummer they had. The *Wisconsin State Journal* had an article on the anniversary of Otis Redding's crash. It was the fortieth anniversary. They had the police reports and pictures of the crash.[8]

"It was the night before the anniversary of the crash,[9] [which happened December 10, 1967, into an icy Lake Monona] a classic Madison rainy thunderstorm day. I had loaded in all my drums and done the soundcheck. No one was there at the club. It was early in the evening, around seven."

O'Cayz Corral jukebox sat near the front door. That night, "(Sittin' on) The Dock of the Bay" came on. Wally walked toward the large windows by the front door that gazed onto the lake.

"It was dark outside," Wally said, "and I saw the lightning striking Lake Monona and onto the other shore. The jukebox was playing, lightning striking, and seconds later, the door opened, and in walked Clyde. He was wearing his hoodie raincoat and said, 'Hey, man.'

"I was putting it all together," Wally said, and asked me, "That's where Otis died, right?"

I responded, "Yes, in Lake Monona."

"It's the fortieth anniversary of Otis's dying," Wally continued. "Clyde played with Otis. It was weird. I mean that things don't get much more, I don't know what the perfect word is. . . ."

"Synchronistic?" I offered.

"Yes. He probably came in to say hi and have a beer, knowing that Pat played on Wednesday nights, or he was going to the Cardinal Bar in the neighborhood. It was raining hard, and maybe he was thinking, I need to get out of the rain."

"Entirely in the groove of life without even thinking about it," I said. "Slim [Robert Eppinger], Clyde's early bandmates in Chattanooga, told me Redding had asked some of the band to go on tour, but he really wanted Clyde. Clyde did tour with him awhile, but it's lucky he didn't join the band, and we're lucky he settled here a few years later."

Wally said, "That's why I think this event fits right in with that. Some vital energy guided Clyde to Madison. So many people have asked him and are surprised that Clyde was living there. When they came to town, every drummer that knew about Clyde tried to reach out to him. They'd go to see him play at the Club de Wash or wherever he was playing. He played at the Havana Club, Club de Wash, the Crystal Corner bar, and the King Club."

One of Wally's favorite memories with Clyde happened on the Horizons of Rock Developing Everywhere tour. "The Blues Traveler started it," he said. "They hired me to run a jam stage called the workshop stage.

I was hired along with Taj Mahal to be the stage emcee, corral people from different bands to play, bring in local guests, organize and manage jam sessions five times a day, and play."

"Like herding cats?"

"Worse. I wanted to bring Clyde in as a guest musician for the show at Alpine Valley [East Troy, Wisconsin]. I told them it was Clyde Stubblefield. We need to offer to pay him, but I think we can get him. I also gave Clyde a good cymbal endorsement and lured him in. We got him five hundred dollars that the Blues Traveler paid for. I can't remember how he got to East Troy. I think someone brought him." Wally remembered it was either the summer of 1997 or '98. "I had two drum kits on the workshop stage and a percussion rig and let all the musicians there that day know Clyde was playing: from Lenny Kravitz's band, Morphine, Les Claypool, and the Black Crowes.

"Medeski, Martin, & Wood were there. I introduced Clyde to them. A line of drummers was waiting to get into that second drummer spot, one after another, to play a song with Clyde. He was holding court, and I had a big grin. I was a hero that day and ensured he was well-taken-care-of, catering, hangout space, whatever he wanted. He liked one cymbal of mine, and I said, 'It's yours, take it.' That day was wonderful and right up there as my best memory of him. We got a lot of hang time and time to play music together.

"There was a parade of drummers and bass players waiting to play with Clyde. Craig Ross, the guitar player from the Lenny Kravitz band, Jack Daley, the bass player, and Cindy Blackman [drummer with Santana, and later Blackman-Santana], may have been there. I'd been jamming with Chan Kinchla [the recent guitar player for Blues Traveler], and Bobby Sheehan, the bass player who passed away, was there. Later, Clyde went on tour with John Medeski and MMW. They brought in John Scofield, who did gigs later with Clyde.

"Clyde could jam with the best of them. Clyde often played with the butt end of the drumstick and slammed it into the drum."

"He had a great grace note touch. It seemed he could grace his rhythms no matter what he used to hit the drum with. His left hand had so much finesse and incredible syncopation that set him up to be the funky drummer, all those in-between sounds [that were almost silent]."

Jazz bassist Christian McBride said, "Clyde had all these subtleties, this kind of bouncy left hand."[10]

Wally said, "Clyde said a million times that he learned how to drum by listening to the trains in Chattanooga."

"Trains, the grain elevator, all the industrial sounds," I said.

Wally said, "You can imagine this kid walking around the streets, the shoreline, and the train tracks. He was a sponge, with his internal clock developed by rhythms and sounds. Trains, it's not necessarily like [mouths the rhythm], especially when it slows down and then speeds up. It's dynamics and tempo variation, not just military march rhythms. It's not square, it's moving, it's a steam engine. An engine of any kind is the best analogy for Clyde Stubblefield's drumming and the fact that the Chattanooga Choo Choo is there. He was the Chattanooga Choo Choo. That was Clyde, complete with blowing the smoke out.

"I think in a drummer-speak way, you feel some unspoken spiritual connection when drumming. Drummers aren't like a lot of competitive musicians. Some drummers are, but often drummers will share with other drummers their skill set. It's like folk music; you've got a story to tell. You're not going to tell them everything, but as far as it seems to be a guitar player thing or a saxophone player in jazz, whatever, they don't show their whole hand to the next guy; the attitude is, 'That's my thing, and I'm keeping it to myself.' Drummers have more of a sharing attitude; this is a paradiddle. Try this stick; try this cymbal. That's why there's the Percussive Arts Society and drum circles. There's sharing of information, drum seminars, and drum workshops, which are very well attended by drummers wanting to learn from other drummers. There's a communal spirituality about it, a sharing."

"Community?" I asked.

"'Community' is the right word for it. I miss him. I can hear his voice in my head and his great laugh. He was a gem of a guy."

Drum Break: Crash Cymbal with the Law

Clyde had difficulty with the law along the way, interrupting the rhythmic flow of his life's path. Slim told me about an incident in Chattanooga in the '60s. One of his bandmates asked him to go to the post office, telling him there was a package waiting there for the entire band. When Clyde picked it up it turned out to contain "some substance." He was busted and immediately left town, and did not return to Chattanooga for several decades, until the Ninth Street reunion in the late '90s.

Several decades passed after this incident. Cris Plata said, "The early to mid-1990s were not a good time in Clyde's life." While living in Madison, Clyde was arrested twice, the first in February 1990. He was arrested on charges of the manufacture and delivery of a controlled substance and pleaded guilty/no contest. In June of that year there was a plea hearing and Clyde received three years' probation with no jail time. Clyde said, "A narc came out of his jurisdiction and begged me to do what I did. I was trying to help a friend and got put in a trap in between. If I'd had the right attorney and a lot of money, I probably would have come out with just a big fine. The newspapers called me a kingpin! A kingpin? God, no! I don't believe in dealing drugs. I can see them moving cocaine off the face of the earth. That's no good for anybody, that stuff."[11]

On April 1, 1996, Clyde was arrested again, on possession of THC and drug paraphernalia. Clyde told Cris Plata what happened: "'Someone asked me to get some drugs, and then I went up to give it to him, and the guy was an undercover cop.' The thing with Clyde was I could see where he got into trouble just by doing a favor for somebody. He was busted in Richland Center but served his time in the Dane County jail." It seemed, once again, that he took the fall for someone, an unfortunate pattern that played out twice in his life, similar to the scenario in Chattanooga. But Clyde kept his spirits up.

On November 8, 1996, there was a plea hearing. Being a second offense, Clyde was sentenced to six months in the county jail and since he had been driving at the time of his arrest he had his license suspended. While in jail, he was eligible for Huber Law, allowing a person to leave jail unaccompanied for work and return to jail at night. Most Huber Law recipients worked regular day hours, nine to five, but Clyde went out at eight in the evening to play his gigs.

"I was one of the people that could go to the jailhouse and sign him out so he could play with me," Cris said. "And at the end of the gig, I would take him back to the county jail. He learned a lesson from that experience."

One time Cris picked Clyde up to play a gig, and at the time, he was playing a lot of shows with Marcy and the Highlights. Cris said, "They made it seem that they were the ones managing him, even though he wasn't still under contract with them. You had to call Marcy's husband and ask permission to use Clyde for a gig. When I went to pick up Clyde from the jail, I asked him, 'What's this deal that I must clear it through him to get you to play?' And he said, 'What?' I said, 'Yes, that's what they're telling me.' 'No,' he said, 'screw them. Just call me up at the jail and tell me when the gig is. You can come to pick me up, you don't have to go through them.' He had a falling out with them over that.

"Three things, he told me: 'I like television, I like reefer, and I like women, and that is all I need.' Simple. He would get really stoned before he played. I don't even know how he did it, but he played excellently. Now, on the other hand, if I even just took a puff, I'd be like, where am I? Almost every time I saw Clyde, he was smoking or doing something like that, but he held it together well."

"I'm sure he had enough of that kind of attitude with James Brown controlling every aspect of his life," I said.

One surreal aspect of Clyde's time in jail was that if you wanted to book a show with him, you had to call the Dane County sheriff. One day, Ben Sidran arranged to have him play and found the sheriff had double-booked him. Ben told me that Clyde realized he was working more when the sheriff booked him than when he was booking his own gigs.[12] Maybe the sheriff should have kept arranging his shows for him after he left jail.

Another incident happened when Clyde was playing a Blue Monday show. An unbelievable show, and yet, it being Clyde I can believe it happened. Tom Strader heard the story from Steve Skaggs, Clyde's keyboardist at Blue Mondays. One night Clyde went outside to smoke a joint between sets. Some cops saw him, came over, and busted him in the parking lot for smoking weed. The police said he could keep playing and finish the show. They told him, "Finish your set, and once you're done, we'll take you downtown."

I thought, well, maybe they were having a slow night, were fans, and just wanted to hear the rest of the show.

Tom said, "They booked him and let him go."

26

"So I Can Go Up and Sing"

David Stanoch was at home in Minnesota, sitting at his drum set, and I was in California, ready to have him demonstrate Clyde's rhythms and techniques, while we spoke via Zoom.

David became a longtime friend and collaborator of Clyde's and witnessed some of the ups and downs of Clyde's life in Madison. He began a major in music performance at the University of Wisconsin-Madison in 1980 to study with Richard Davis, the great jazz bassist and head of the jazz department. David told me, "I wasn't as tuned in to what it took to function as part of a rhythm section, what to listen for, how to lock into a groove, things that required a strong hook-up with a bass player. But I knew that's what I had to learn, and Davis was the obvious choice because I had so many favorite records he played on—and he was available!"

Stanoch said that after he was in town a short time, people he met would ask, "Are you hip to Clyde Stubblefield?"

"I had no idea Clyde was living there. I was aware of Clyde because of David Garibaldi from Tower of Power, Mike Clark from Herbie Hancock and the Headhunters, and Jim Payne, a well-known drummer, educator, and record producer. The reason these fellows knew who Clyde and Jabo were, particularly in the case of David Garibaldi and Mike Clark, who grew up in Oakland, was that their bands were playing on the same bill as James Brown at places like the Fillmore West in California in the late '60s and early '70s."

"You'd hear James Brown say somebody's name on a record. Brown often called out Fred doing it to death, 'Hit it Fred' [also the title of Fred Wesley's book], and Bootsy. I don't think he ever said Clyde's name when he called out, 'Give the drummer some,' which is one of the most famous taglines ever, but he once called Clyde's name on the second recorded version of 'Give It Up or Turnit a Loose.' The song was released in 1969 with Clyde playing in tandem with congas and was released around the same time as 'Funky Drummer'—March, 1970.

"As a kid, I distinctly remember two articles, one by Mike Clark in *Musician* magazine, with transcriptions of Clyde's James Brown's rhythms, and another in *Modern Drummer* magazine, by Jim Payne, that broke down 'Mother Popcorn.' I could decipher them, and I thought they were so cool! This was the beginning of them [Clyde and Jabo] getting their due. They weren't credited on records. Jabo played on 'Sex Machine,' Clyde on 'Cold Sweat,' and Melvin Parker on 'I Got You,' but nobody knew who played drums on those records out in the world."

David went to a gig in town where Clyde played weekly at Morgan's on Sundays on Madison's east side and Mondays at Club de Wash on the west side. "It was 1980, and I watched him play, and after the show, I introduced myself. He was very welcoming. I asked [as so many have], 'Could I take lessons from you?' He told me that he did not teach but said [David talks in Clyde's voice], 'Listen, man, come to my gigs and sit in and I'll come to your gigs and sit in, and we'll do it like that!' I hear his voice in my head. He called me Davy. 'How you doin', brother?' I'd say, 'How you feeling, Clyde?' He'd say, 'With my fingers and my toes, brother.' That was the fall of 1980.

"I took him up on attending his gigs and learned a lot by having what I call the bandstand education from Clyde. I studied at school, played jazz gigs, and joined bands in town, including Pat MacDonald & the Essentials, which later became Timbuk 3. I was Pat's drummer before my pal Wally Ingram joined Pat and Barb after they dropped the boom box in Austin. I made it a point to go almost every Sunday and Monday to Morgan's and Club de Wash. Clyde could hear my potential and knew immediately that I wasn't a funk drummer but a jazz drummer. I could swing, and I could rock, that's what I grew up doing. To me, funk beats sounded like rock beats, but funk beats have a different level of nuance that I didn't understand then. Clyde would have me sit in, and at first, those cats on the bandstand would give me dirty looks, not make me feel welcome, shake their heads, and turn their back to me.

"Clyde made it possible for me to keep coming, and as important as playing was the ability to watch him move when he played and to listen to him and the band. I began understanding the nuances and techniques of playing in his drumming style. I worked on it, and, after a while—and I'm not talking a couple of weeks, I mean after over several months or a year—Clyde started calling me to sub for some of his gigs. I kept showing up, and it wasn't long before those other cats in the band warmed up to me and called me for gigs. That was my rite of passage."

David didn't remember who were in those early gigs but said, "Over time I got to know cats who were in and out of the bands like Reverend Dippermouth and Bruce Koenig on keyboards. Mark Davini, who was in Tina and the Tigers with Clyde, might have been there, along with Robert J. [Conaway], a singer/songwriter. Robert J. was a staple of the Madison music community for decades. Those are the cats I remember.

"When Clyde put together the first Clyde Stubblefield band to play at Bunky's, around 1984, I lived three blocks from there. I wanted to go as a fan. Clyde called on Tuesday and said, 'What are you doing Friday night?' 'I'm coming to see you.' 'Good, man, because I want you to play the drums.' 'Did you say play the drums? Why?' Clyde said, 'So I can go up and sing, fool.'" David laughed and said that he replied, "'It would be my honor.'"

"I was jamming, listening, getting mentored on the bandstand, and suddenly backing him in the Clyde Stubblefield band. I gave Ben Sidran's son Leo lessons during those days. Years later, Leo produced an excellent record for Clyde called *The Original*."

In later years, when visiting Madison, David would go to the King Club or the Lounge at the Concourse, and Clyde would tell him, "Davy man, come on up and play." When that happened, David said, "We wouldn't see him until the end of the night. He'd split."

Kathie Williams, his manager, told me that with Clyde and Jabo, she'd be the last one through the door behind them, because if she was the first, Clyde and Jabo might look at each other, turn around, and split. So, she said she learned to follow them through the door. She told Clyde, "I know your history."

David said, "He was a rascal, a very lovable rascal."

"Back in my college days, after I'd been in Madison a couple of years, David Garibaldi from Tower of Power conducted a clinic at Ward-Brodt Music.[1] Clyde called me and said, 'Davy, are you going to see Garibaldi?' I said I was. He said, 'Man, give him my phone number. He's the only person I know that mentions me by name, and I want to thank him for it.' I said, 'Clyde, you got it.' After the clinic, I introduced myself and said, 'I'm here as a messenger as much as a fan. I was asked to give you this from Clyde Stubblefield. Clyde lives here, but he's gigging out of town today and couldn't be here. He wanted me to make sure to give you his number. He wants to thank you.' Garibaldi replied, 'That's incredible. I didn't even know Clyde was still alive, where he was, or anything.' It was beautiful to be a catalyst for that. That's one of my favorite Clyde stories."

Many years later, in a tribute to Clyde, Garibaldi said, "I had the pleasure of meeting [Clyde], which is a highlight in my music career." And then said, "His drumming is still sounding as fresh today as it did when I first heard 'Cold Sweat' in 1967. I was in the military and that record was in the jukebox at the base cafeteria . . . it was mind-blowing at the time. Then came 'I Got the Feelin'' . . . to me, that one is still his very best performance and is my all-time favorite JB track. . . . Clyde is blowing his heart out and it's still something to learn from for anyone who is interested in what creative funk drumming is about . . . it's like a great jazz performance." He then added, "I certainly wouldn't be the drummer that I am today without his influence."

Clyde Wasn't Trained That Way

"I teach people in my studio by sitting with my student at our drums," David said. "Demonstrating techniques, styles, and musicality and answering whatever questions they have, building them up in the traditional way. Clyde wasn't trained that way. When Clyde talked about how he didn't teach, he would tell me the story of his upbringing in Tennessee, walking to school; there was a rhythm over here and something different over there. He'd listen to each one and piece them together. When he got home, he tried to play what he had heard on the drums. His contribution to drumming is unique because of this way of interpretation. He would say, like in *Soul of the Funky Drummers*, 'I don't know anything, just 1-2-3-4, and I mean, that's it.' But that wasn't true."

Whad'ya Know?, Michael Feldman's radio show, came to Minneapolis in 2000, when David Stanoch was living in the Twin Cities. He was the original drummer on the show from its earliest days, broadcast early Sunday mornings at the Club de Wash in Madison. "One day, not long before the show in Minneapolis, my phone rang," David told me. "It was Jeff. He said, 'Hey Dave, the *Whad'ya Know?* show is coming to town, and the rhythm section has a gig at the Dakota the night before. We're wondering if you can play the second or third set.' I was a little confused because Clyde was then the drummer for the show.

"Apparently, Jeff had booked the gig at the Dakota, a prestigious Midwest jazz club, with the *Whad'ya Know?* band. Clyde's name was prominently displayed on the marquee as the main draw, but they didn't ask Clyde first. Members of Jody's family lived there, and they had plans to spend time with them on the night of the gig.

"Clyde was pissed, but he told Jeff, 'I'll play the first set on the drums, but then you need to call David Stanoch, and if he can play drums on the second set, that's when I'll sing. He can play the third set because I'm out of there.'

"At the Dakota, when Clyde was ready to leave, Clyde poked me hard with his finger and said, 'So I heard Katy's making a record down at Jay's.' I said, 'Yes,' and he said, 'Who the hell is playing drums on the record?' I said, 'You want in on the record? That would be my honor.'"

In Madison, which was in many ways a small town, a close friend of Wally's, Jay Moran, operated his own music studio called Wakefield Mines. It was the year 2000, and David was making the record *Fall* with his boys' mother, Katy Tessman, a folk singer-songwriter. David said, "Clyde did a track for us, but what was beautiful was not only that he played on the song ["Odd Timing"] but what he taught me in the recording studio by sharing his knowledge and skill.

"It's memorable and special for me. Clyde was on drums, and Wally and I played percussion—it's the only track the three of us ever made together. In the session, Clyde demonstrated how he shaped ideas, which made them better and improved the song we were recording. He would claim that he doesn't teach—he didn't want much responsibility—he just wanted to play."

Clyde and David played for many years with Randy Sabien, a jazz violinist and educator. Sabien's website describes him as "a bluesy, rockin', swingin', funky, jazz violinist. With an intensely rhythmic, vibrant, and inventive style."[2] Just the kind of musician that Clyde would find along his rhythmic road of expanded musical genres. Stubblefield played on Sabien's "Fiddlehead Blues," "Paintin' the Canvas (Live at the Big Top Chautauqua)," "Rhythm and Bows," and volume 1 of the play-along CD for Sabien's jazz string method book *Jazz Philharmonic* (Alfred Music). Clyde and Randy traveled together playing gigs from Florida to Alaska.

When Clyde was unavailable, David filled in. As time went by, they split the gigs; Clyde played throughout Wisconsin and east of the state, while David played Randy's shows west of the Mississippi River. Later Randy formed a band called Rhythm and Bows, "with three different fiddle players, including Randy, a complete rhythm section with double drums. Initially, it was Clyde and someone else. It might have been Dane Richeson, a fabulous drummer who teaches percussion at Lawrence University. At some point, Dane left, and Randy asked me to play. It was after our first gig together that Clyde told me, 'You're my favorite drummer to play with when I have to play double drums.' That blew me away, but there's some context that needs to be explained."

David said when they performed together, he metaphorically became the two poles holding the solid structure for Clyde so he could explore the rhythmic world between them. It worked similarly to what Clyde once expressed to Ann Plata about her being there on the One when he came back from outer space.

David explained, "What made it work for me to play with Clyde when he sang and we double drummed was how I played differently for him.[3] If he was singing, I would play more in his style, which was dynamic, inter-dynamic, and intricate. That's a whole different thing than if I'm playing my drum set with Clyde. And there were tunes where I played hand percussion. We didn't need the double drumming on every song.

"In his later years, Clyde had big, thick, heavy-sounding drums. He had a dynamic touch, and his sound was intricate, like in the song, 'Mother Popcorn.'" It sounds to me like a driving funk tune with regular interjections simulating the feel of popping corn—irregular, loud then soft sounds. "So, when playing with him, my beats would be big and wide, and my drums were smaller and tuned higher and jazzier. There was a contrast in our timbre, so when he was playing in his style, I played in a way that outlined a framework for him to play through. It was like a fence. I would be the posts, and he could be the mesh in between. We didn't talk about it; I just did it. Maybe he couldn't explain why, but I knew I wasn't getting in his way, and he loved it. So, when he said after the show, 'You're the best drummer I ever played double drums with Davey.' Wow! I was thrilled at the compliment simply because I respected him and knew how to make that work. I knew what he did, how he did it, and what not to do myself."

"You were the supportive structure."

"If it's me playing with Clyde, nobody cared about me being there—it's about him. I thought to myself, 'I'm not sure why I'm doing this, but I won't say no. I'll take on the challenge.' We succeeded and scheduled more dates with Randy around 2009."

David's poles and mesh analogy intrigued me, and I asked him to tell me more.

"If you think of a tempo [bangs on a beat], that's the quarter note. Clyde would play something like"—David plays a very intricate fast rhythm.

"I'd target the essential notes. I knew Clyde would play with his foot that would go with the bass line and the backbeats. I'd play those with him to anchor the beat but then leave the space in between for Clyde. In putting this concept together mentally, I drew from my experience growing up watching bands with double drummers like Earth, Wind and Fire; the Doobie Brothers; and the Allman Brothers, and observing their different approaches. There was precedent for this approach. I'd read Andy Newmark's description about him and Joe Vitale drumming together in Joe Walsh's band. Jim Keltner also shared pointers on how he optimized his approach for double drumming with Ringo Starr at George Harrison's Concert for Bangladesh. All of this helped me arrive on the bandstand with Clyde with a fully formed approach for a concert where we double drummed together all night with no prior rehearsal, and it worked wonderfully!

"I learned from Richard Davis that you don't want everyone in the same end of the boat. When I was studying with Richard at the UW and would be walking down the hall in school . . . he'd say, 'Stanoch, I'm up there, and I'm playing [mimes playing bass] be do ba de boo ba pa—what are you doing?' And I'd say, 'I'm keeping time so that you can do your thing,' and he'd say, 'Right!' and walk away. I'd see him a couple of days later, he'd say, 'I've got my bow out [mimes playing like a violin] scheennigh, ahhhh—what are you doing?' I'd say, 'I'm filling up the space between beats. I'm [David does intricate rhythm on the drums]'—and he'd say 'Right!' and walk away. He was conveying not being in the same end of the boat. There's a time and a place for that. Playing in unison can be effective, but if you do it too much, it's simply mimicry or lopsided, like a conversation with only questions and no answers.

"I knew how Clyde played, and I wanted to wrap my arms around that and help the ebb and flow through a solid foundation and framework, so we don't take up all the space. We were two people in a band with a bass player, a piano player, a guitar player, and three fiddle players. Clyde played dance rhythms dynamically, so it didn't feel like an onslaught. It feels like popcorn popping, and then something's happening over here, and something is happening over there, but because of his dynamics, he doesn't take up all the space. These are things I learned watching him play that was helpful to me in adapting his style of playing to my own."

David loved playing those gigs with Randy and Clyde, but his wife at the time, and mother of his children, Katy, developed cancer. "Thankfully, she survived," David said, "but I had to cut back on my gigs." He stayed close to home and didn't play as many out-of-town gigs. Clyde continued to play with Randy.

In September 2015, Kathie, Clyde's manager, called David about playing with a star-studded lineup for the Clyde Stubblefield Day at the Barrymore Theater on the east side of Madison. David said, "The last time Clyde and I played together was at the Clyde Stubblefield Day. Kathie called me and said Fred Hopkins, Fred Wesley, Jabo, and Clyde would be playing, and Wally would be there. She said, 'Clyde wants you to play,' and I said, 'Play what?' [Laughter.] I said I'd pick up a tambourine and stand between them [Clyde and Jabo]. I'll do that. And that's what I did. That was the last time we played together. What a thrill to play together with all those cats at once! It was magnificent.

"Dave Jewell and I were in a percussion ensemble together. Dave and I met in college, and he later managed Milano Music in Scottsdale, Arizona, and was hired as a Yamaha artist rep for drums. He secured having Clyde and Jabo signed to Yamaha as drum artists. Dave then became Yamaha's drum product manager and later global music manager. One day, around 2009, he called me and said, 'Dave, I want you to come and do a clinic with me for Yamaha at the Wisconsin Music Educators Association Convention in Madison. While we're there, we'll be able to hang out and see Clyde.' Yamaha gave legacy awards to some of their heavy hitters, and they would present them in person on various occasions. I said, 'Dave, if we're going to Madison, we should get Clyde there, and you could get him a legacy award.' Because he's brilliant, Dave took it one step further, had Jabo come up from down South, and gave them both legacy awards at the convention. It was a beautiful thing. I brought along a famous CD box set[4] called *Star Time* (A Tribute to James Brown), by Tower of Power, a career retrospective of James Brown hits, and I had Clyde and Jabo autograph it (see FIG. 18). I cherish it to this day.

"At our clinic, Dave and I presented together, Dave talked about tuning, and I spoke about playing. Richard Davis was also there. Dave had played in Richard's jazz ensemble before I did. The day was memorable, honoring both Clyde and Jabo.

"Around 2014, when Clyde had kidney failure, I recruited two of my friends, Stanton Moore, the New Orleans funk band Galactic's drummer, and Johnny Rabb, the drummer for Collective Soul, who is a pioneer at playing drum and bass music live. It is a style that took many things from 'Cold Sweat' and other beats of Clyde's. They sampled them and then sped them up. Johnny wrote a book on that style. He gave Clyde a lot of props in his book [*Jungle/Drum 'n' Bass for the Acoustic Drum Set: A Guide to Applying Today's Electronic Music to the Drum Set*].

"We created the Coalition for Clyde Stubblefield, with backing from Yamaha and Vic Firth. Questlove and many others helped us put out the word that Clyde needed help with resources. In those days, it was called a chip-in campaign [an early Go Fund Me]. We raised $30,000. Jody and Clyde were very appreciative."

Bernard Purdie, an earlier drummer with James Brown, was described by Stanoch as "an innovative funk drummer. Purdie was well known in the music world, but neither Clyde nor Jabo was. Many people in the day assumed Purdie played the rhythms Clyde and Jabo actually played. People knew Bernard had played with Brown, Clyde and Jabo's names were unknown, therefore, they assumed Purdie was playing their parts.

"Clyde, Jabo, and Purdie were all friends. Purdie would tell me Clyde and Jabo would tease him when they were at trade shows. He'd say, 'I would always know when Clyde and Jabo were around because they would come up behind me and put their hands in my pockets!'—a kind of joke on how they felt he had gotten the glory and not them, so they were going to take it back.

"Purdie called me and said, 'What you're doing with the coalition is beautiful.' It wasn't only a question of whether he needed money for the treatment, but instead, the loss of work and bills that needed to be paid when Clyde couldn't go out and work every day. Purdie understood that.

"My relationship with Clyde was special. We would talk often and remember each other's birthdays. Jody told me how much he looked forward to that. It was a tradition and I consider myself very fortunate. I know he loved me, and he knew I loved him. I was able to show that to him in many ways. After all, he's Clyde Stubblefield, and all those amazing things that we talked about that he accomplished will be known forever. Beyond that, I'm extremely grateful he gave me a chance to sit in at his gigs. I kept going back every week because I was getting nurtured. That was better than sitting in a room alone because he taught me how to play music with the band in his style and gave me a chance to make mistakes and get them right in real time. That's one of the reasons I'm still working. To me, that's invaluable, and I will always honor him because he was kind to me and was my friend.

"It delights me to think that people in every corner of the world have heard Clyde play. They might never know his name or know they listened to a sample by him, but what he did was strong and timeless. It had that impact. How many people can say that?"

Drum Roll: Truck Stop

Despite having a major influence on contemporary music, Clyde was a very down-to-earth and approachable man. Drummers are used to packing up their own equipment. David Stanoch met Jabo at the Wisconsin Music Educators Association clinic. They hit it off and spent time together. "He was a sweet man," David said, telling me about the time Jabo asked him, "'So, you're from Minnesota? I used to drive a truck up by International Falls. It was cold, but I liked it up there—the people and the countryside.'

"You're from the South," David replied, "and you were in International Falls [the coldest climate in the country] and liked it?"

Jabo said, "Yeah, it was all right."

Tom Strader shared that "Clyde loved packing up trailers. He was very good at it. Whenever there was a trailer, he pushed people out of the way. He must have driven a truck at some point in his life."

Reminiscent of the days Clyde would move the equipment around for the Cascades in Chattanooga.

There was a story I heard, that musicians in the James Brown band would take turns driving the tour bus when the regular driver was fired. Maybe they enjoyed the experience. Maybe both Clyde and Jabo had memories or dreams of getting out on the road, skimming the borders, and being free to drive away to the places they heard in their rhythmic universes.

Although it wasn't until the early 2000s, as Rickey Vincent told me, before he and Jabo did their collaborations and double drummed together, a story forms inside my head.

Clyde is packing up Jabo's truck, and the two drive off along the shores of the largest Great Lake in the United States, the 32,000 square miles of Lake Superior. I imagine them making their way along the Canadian border, past Thunder Bay, listening to the crashing waves on the boulders and metamorphic rocks, hearing the rhythms of the big wheels under Jabo's truck down a two-lane back road, complementing each other's stories, in rhythmic sync, smiling, sharing a laugh.

27

"Echoes of Africa"

Dr. Rickey Vincent is a scholar, educator, KPFA radio host of *The History of Funk*, and the author of *Funk: The Music, the People and the Rhythm of the One*. We spoke on Zoom and he enlightened me about a history I knew only slightly.

"Every time I've come across Clyde, Jabo, or Fred [Wesley]," Rickey told me, "they have their public personas and style well established. They showed up clean even if their craft is low-down dirty funk, and they'd walk onstage dapper. They're from the jazz school, the old school, [and], especially Clyde's generation, was trying to portray a civilized art form, an intellectual craft, but they have to 'get down.'

"Even if their craft is the wild and crazy funk, Maceo Parker's book, titled *98 Percent Funky Stuff*, was making light of the business they were in. The recording is 98 percent jazz and 2 percent funky stuff, but when they go live, it's 2 percent jazz and 98 percent funky stuff. Jazz is the craft, but you reach the people, give them what they want, and everyone wants to cut loose.

"Fred Wesley did the best breakdown of the difference between jazz and funk I've heard of in his book, *Hit Me, Fred*. The two styles of music come from the same place, but jazz is more for the intellectual and the mental listener; funk has got a little more attitude. Wesley wrote, 'I've always believed that funk and jazz are the same, with emphasis on different elements and playing with different attitudes. Jazz is cool and slick and subtle, emphasizing the melodic and harmonic side of the music, and appeals to the more cerebral listener. Funk is bold, arrogant, and aggressive, emphasizing the music's hard downbeats and tricky rhythms of the music, and tends to appeal more to the booty-shaking listener. I submit that there is a very thin line separating the two schools of music appreciation.'"[1]

Rickey continued, "Many jazz musicians are naturally funk players; the two are organically connected. There are bits of biased prejudiced assumptions around the different styles of music. [Musicians] get boxed in and must work against that grain to avoid being categorized. The JBs were pioneers; they should have been headliners at any jazz festival in the Western hemisphere in the last fifty years. In Europe, people accept R&B and jazz as part of the same family."

I used to think there were boundaries between the styles of music, rock and roll and psychedelic on one end, and blues, R&B, and soul on the other. I said, "Growing up in the '60s, I saw African American musicians well dressed, wearing suits and ties, nice dresses, presenting a cohesiveness in their clothes and mannerisms. White musicians were the opposite, wearing torn clothes, and ripped jeans, being wild, and dropping out. Blacks were trying to get into society while whites were trying to get out."

Rickey explained, "That's true, but there was musical study across that imaginary boundary. Many counter-culture artists would study jazz masters. Still, open-minded jazz masters like Miles Davis, Herbie Hancock, and Chick Corea studied psychedelic artists and free-form music. It doesn't take long to tell which artists are open to that. Funk emerges as an institutionalized self-liberation in that the music is open. The craft is open to studying technical forms, free forms, and higher chemical consciousness creative forms. It's fair game, welcome, and, at some point, is expected in 1970s funk. It never strays far from the tree, which is that pocket, the rhythm of James Brown's sounds, the backbone of it all—the funky drummers and the funky drummer.

"The great rhythm masters understand whether they're conga or other types of players. An artist can create depth perception. There's something in front, a background, and distant background. All of them can hit it on the front so the band can follow, then there's a shadow behind that main skeleton of the beat that works around it; it floats around the music.

"You need to use terms that are somewhat in the abstract. George Clinton has a description when he talks about rhythm. He would talk about a groove and how the groove masters work, or any 'rhythm master' works around a beat. There's the expectation of exactly where the beat is, where the beat is supposed to be, and what time. A metronome or a computer can pinpoint it and tell you, but a master gives you something infinitesimal around that beat so that your mind, body, and soul must reconcile where that will be and where it belongs. The listener becomes an active participant."

Rickey continued, "George Clinton would say it's a silly millimeter when you're off by a little. It explains what happens when used in music with multiple concurrent rhythms, and it never gets boring. They're playing within an infinitesimal amount on and off the beat, depending on how they see, feel, understand, and witness it when the audience is there. It's anything but a specific data point. They are coming together and coming apart on many layers of energy. They talk about this in jazz, around melodies and the expectation of a note. Rhythm masters do the same thing."

"I'm having these flashes of atoms bouncing around," I said, "which is rhythm, patterns, the process of creating energy."

"That's Coltrane," Rickey responded. "His book *Jazz of Physics* is in the adventurous territory and hard to describe. The book *Presence and Pleasure* tried to explain the rhythms of James Brown academically but, in my opinion, fell short. When you feel it, it's not something you can draw data points around. It's out of bounds, and rational thought has limitations. Even Mr. Spock would say that at some point, intuition, emotion, rhythm, and the groove take over and enter a domain that defies rationalization. Clyde lived there.

"I saw Clyde play this song ['Sookie, Sookie'] at the Elbo Room in San Francisco. You need to hit the hi-hat and stay on top for a long time, making it a difficult song to play. Then at 9:50 minutes into the song, he hits a stride that still strikes me how deep into me that groove went. It took me to another place where I had to remind myself where I was and snap out of it. I looked at Clyde, and he was sitting there with a big grin on his face. He was inhabiting that place with ease. He created rhythms in that pocket that other drummers might have to work their way into, but Clyde was already there and inhabited the joy of that moment in a way few people could reach.

"Clyde was unbounded. He didn't boast or show off like other masters. He conveyed: I'm not a master; I'm just trying to reach people. He could hit transcendent next-level layers of rhythm all at the same time.

I know other drummers struggle with it, but to him, it was natural. He knew that was his place; it was his calling, his zone, and it was a delight to experience it. As much as he's gone through, I don't remember meeting anybody with a warmer disposition."

"I heard you saw Clyde play with Grant Green Jr.?"

"When I first met Clyde at the Elbo Room, it was with the Grant Green trio on November 11, 2005. The trio was Clyde Stubblefield, Grant Green Jr., and Reuben Wilson—the Masters of Groove.[2] I was the DJ that night and opened for Clyde, and I thought if I were to DJ a set before Clyde Stubblefield, I would play songs with the most active funk drumming, not some electrofunk. I opened with 'Time Is on My Side,' 1977, the opening track from Maze featuring Frankie Beverly's first album. Eventually, it sold over 4.5 million albums in the United States but got overlooked because of radio hits. Somebody from the dressing room came over to me and said, 'Clyde wants to know what you're playing. Who's the drummer on that song?'

"For a DJ to hear that is heaven. I said, 'Well, I'm not just going write you a note; I have to tell him in person.' That was my way to get backstage and meet Clyde. He wanted to know who the musicians were on that song and what the upbeat polyrhythm jam was. I told him the song and that the drummer's name was Ahaguna Sun. That was how I met Clyde for the first time. He was wearing that little black leather jacket that was low-key but cool at the same time. It was amazing for a master to recognize those rhythms from a record and immediately connect the dots. Meeting him was a magical moment for me. That's what I play these rhythms for, and it was all worth it.

"In the early '90s, Maceo, Fred, and Pee Wee made *Life on Planet Groove*, which helped elevate their visibility. It gave space for all the JBs to be better recognized. Not just legends in a museum but living legends with which you can have a life-transforming moment like I had with Clyde.

"They played in San Francisco twice with an all-star line-up, at the Elbo Room and the Mezzanine [a San Francisco music hall with a large dance floor that closed in 2019]. There was also a James Brown symposium in 2007, but I don't think Clyde was there." After thirty-seven years, he still did not want to be in Brown's presence.

A New Way

The entire experience was changing when the genre shifted into the realm of psychedelic music, from the sounds and light shows, to the clothes that musicians and fans wore. But it went beyond that.

Rickey said, "The band War gave writers credits to all seven members. In the '70s, a new way of collective grooving was being represented, different from military control of an operation. The old method wasn't working, and people stood up to Brown. They left. They couldn't find gigs partly because of his efforts. He knew every DJ in the country, and he essentially said to them, 'If you play Maceo, you're not getting the next JB album.'"

"He owned three radio stations, a publishing company, and his own Learjet," I said.

"When you listened to soul radio, which was Black radio, you not only got the music but the news and public affairs a few times a day. It was part of the Black experience. James Brown stayed on top of everything, became his own manager, and knew everyone, and they knew him. It was tough for any former JB to go out independently. Marva Whitney, Lynn Collins, and other women who recorded solo albums with him had it much harder. It was a Napoleon complex. People grew and were ready to refresh the vision of music he had established, but he was not prepared to let go of the control he held."

Rickey explained how hip-hop stole Clyde's rhythms: "The hip-hop DJ existed as a purveyor of mystery, as somebody with those beats that came out of nothing, they could create beats on top of beats that were already recorded. That's what good DJs can do. The early hip-hop DJs, back in 1973, cut the labels off their records. They did not let people know whose beats they were playing. That was part of their turf battles before any rap music recordings began in 1979. In 1973, that is how the local kids who were DJs were operating. Everybody knew James Brown was the centerpiece of the sound they were making in New York. They all knew, but not everybody had the extended remix before the 12-inch single. You made sure nobody else would know where it came from if you found something."

"Why?"

“Think of DJing and breakdancing as elements of hip-hop. They wanted you to deal with the mystery of their greatness, but they had a shortsighted sense of their value. The ethos was all making something out of nothing and saying, ‘That’s ours.’ Hip-hop had no elders. They didn’t want to apprentice with anyone twice their age. Someone saying, ‘Let me show you how to scratch mix these two older records’ didn’t happen. Their elders were their record collection, which guided them and shaped their rhythm, tone, and attitude. The James Brown collection was a standard.

“The flow is how and why Clyde’s funky drummer beat made its way into the mainstream, DJs feeling and thinking about what would keep people dancing. Once people start putting it in their raps, you can extend that song’s entertainment by putting the funky drummer on top of it. It’s the same drummer pattern and beat, but they kept adding to it, and to a large extent, those beats weren’t people, they were records. Many said they did it without adult supervision and didn’t recognize their elders; however, a few did. Public Enemy, for one. For the most part, it was a celebration of creating something from nothing. Unfortunately, because of that, Clyde became one of the people that missed out the most.

“Nobody has ‘rhythm awards.’ The Grammys have awards for jazz, rock, country, songwriters, lyrics, and melodies, but nothing for rhythms. The reason goes deep into our contrived Western construction of music and its value. The beat and the groove have always been tied to Black music, which has been linked to lower forms, the primitive. Not sophisticated music, nor the genius of it. If there was, Clyde would be at the top of the list. That’s where we are now.”

“Do you think the reason is, all the rhythms go back to Africa, and those rhythms in America are not recognized and valued?”

“‘Fear of a Black Planet’—that’s how Public Enemy said it, using funky drummer in the song. Even though hip-hop and that beat [Clyde’s] have taken over the world, it isn’t recognized. I frame it that way because being left out, it’s part of power and money. When I teach classes in the music business, all these things happen. It’s racism and capitalism, they work in tandem. We have originators from the Black community who create something that gives people a lifetime of enjoyment. You have another element that profits off it and gives them lifetime financial rewards. The innovators were out.”

Similar to the innovative musicians of Clyde's early days in Chattanooga, the creators of those rhythms were left out in the cold without recognition, without acknowledgment of their names and accomplishments, and without financial compensation.

28

Promoting Funk in the Bay Area

> I love them. If they asked me to, I'd fly across the country to take in their groceries. I feel that way about Clyde and Fred [Wesley], and I probably would about Jabo if I got to know him a little better.
> —**ROBBIE KOWAL**

The first time Robbie Kowal met Clyde, he was playing with Masters of Groove. He said, "There was Clyde, Grant Green Jr., Marc Cary, and Reuben Wilson. The best way I describe him is bubbly, effervescent, and joyous—the sweetest guy ever. After I met him, I thought I should get them out to play at my festival. We had Funk Fest and worked on North Beach Jazz, an annual free event in Washington Square in San Francisco."

Robbie grew up in Newton, Massachusetts, and arrived in San Francisco in 1997 after attending college in New Orleans. He worked as a DJ and, in his words, "was a funk zealot." He told me, "George Clinton radicalized me in New Orleans into the church of funk." Robbie started a promotion company, Sunset Promotions, and brought bands to the San Francisco Bay Area, like Rebirth Brass Band and George Porter. He told me how he wanted to put Rickey Vincent's book *Funk* into action as a funk festival.

"In the early 2000s," Robbie said, "the Bay Area was a hotbed of underground hip-hop, the height of West Coast hip-jump [a reset of the previous groove]. I felt nobody was paying attention to funk. In 2000, we had our first funk fest with the headliner Mandrill [an eclectic funk rock and blues band from the late 1960s] and had a Family Stone reunion without Sly. The following year, we had *The Art of Funk* art show in November 2001, with George Clinton and all the P Funk painters,[1] with three movie nights at the old Red Vic theater. We felt so hopeful; we thought we would change people's perceptions of what funk was. It lasted three years but lost a lot of money.

"I was a promoter. Young white people played funk music in their shows, especially those who had gone to school in New Orleans, where people got inundated and radicalized into the funk movement. It wasn't cool if you didn't play the music or were getting your culture from mainstream radio. There was a cross-section of people coming to these events, but had it not been for the jam band movement playing funk, many funk artists would have fallen into obscurity. The Grateful Dead ['Shakedown Street'] and Phish [1997-to-1998 era "cow funk"] played funk tracks, and the Talking Heads is the greatest white funk band of all time. [I would include the Average White Band, a Scottish funk and R&B band, and, of course, Miles Davis was keeping the funk alive.] The movement out of Berklee College of Music included many young people studying fusion jazz, then becoming funk musicians. So, it was primarily white funk players keeping the funk alive. These are white kids from more congenial families who grew up going to jazz school.

"John Medeski was a big part of that community, along with Berklee offshoot band Sam Kendra. I started DJing and ran into Masters of Groove at the Berkshire Mountain Music Festival, an offshoot of High Sierra in Butternut, Massachusetts. It's a big jam band festival with headliners String Cheese Incident and Widespread Panic. I met Adam Deitch of Lettuce and many incredible East Coast funk musicians.

"We had a festival on August 6, 2006, called FOGGfest with James Brown and Bernard Purdie playing drums at Fort Mason meadow in San Francisco.[2] None of James's old friends wanted to be with him. Maceo still had enormous respect for James Brown, but some of them wouldn't even mention his name without shuddering. We lost tons of money. Soon after [December 26], Brown passed away. I started calling around. My idea was to create a tribute and do another funk fest. I talked to Rickey and said, 'Let's honor James Brown and have everybody that played with him.' Rickey said it wouldn't fly. I asked why, and he said, 'Some of them hate him, and some feel they never got the respect they deserve.' I said, 'OK, why don't we frame it as a tribute to the music of the James Brown era, the James Brown family of musicians, a JBs reunion?' I wanted Clyde, Jabo, Purdie, I wanted everybody.

"Clyde was on the fence. I talked to his agent Kathie Williams and asked why. She said he had a rough time with James Brown as part of the band and wouldn't do it. Our investors pulled out. It was heartbreaking that we couldn't put it on. We had everybody. I was even talking to Bootsy's manager, who was also his wife; he was going to bring his brother Catfish. It was going to be the biggest JB reunion of all time, and then it fell through. Bobby Byrd died a month later.

"I'm a historian at heart. I wanted everybody to understand the truth and the real legacy of the JBs before everyone was gone. Six years after our original attempt, in 2012, we pulled together a funk fest: Fred Wesley and the New JBs, featuring Clyde Stubblefield, Jabo Starks, Fred Thomas, and Fred Wesley, were all on board. Fred was a linchpin of the whole venture, he came with his band, the New JBs.

"Clyde and Jabo came through. Kathie managed it well and made it easy to work with them. She also helped me get in touch with Fred Thomas and get him on the bill. We had four of the original JBs. We struck out on Bootsy, who was touring, and Maceo and Pee Wee were in Europe. I had Johnny Griggs, the conga player. They all came together, we had a big dinner at the venue, where everybody sat down and hung out at the Mezzanine. Those were the best moments, the quiet moments sitting with them all backstage. I sat down with Fred, Clyde, and Jabo and listened to them talk about music. If someone asked Clyde about Brown, he'd say, 'No, I don't want to talk about Mr. Brown.' Jabo talked a little bit, and Fred was always polite."

Rudiments: At the Wheel

Robbie Kowal told me, "The Masters of Groove band included Reuben Wilson and Grant Green Jr., either Clyde or Bernard Purdie played on drums. We had booked some shows with them in 2005 at the Elbo Room, and I picked them up at the San Francisco airport. Being with them was one of the best days of my life. They were funny, and Grant, Reuben, and Clyde spent the whole car ride from SFO to the hotel ragging on each other and talking about, 'Oh no, you didn't play on that record. You played on this other one. You didn't play there. Nobody knows who you are, Grant. Everybody thinks you are your dad.' It was hilarious. Reuben, Grant, and Clyde went at it and ragged on each other for three straight days."

Tom Strader told me another story of driving Clyde and Jabo. "I was asked to pick up Fred Thomas, Clyde, Fred Wesley, and Jabo from the airport in Madison for the scholarship concert and get them some food. I was driving Kathie's car, and she had on Sirius radio, which was on the soul station. On the radio, there was a song they had all played on; they weren't paying attention to the music. They were going on and on—'Do you remember this, you remember that?' They're going back and forth. I mean, this is so cool, I'm driving along, and I wanted to take a selfie but had to stop myself. Maybe I should have because it was so fantastic."

"Do you remember what song was playing?"

"I think it was 'Cold Sweat.'"

29

Her Idols

> Every second I was with them stands out to me.
> —**KATHIE BOWMAN WILLIAMS**

Kathie Bowman Williams was Stubblefield's manager for twenty years beginning in the mid-1990s. Clyde lived and played music in Madison for forty-seven years, but, Williams said, "He's an international artist."

During those years, Williams was also Jabo Starks's manager. She first met Jabo at the Red Bar, in Grayton Beach, on the Gulf Coast of Florida. Jabo, whom she knew as John Starks, was playing there one night while she was having dinner with a friend at the restaurant. In 2015, at age seventy-seven, Jabo was still playing with the Red Bar Jazz Band five nights a week, then he'd drive to Mobile to play drums on Sunday at his church.

Kathie referred to Clyde and Jabo as her "childhood idols." The three of them became friends, and it wasn't long before they asked her to be their manager. She thought of them as her kids and was protective, ensuring that they were justly compensated for their time and talent. "I loved those two guys," she said. The arrangement worked well because they kept the lines of communication open, and she told them to question everything she did. Early in Kathie's tenure as their manager, Clyde recorded *The Original*, a CD that was released in 1998.

Kathie traveled with Clyde and Jabo to Japan, Scotland, and Germany. On their first trip to Japan, in 2004, their group included Fred Wesley and Sam Williams, a sax player out of Montgomery, Alabama. Waldo Weathers, a sax player with James Brown for fifteen years, joined them for one of the trips to Japan. Also with them was Robert Orr, from southern Alabama, who sadly died of Covid in 2020. Wesley called him "the greatest guitar player nobody has ever heard of." Orr also joined them in Europe.

After one of their shows in Japan, they flew directly to Scotland and performed within six hours of landing. On the plane, Clyde said, "Hey, Jabo, remember when we wanted to tour the world?" Jabo's reply: "Yes, but I didn't want to do it all in one day!"

When they arrived in Scotland, Clyde loved discovering there was a river with his name, the River Clyde, which flows through Glasgow. Along with them were Bernie Worrell on keyboards, George Clinton, and Scottish bass player Harold Adams. They played three performances in Scotland over three days. "They were great every single performance," Kathie said. They also toured in Germany a few times, playing with local musicians.

Kathie made sure they were not playing, as she said, "for nickels and dimes." One time, when the payments weren't going to be met, she gave up some of her manager's salary and asked the promoter to part with a portion of his commission to ensure they were correctly paid. She was happy when he complied with her request.

Clyde and Jabo never went on a U.S. tour outside the James Brown band, but they played at the Red Bar in Grayton Beach a few times. They also played shows in Montgomery, Alabama, and with Johnny Griggs, who had been a percussionist for James Brown.

"When Clyde and Jabo played with Brown, they complemented each other as if they were connected at their souls," Kathie said. And that's what made the music so great.

Single Stroke: Hearing Clyde the First Time

That connection and feeling the soul of the rhythms was what I experienced when I met Clyde at the Chamber, later the King Club, on a street of the same name in Madison. He was there for a Blue Monday, one of the weekly gatherings of his band, which occasionally included the blues great Luther Allison, who had also settled in Madison. On any Monday, for five dollars, I could stop by the club to be uplifted by its music: I'd either join in the dancing or sit at a table, tapping my hands to the beat. Clyde's rhythms inspired me, and in a couple of years, my tapping grew into drumsticks with a complete drum set of hi-hats, cymbals, bass, and snare drums, along with lessons.

When Clyde sat on his drum throne, the neon light from the sign of the King Club with a crown on top glowed through the window and over his head like a halo. He was striking, with his muscular frame, warm smile, wire glasses, and short, curly black hair. He wore a look that said more than he would ever give voice to, except through his music. A glow seemed to emanate from his red drum set. In that club, my inner rhythms found a home with Clyde's polyrhythms.

I would finish an evening shift at the sleep research lab in the middle of the Wisconsin winter, where the temperature was usually between 20-below and 20 degrees. I arrived just before midnight, and the stars were visible on a clear cold night after the moon had gone down.

Springs and summers were special because we would sit outside when the band took a break. We'd talk about music, politics, and the weather, and listen to the quiet streets that, during the day, were filled with state politicians and university students. It was half a block from the Capitol, with its white dome and statue of "Wisconsin," a stately woman facing Lake Monona.

And it was on King Street, listening to Clyde, where I first heard the call of drumming.

30

Spiritual Grandson

"Clyde and, of course, Jabo were responsible for waking me up for school growing up! My mom would BLAST James Brown in the house at 7 a.m. to get me up. I loved it, and it worked! I spent countless hours playing along to his recordings," Adam Deitch wrote to me.

Adam Deitch is the drummer for the band Lettuce, a funk band that originated in Boston in 1992. I reached Adam through email in 2022, as he was preparing to go on tour.

"Robbie Kowal described you as the 'spiritual grandson of Clyde.' How do you see Clyde's legacy influencing the various genres of your music—funk, jazz, jam band?"

"I'm honored to be called his 'Spiritual Grandson.' I have been a devotee of Clyde's style since I was twelve years old in the basement of my parents' house playing along to the *Star Time* compilation.[1] Clyde was an innovator whose grooves would stand the test of time. The whole concept of my band, Lettuce, is hard-hitting Clyde-style breaks that get people moving! Clyde's legacy is forever alive and well through multiple artists and genres."

"You said in *Drum Magazine* about funk rhythms, 'It's a feeling that can be thrown into any beat and genre.'[2] Would you say that Clyde's rhythms bridge those various genres in Lettuce's music, and how?"

Deitch replied, "Clyde's feel, sound, and inventiveness are the cornerstones of Lettuce's concept. What if Clyde was just in an instrumental horn band with long solos and no JB to cut him off? That's where we come from, in a way."

Adam described Clyde's legacy in the music that came after him. "Clyde's concept of a SUPER high cracking snare and his almost robotic 16th note hi-hats ('Funky Drummer') pretty much inspired the genre of hip-hop. Hip-hop is the most listened-to genre on planet Earth. His grooves are the backbone of hip-hop and funk music."

Adam met Clyde one time. He said, "We got to hang out when he visited John Scofield backstage in Madison. John introduced us, and I bothered the shit out of him for the day. We had a great time talking. I played my ass off for him that night. He was also a great human. The day I got to hang with him in Madison . . . I found that his laugh was infectious! Clyde4ever!!!!"

On February 21, 2017, Lettuce was playing a show at the Capitol Theater in Port Chester, New York, the day after Clyde passed. Adam honored Clyde as he announced, "Lettuce dedicates this Funky Capitol Theater Performance to the late great Clyde Stubblefield."[3]

Double Stroke Roll: Poker at Fuzzy's

Lakeside Pottery studio, owned by Steve Becker (Fuzzy), was the location of a poker game that occurred over a span of decades. Its participants called the game "Guts." The tables were filled with people who played music with Clyde and were friends of his or Eastside Johnny's. Throughout the years, sitting around the tables were Clyde; Diane Neukirch (whom Clyde called DeeDee); Tom Strader; Joey Banks; Reverend Dippermouth (who jammed often with Clyde on Mondays at the Club de Wash); Steven Staggs (from Clyde's band) and his girlfriend Paula, who played on and off for years; and Eastside Johnny (John Mehne, guitar) and his wife, Marge. Even Clyde's dentist joined the group in later years. In its heyday, two tables were in swing with betting, winning, losing, drinking, and fun.

Tom Strader told me, "You needed at least five people to have a good time. We played once a week, mostly on Tuesday nights. There are two things you don't do with Clyde—play poker and play ping-pong. Clyde was reckless—he'd rip off a piece of the white paper that remained from the day's pottery work. We'd called them Stubblebucks [Clyde's IOUs]. It was looking like he was going to win. I was waiting and waiting. I kept one and put it back in the pot, then Clyde lost the bank."

When Diane joined the card game in the late '80s, the game had been running for several years. While attending grad school at the UW and working as a waitress, she met Marge, Eastside Johnny's wife at the time, who invited her to play. She said it was nice to have another woman at the table. Diane described herself: "I was in my early twenties, a visual artist, and in awe of all these blues and funk musicians with huge personalities. They were everything this shy girl from Missouri was not."

The poker games continued for decades at Fuzzy's Pottery studio and later at Clyde's home. Diane described their game, "All players had two cards, including the center [dummy hand]. If you thought your hand was better than everyone's at the table, including the center's card, you declared that you were going 'pot.' If you didn't beat the pot or anyone else going 'pot,' you had to match it. Three people going 'pot' at once could significantly boost the amount. Clyde always wanted to ante five dollars, but I would lobby for two, which exasperated Clyde, who tried to get me to start with a bigger ante. Clyde was willing to go all in with an ace or king high. I was nervous going 'pot' with anything less than a pair of eights. Clyde often got beat by the two cards in the center, which meant he had to match the pot. We joked that he was chasing his money because he went 'pot' so much. The pots often were large, especially when they were already full of Stubblebucks—but anyone could add a marker.

"During the day, the studio's wheels were spinning with clay, making pots and bowls with an array of ceramic pigments lining the shelves. At night, when the card players arrived, the white butcher paper Fuzzy covered the tables with had pieces of clay stuck to them, and dust hung in the air. Markers were allowed in the game when we could not cover what we owed in cash. By the night's end, the edges would be dog ears with small torn pieces written with the amount owed and the player's initials. We would hold on to our markers [for the week], most likely they were Stubblebucks—and present them right away the next time we played. This would irk Clyde. He preferred to win some money before he paid off his markers. It was always fun and friendly, and Clyde loved it and took any ribbing in good stride. I think I still have a small marker from Clyde with his C. S. initials. Clyde was great at bluffing, but it took about a year to catch on. Once my winnings increased, it was more fun.

"The Reverend Dippermouth hated to lose. Steve, Tommy, Clyde, Eastside Johnny, and I were the core group during the years we played at the pottery studio. I would draw and sketch on the butcher block paper covering the table. We had the blues or classic rock playing in the background as we played cards, drank a bit, and breathed in the pottery dust. Luckily, Steve did not allow smoking cigarettes inside the studio, a staple in the earlier years when all the musicians chain-smoked.

"The table talk and stories were great fun. When Clyde was winning, the stories were long and drawn out, and the game's pace slowed. When he lost, he would tell us to shut up and play, but he was never mean-spirited. He would say it with a laugh. He would kid Tommy about Tom's long stories. I soaked it all up, mostly stayed sober, and won many hands. When Steve sold the pottery studio and moved to Florida, Joey started to play more. By this time, Eastside Johnny had passed away. Joey was such a great friend to Clyde, and it was great to have him join the group. During the last few years, as Clyde had more health issues, we played increasingly at Clyde's home—the consummate host. Many of the past years' characters were not playing anymore, but our smaller group was still a joy. I think Clyde's dentist started playing around that time.

"Clyde loved poker, Madison, and, of course, the music. He was so full of life, and we loved him. He always brought warmth and laughter to the game unless the pot got him too many times in one night."

Encore

31

Returning to Chattanooga

When Clyde returned to Chattanooga, Slim and he drove around and couldn't find any of the old places open. "I can't believe all the places we used to play around here. You mean, there are no clubs?" Clyde said, shocked. Slim answered, "That's it, this place died as far as live music in town. Nothing is going on now."

The once thriving Chattanooga music scene along Ninth Street and its surrounding areas were gone. Its streets had reverted to the industrial and natural sounds of the city—the clickety-clack of trains on steel tracks, the rolling of rubber and their engines revving, sounds of shoes in a hurry, and the gentle lapping of the Tennessee River. The sand bars in the river came and went with the seasons, but the music scene stayed submerged, waiting, silently underground. Slim had showed me on my visit to Chattanooga where the venues once stood hosting famous visiting acts, local talent, and future famous musicians, along with the people who came to listen and loved their music. A musical land of R&B, blues, and funk music that once permeated the air with song, voices, rhythms, and notes from the clubs and halls that poured into the streets.

"The late sixties and seventies were dominated by disco," Slim said with an air of sadness. "There would occasionally be live music, and I'd get back together with a group that would last two or three months, but nothing like the old days."

The Ninth Street Revival is a reunion of local musicians that the city calls "Live on the Big 9," which continues to present day. Slim said, "I managed to get five of us from the old group together, including Clyde. Joe Burke came up onstage while Clyde took down his drums. Joe saw

Clyde's unique foot pedal. Joe grabbed it and put it under his shirt and started off the stage. Clyde yelled, 'I see you. Come back here!' Joe yelled back, 'Man, this is a *machine* here.' Clyde said, 'Well, we'll get you one, I have some connections.' Slim said, 'Joe, what are you going to do with it? Hang it on your wall or something?' And Joe said, 'Yeah, that's right, this comes from Clyde Stubblefield.'"

"We used to worship him," Slim said about Joe. "Now he doesn't do anything. He feels like he missed something back in the era when the drums played a lot of melodic tunes and continuous rhythm, as Clyde did on 'Cold Sweat.' Joe couldn't do those things. Technically, he knew all about drums, rudiments, and rhythms. He's a great drummer, but he won't play."

Joe was revered and respected by musicians who knew and played in bands with him, and there was sadness and regret among Clyde and those who were closest to him that Joe had stopped drumming. He had played with the Blue Shufflers, the Cascades, the Midnighters, Chubby Checker, *and* Bill Doggett. Joe had given Clyde his first drumsticks and taught him his first rhythms.

But Joe's belief in himself, his abilities, and his talents had fallen away over the years. He felt he could not keep up with the changes. He watched as the teenage Clyde, who once told him, "Joe, someday I'm going to be better than you," rose above him and everyone around him. And in the end, Joe, who had formed the backbeat of Clyde's early rhythms, admired Clyde the man, his talent, and his accomplishments so much that he wanted his foot pedal to hang on his wall.

32

Clyde's Beat

Hip-Hop

Funk is the DNA in hip-hop.[1]
—**GEORGE CLINTON**

Fifteen years after "Funky Drummer" was released in 1970, Clyde's drumbeats began appearing in hundreds of songs. It was the beginning of hip-hop's widespread popularity, legacy, and financial success. In the documentary *Copyright Criminals*,[2] music historian Jeff Chang said, "No one took hip-hop seriously until it started making a lot of money."

The roots of hip-hop block parties reach back to the late 1960s, when Jonathan Cameron Flowers, from Brooklyn, named himself the first Grandmaster. He mixed funk and blues music and used up to three turntables to spin his sounds. In 1969 he opened for James Brown at Yankee Stadium, bringing his music to a huge audience from across the five boroughs of New York City.[3] Playing from the baseball field that day, Clyde had no idea that decades later this concert would foreshadow a merging of his rhythms with a new genre.

Cindy Campbell, a high school student in New York, promoted a Back to School Jam on August 11, 1973, with her brother Clive, the future DJ Kool Herc.[4] The jam was held at the siblings' home, at 1520 Sedgwick Avenue in the Bronx. The address became synonymous with the birthplace of hip-hop and was commemorated by a sign in front of the 102-unit apartment building on what is now called Hip Hop Boulevard. The jam cost 25 cents for women and 50 cents for men.[5] Its party soon expanded outdoors into Cedar Playground. "Simultaneously the historical jam session became the first in a series of popular block parties,"

Briana A. Thomas said.[6] Soon, multicultural gatherings occurred with African American, Caribbean, African, and Latin American communities coming together for block parties in increasing numbers. New DJs of the genre appeared on the scene, including Grandmaster Flash and Afrika Bambaataa, who soon overtook Grandmaster Flowers in popularity. The growing explosion that gathered and recombined pieces from many types of music left Flowers behind. Sadly, Flowers died homeless in 1992. Also forgotten for much of the rise of hip-hop's popularity was Clyde's place as the constant backbeat in the evolution of what the first DJ Grandmaster had begun.

The block parties were organized and run by MCs with microphones and DJs who created infinite drum loops on turntables. The DJs later became the original hip-hop producers, among them Kool Herc and Grandmaster Flash. The DJs would play the same record on two turntables, then rewind one while the other was playing, creating an infinite drum loop as they rapped on top of the beat. The DJs searched out drum breaks on records and put them together with different parts of several songs. The lyrics from one song, a guitar riff from another, a drum break, a trumpet solo—whatever sounded good to them. This sampling became the foundation of hip-hop.

James Brown knew the DJs were looking for drumbeats to sample, so he made an album released in 1986 called *In the Jungle Groove*, a compilation of his old tracks. Featured on Side 1 was "Funky Drummer"; on Side 2 was a three-minute track of the looped "Funky Drummer" solo. That year, three hip-hop songs were released sampling the loop: "It's a Demo," "South Bronx," and "Eric B. Is Present." As the genre grew from 1986 to 1987, Clyde's rhythms were being heard everywhere. His name, however, wasn't. "'Funky Drummer' has done miracles for hip-hop," Questlove said on the blog Crimes Against Music. "It's the traffic cop. The greatest hip-hop album of all time, *It Takes a Nation of Millions to Hold Us Back*, by Public Enemy—it's all over that record. Funky Drummer was essential for that classic hip hop period. Everybody used that sound."[7]

Clyde said in *Copyright Criminals*, "I didn't even know what sampling was until someone said [to me] they're sampling your drums. Next thing I know all the rap artists are using it for their sampling. I never got a thing, I never got a hello, how are you doing from any of the rap artists . . . not a penny for it. So many groups that sample my stuff, they say I'm the world's number one sampled drummer."

"Hip-hop sampling came out of the DJ culture," explained Hank Shocklee of Public Enemy.[8] "You would have a drum beat and then we would scratch a horn hit on top of the drumbeat."[9] In *Copyright Criminals*, Steve Albini, a musician and recording engineer, said, "The argument that a sample is not different than any other instrument is absurd. It's absurd because no other instrument allows you to simply and easily take someone else's life's work and put your name on it."

The beginnings of an early type of what might be considered sampling go back to the 1940s, to *musique concrète*. French composer Pierre Schaeffer recorded natural and man-made sounds around him—falling rocks, a metronome, a bird song, pounding rain, a pan being hit—and then spliced the tape so one sound would run into another.[10]

It occurs to me that modern hip-hop is essentially an updated and highly technical version of Clyde's innate genius at turning sounds from his world, both natural and man-made, into polyrhythmic drumbeats, and *musique concrète*'s combining and recombining sounds on tape. Modern sample-based hip-hop exploded when it turned from turntables to digital samplers, which allowed the construction of entire songs from complex assemblies of fragments assembled from large vinyl record libraries.

Copyright Criminals describes sampling as making a game of the process and having everyone try to figure out where each part of the song came from. Part of the reason for the "game" came in an attempt to protect the DJs from lawsuits. In the film, Clyde admits that after hearing a cut, "I can't be sure if that's my drum pattern. If it's a little snap, I can't be sure. That's where honesty comes in, if a person comes in and says 'Yes, that's yours.' Then we discuss things. Otherwise, I can't go anywhere saying, 'Hey, you're using my drum pattern,' a little da-da-da—I don't know what was me."[11]

"[Clyde's] name has never [appeared] on any of the compilation credits," media professor Siva Vaidhyanathan says in *Copyright Criminals*. "His name is not part of the legal legacy of all of those great tunes he played on. He doesn't get royalties, he got paid for time in the studio." And that was it.

The same year *Copyright Criminals* was released, in 2009, Tower of Power released *Star Time* on their album the *Great American Soulbook*. In David Garibaldi's tribute to Clyde he recalled, "I try to channel Clyde every time we play it . . . my tribute of love and respect for one of the greatest drummers in the modern era."

According to the website *WhoSampled*, "Funky Drummer" has been sampled in 1,783 songs. Even the theme song of the Cartoon Network's *The Powerpuff Girls* sampled the drumbeat heard on seventy-eight episodes from 1998 to 2005. But Clyde never saw royalties from any of the songs because he wasn't credited as a songwriter.

A Partial List of Songs That Sample Clyde's Drum Breaks

"Rebel Without a Pause," Public Enemy
"1 (PEace)," Public Enemy
"Mortal Combat," Big Daddy Kane
"Fuck tha Police," N.W.A.
"It's a Demo," Kool G Rap and DJ Yolo
"Have a Nice Day," Roxanne Shante
"I Am Stretched on Your Grave," Sinead O'Connor
"Say Kids," Coldcut
"My Name Is Prince," Prince
"Fight the Power," Public Enemy
"Mama Said Knock You Out," LL Cool J
"Run's House," Run-DMC
"Save Me," Nicki Minaj
"Kick the P.A.," Korn and the Dust Brothers
"Drug Fits the Face," Moby
"Freedom! '90," George Michael
"2001," Melissa Etheridge
"Shirtsleeves," Ed Sheeran
"Popcorn," Aphex Twin

A few hip-hop legends did eventually acknowledge Clyde's contributions. Among them were Flavor Flav and Chuck D of Public Enemy, and Questlove of The Roots. The singer-songwriter Melissa Etheridge also acknowledged his contributions to her music.

Public Enemy featured Clyde on the song "1 (PEace)" in 2012 on the album *The Evil Empire of Everything*. From 2006 to 2007, Clyde went on tour with DJ Kool Herc. An excerpt from the *Madison Isthmus* newspaper reads, "This Friday at the Memorial Union Terrace, DJ Kool Herc won't have to sample Stubblefield's beats. The two perform live on the same stage in an encore of their 2006 Madison appearance. The show will serve to welcome to campus the fourth cohort of UW-Madison's First Wave Spoken Word and Hip Hop Arts Learning Community."[12] Clyde also performed with DJ Kool Herc on October 31, 2007, at the UIC Theater at the University of Illinois in Chicago, a performance that was sponsored by the departments of performing arts and African American studies, Jane Addams Hull-House Museum, and the Public Square.

Etheridge, who used Clyde's beats on her 1992 song "2001," honored Clyde and his drumming during a July 4, 1994, concert at the Civic Center in Madison. According to Tom Alesia's blog, she and Clyde went out bar-hopping afterward.[13] Clyde also appeared on *The Tonight Show Starring Jimmy Fallon* on March 3, 2011, performing "Fight the Power" with Eclectic Method with Chuck D and The Roots, the show's house band. Normally Chuck D would rap over a sample, but that night he didn't have to—he had the real Funky Drummer onstage playing drums with him.

Clyde is on the cover of the *Copyright Criminals* boxset, which includes two DVDs and a vinyl LP. He capitalized on his hip-hop resurgence with his solo album *Revenge of the Funky Drummer*, released in 1997 by Interaction Records. The title of the album says it all.

33

The Heartbeat of the Drum

The Prince in the Shadows

I still don't believe it, but I am honored.[1]
—**CLYDE STUBBLEFIELD**

There had been discussions about Clyde and Prince collaborating, but it never materialized. However, Clyde recorded once in 1992 at Prince's Paisley Park when he traveled to Minnesota to play on three songs of Phillip Upchurch's (jazz guitarist and bassist) album *Whatever Happened to the Blues*. The album was in the genre of jazz, funk/soul, and blues with its fusion and modern electric blues and funk styles. Clyde played double drumming with Michael Bland (a drummer for Prince and later Soul Asylum) on "I Don't Want Nobody to Give Me Nothing," a James Brown song, and drum soloed on "I'm Going Down Slow" and "Sweet Woman Blues." Bland said in *Modern Drummer*, "As soon as he started playing, all I wanted to do was put my sticks down and listen. The anatomy of all those JB records was just there in the raw."[2]

"Who knows what the Clyde-Prince relationship was?" Tom Strader said. "Someone asked him if he had met Prince. In a TV interview, Clyde said he saw him in the hallway at Paisley Park, but they didn't interact much. However, the urban legend recounts someone coming into Clyde's recording studio and saying, 'Prince would like to talk to you.' It was well known that both Prince and Clyde were exceptional ping-pong players and very competitive. The legend recounts Prince saying, 'You think you're a better ping-pong player?' Clyde said, 'Maybe, maybe not.' Then they played a game and found out who was better."

Ping-pong being a *tink-tink, ping, tink-tink, ping*, back and forth, a rudiment rhythm, it makes sense Clyde would be a good player. Whether they only talked or also played ping-pong, Clyde influenced this musical giant of Minnesota.

The last fifteen years of Clyde's life were plagued with struggles. His wife, Jody, said he remained strong throughout the last few years of his life. She said, "He would have liked to continue playing as much as he always had." He sadly experienced many challenges, both physically and financially. In 2000, Clyde received a diagnosis of bladder cancer, which he survived. He underwent two surgeries and other cancer treatments in the summer of 2002 but kept playing music fourteen months after being diagnosed. He said, "I'm feeling just fine. I have a checkup every three months and I have one more of that, then it's down to a check-up every six months. Everything looks good so far."[3]

Two years later he had surgery to remove a kidney, which required him to have dialysis three times a week. He received countless calls and emails from family and friends who offered to be tested for a kidney match. "It's a humbling response for Stubblefield. People care about him. He looked up when told that and smiled. I care a lot about the people, too."[4] The dialysis dragged on for seven years. Cris Plata said that while on dialysis Clyde burned his thumb on a skillet, which caused him to lose feeling in it. This caused complications, and the dialysis probably prevented it from healing.

"It was miserable," Jody said. "One day he pulled some cornbread out of the oven and hit his hand and burned it so badly his thumbprint was left on the cast iron." He wasn't able to get proper medical care soon enough and it became a huge problem. It became infected, causing gangrene. They eventually had to do surgery, having both his thumb amputated and the entire joint to the wrist.

"Oh my God Kathie," Jody cried to his manager, "how is he going to drum?" Kathie replied, "I've seen Clyde do more with his left hand than three bad drummers, and everything he did was with his left hand, so he just hit the hi-hat."

He was able to continue drumming his unique rhythms by using his ingenuity. He made a drumstick out of the thick padding and a stretchy foam rubber that he put over a maraca handle and attached it to his drumstick. He used that in his right hand so he could still hit the hi-hat. Despite all this, Clyde proclaimed, "I never expected all the stuff I've experienced. I just play from my soul and heart and feelings, and I love it. Like I say, I'm a very happy man."[5]

The first gig he played after getting his thumb amputated was the Hollywood Bowl, on August 13, 2014, to fifty thousand fans with some of the musicians from the old James Brown band. It was led by Christian McBride, with D'Angelo, Pee Wee Ellis, Fred Wesley, Clyde, and Jabo. It came on the heels of the movie *Get On Up*. Jody said, "No one even knew anything was wrong." He played with the same power and enthusiasm as he always had, despite missing his thumb.

Clyde and Jabo were going to breakfast the day of the Hollywood Bowl show. Clyde didn't step up high enough for the curb, so he tripped, and he had a big gash on the top of his head. "When they got back," Jody said, "I could barely see the Band-Aid. I said, 'You tell me in California they sell brown Band-Aids?' Kathie had put on a Band-Aid and colored it with her black marker. Nobody knew."

In speaking about his recovery and road back to playing, Jody said, "He took it in stride. He had never asked me to zip or button anything; he never asked for help when he was training himself to do things with his hands. The last couple of years of his life he was getting sicker and sicker and all his players—Doc, Dave, and Jimmy—went wherever Clyde needed them, even if they had to cancel other gigs. He would say to them, 'If you want to be with me, you are going be with me.'"

In 2016, Clyde traveled to the Ardmore Music Hall in Philadelphia to play a James Brown Dance Party. "I'm not doing too many live shows anymore," Stubblefield said, "so if I'm going to do it, I better like the people I'm with and the talent they have, because it's the music that matters most. Always did."[6]

Clyde was not old enough for Medicare and had no medical insurance. The bills mounted. He and Jody had no idea how they would pay the rising hospital and medical costs. The numbers rose to over $90,000. Madison musicians held benefit concerts and well-wishers contributed, but that only covered a fraction of the bills.

Then, one day, there was a phone call with an offer to pay Clyde's debts. The only stipulation was a request not to reveal who paid the bills to anyone until the donor had passed away. We now know the phone call came from Prince, the prolific singer, songwriter, and guitarist who anonymously paid all of Clyde's bills.[7] Prince, a musician known and loved around the world, a Jehovah's Witness, a vegetarian, and a behind-the-scenes philanthropist, had a practice of secretly donating money to people and causes.[8]

Jody said, "The medical bills were rising. . . . We were worried about how we would deal with the rest of this. I got a call from Clyde's manager at work, and she said, 'These people want you to call them back.'" Jody did.

When Clyde heard about it, he said, "I still don't believe it, but I am honored."

"It's a house," he said with a laugh. "So many people donated to my medical cause and I'm paying the bill every month. It's my fault. I didn't have health insurance. I'm going to get it. I learned my lesson."[9]

Clyde had played for the "hardest-working man in show business," but Prince admired Clyde's contribution to music and cared for him in a way the Godfather of Soul never had.

Jody said, "He did everything he was supposed to do. He didn't want to die. In his final days he was very tired. He was sleeping twenty-three to twenty-four hours a day. He was very sick, but he would lift himself up and he'd go out because his name was on the marquee." After a while, he had his nephew Brett do the drumming. Clyde Stubblefield's kidneys finally failed him on February 18, 2017.

In looking back to how they met, Jody said, "He came to my restaurant, I cooked food for him, watching him eat. . . . I lived with him the last twenty-five years of his life, and it was pure heaven." Jody said her husband loved Madison. "He chose to settle down here because he loved the people, and the people loved him."[10]

"When he was in the hospital, I was with him all night until two in the morning," Jody reminisced with sadness. "He hadn't said much. I went out to get coffee somewhere, and as I got up and walked away to the door, I said, 'I love you, Clyde,' and in this big booming voice he said 'I love you too, baby.' I'm grateful for that; he lived maybe another ten hours."

Jody continued, "Clyde was strong until he couldn't be anymore. His was a very gallant death. I was right by his side; one moment there was a heartbeat and then next there was nothing."

The heartbeat of a man who knew and lived his life embodying and expanding the boundaries of rhythm, the heartbeat of the drum, the heartbeat of the world, had stopped.

FIGURE 24. Dr. Stubblefield poster from when Clyde received an honorary PhD from University of Wisconsin-Madison. Illustration by Brent Nicastro.

ON THE DRUM THRONE

Honorary Degree: Dr. Stubblefield

It was a slightly cloudy, breezy day in Madison, on May 12, 2017, one day shy of twelve weeks after Clyde passed away. As part of the University of Wisconsin's commencement ceremony, Clyde was being posthumously granted an honorary PhD; thankfully, he knew before he died he was to be granted the honor.

Several prominent university and close music associates of Clyde wrote letters of recommendation for the award. Thomas E. Strader, MS, honorary associate fellow at the UW-Madison School of Engineering, was key in organizing the process. He secured letters from Dr. Anthony Di Sanza, professor of percussion; Richard Davis, emeritus professor of bass; Johannes Wallmann, associate professor of music; and Steven G. Fisher, marketing manager with Yamaha Drums and cymbal maker Meinl.

"It is impossible to overstate the impact Stubblefield has had on the world of drumming," said Anthony Di Sanza in his letter nominating Clyde for the degree. "He has inspired generations of drummers with his syncopated yet flowing rhythmic grooves that combine effortlessly with his unique musical taste and sensibility. For many of us living in the world of drums and percussion, he is a trailblazer and a hero."[1]

Along with the long list of honors, musical associations, and accomplishments, the university's commencement program read: "All of the accolades aside, Stubblefield perhaps made his biggest impact by inspiring numerous musicians with his music and also made a point of helping young musicians learn the ropes and establish their careers, whether with words of wisdom or inviting them to join him onstage. Stubblefield's music is still enjoyed by people throughout the world and is a musical example of the Wisconsin Idea."

Highlights of Clyde's Career

1958: Clyde joins his first band, the Cascades, in Chattanooga
Early 1960s: Plays with and tours with Otis Redding
1965: Clyde joins James Brown's Famous Flames
1967: Records "Cold Sweat" with James Brown's band (no. 1 R&B, no. 7 Pop)
1968: Goes on tour of Vietnam with James Brown
November 20, 1969: Records "Funky Drummer," destined to be the unofficial "most sampled track ever"

1971: Leaves James Brown's band and settles in Madison, Wisconsin
1990: Named "Drummer of the Year" by *Rolling Stone*
1997: *The Revenge of the Funky Drummer* is released
2000: Inducted into Wisconsin Area Music Industry Hall of Fame
2000: Clyde's drumsticks are displayed at the Rock and Roll Hall of Fame
2002: Prince pays Clyde's medical bills
2002: *The Original Funky Drummer Breakbeat* Album, with twenty-six tracks, is released
2003: Clyde's third solo album, *The Original*, is released; all compositions are based on his drum grooves
2004: Receives lifetime achievement award at the Madison Area Music Awards
2009: The documentary *Copyright Criminals*, featuring Clyde, is released
March 29, 2011: Clyde Stubblefield plays as guest artist with Chuck D and The Roots with Questlove on *The Tonight Show Starring Jimmy Fallon*
2013: Awarded Yahama's Drums Music lifetime achievement award
November 8, 2014: Clyde Stubblefield Day is declared in Clyde's hometown of Chattanooga, Tennessee
November 11, 2014: Named no. 2 in "Top 20 Drummers of All Time" by *LA Weekly*
October 10, 2015: Clyde Stubblefield Day is declared in Madison by Mayor Paul Soglin
March 16, 2016: Clyde and his longtime drumming partner Jabo Starks were named the sixth-best drummers of all time in *Rolling Stone*
2016: Awarded honorary PhD from the University of Wisconsin-Madison
2019: Bench with plaque dedication in Brittingham Park, Madison

Take a Bow

> My music is my life—my music is my breathing.
> —**CLYDE STUBBLEFIELD**

REMEMBERING CLYDE

from the family of Sir Miles Dewey Davis

Play On.
We love you, The Real Funky Drummer.
Vince, nephew of Miles
Erin, son of Miles
Cheryl, daughter of Miles

FIGURE 25. Clyde at twenty-fifth anniversary for *Whad'Ya Know* radio show, Wisconsin Public Radio, August 2010. Photo credit Brent Nicastro.

“We lost another Pillar Stone that held up the Foundation of Funk. Mr. Clyde Stubblefield has left our frequency. I am lost for words & Rythm right now. Dang Clyde! U taught me so much as I stood their watchin’ over u & Jabo while keepin’ one eye on the Godfather. We all loved U so much. (SENDOUT YR LOVE TO HIS FAMILY & friends)! Then share yr stories about this Fire breathin’ Drummer, (THE FUNKY DRUMMER)! R.I.P. From all yr Funkateers. . .” —Bootsy Collins

“When I woke up this morning and saw the news that Clyde has passed away, my heart sank. He was one of my favorite drummers and a hero. I learned a lot from listening to him and even today I still study his drumming from time to time and always am amazed at how futuristic his drumming with JB was. So creative, and definitely in that category of drummers who were at the vanguard of a rhythmic revolution in the late ’60s. It’s with much love and respect that I offer TOP’s most sincere condolences to Clyde’s family . . . and from me, Clyde my brother, RIP and thank you for all you’ve given to those of us who wanted to be like you.” —David Garibaldi of Tower of Power

On the CD *Dan Trudell Fishin’ Again: A Tribute to Clyde Stubblefield & Dr. Lonnie Smith* (February 17, 2023), Trudell said, “What strikes me about these two musical geniuses is the similarity in their spirit of love and joy. They shared it effortlessly to those around them not only in the music, but in the way they interacted with everybody they were around. How fortunate I have been to have had them in my life!”

POEM TO CLYDE
by Cris Plata

Well, I said goodbye to an old friend of mine.
We both circled that old sun for a long, long time
When the hour is late, and the light grows dim
These are the times I remember him
Oh, he could roar like a thunderstorm
Thunder and lightning in a human form
You never knew what was behind his eyes
He was the devil in an angel disguise

"The fun thing is, you can listen to him play and we can always recall his musicianship and malaprops. I'll always have fond memories, and even after we stopped playing together, we didn't stop being friends. We would hang around with him, watch Packer games, or go out to eat. He'd always come out here to the farm and raid our garden. I like to listen to my CDs, cause he's on there all the time." —Cris Plata

Pauli Ryan, a medical professional and Clyde's percussionist for thirty years, was with Clyde at the end of his life. "He taught me so much," Ryan said, "and I miss him as a dear friend."

Joey Banks echoed what so many have said: "Clyde was a super, kind, iconic individual and should have been treated with the most grace and respect but wasn't always. My life would be much different if I hadn't met Clyde. I felt privileged and honored to have a relationship with him. His legacy is alive forever. He would always sign his autographs 'peace and love.'"

FIGURE 26. Clyde waving with drums and stuffed toys. Vilas Park, Madison, 1996. Photo credit D. Leah Steinberg.

FINAL NOTATION

Clyde was born and raised in a city on the Tennessee River with Lookout Mountain peering down on the place that birthed the Empress of the Blues. He had ridden that train of legend, the Midnight Special, and taken the rhythms of the industrial age, transforming and creating them from rhythms of the past into a fusion of his internal understanding, leading to new forms of music. The *clickety-clack* of the rails, the rhythms of the Tennessee River, the sounds of factories, and a young man's footsteps in a Southern city were all part of his DNA that developed into an integrated synthesis of rhythms in his heart and soul. Everything united to produce an exceptionally talented, gentle, and giving man who would change the face of American music, giving it new breadth and depth.

Along with the rhythms he absorbed from the industrial sounds around him, older African American musicians took Clyde under their wing. With kindness and compassion, they nurtured him with ideas that fed Clyde's own musical creations, leading him to branch out into new terrain that was rooted in the musical Delta. Clyde put his rhythms under the freshly polished shoes of the Godfather of Soul, powering him to dance his way to a brand-new bag. He brought rhythm and blues to southwestern Wisconsin and seamlessly blended R&B, blues, jazz, country, Tex-Mex, and rock music into the rhythmic seasonal groove of a northern capital city where he found a quiet life with friends and family.

In 1969 Mayor Dyke presented James Brown with the key to the city of Madison.[1] Clyde Stubblefield and Jabo Starks, the remaining two drummers after an original line-up of five, were the ones keeping the polyrhythmic beats under Brown's dancing feet. Less than two years later, Clyde settled down in the northern city. After owning dozens of keys in the capital city and opening doors for dozens of musicians, it took another forty-five years for Clyde to receive the same honor of the key to the city from Mayor Soglin in 2015.[2]

Meanwhile, Clyde Stubblefield, the drummer who changed the face of music, who got his start on the streets of the Southern segregated city of Chattanooga, left the door open for everyone.

Clyde opened up the intricate polyrhythmic sounds of Africa to this author, rhythms of drums falling in sync, like the brain and heart waves I interpreted for a living, creating the music of a good night's sleep. For it was in that small dark smoky club with a stage barely large enough for a band that I discovered a rhythm that was missing in my life. He helped me find new rhythms of my own, awakening me to the soulful daylight of the blues and funk.

Two thousand miles away, upon hearing of his passing, near a dock of the San Francisco Bay where Otis Redding wrote "(Sittin' on) The Dock of the Bay," I pictured Clyde singing the song, his voice coming through just as it did when I listened to him sing in Madison, less than a mile from Otis's memorial: "Two thousand miles I roam, just to make Madison my home." I hung my head and cried and watched the tides roll away.

I hope Clyde will nod his approval with this effort to honor him and give me a big smile and hug when I see him again.

CODA

Random Synchronicities, Thoughts, and Memories

My father used to speak about wandering Maxwell Street in Chicago, the home of the Chicago blues, with his parents in the 1920s and '30s, hearing music playing on every corner. It was the place he bought his first clarinet. That was the first live music I remember hearing in our Chicago suburban living room.

The snow falls, I stomp my boots and walk into a café in Madison, Wisconsin. It is the early 1990s and the music of Clyde Stubblefield and Ben Sidran fill the warmth of the room, spilling onto State Street. A hot delicious meal, the music, the falling snow, me and a friend drifting away into a wintery afternoon.

I was inspired by Clyde and decided to take drum lessons a few years after first hearing him play. At the time, I worked in a sleep research lab at the University of Wisconsin Hospital and Clinics. I began contemplating all rhythms intertwined, sleep, circadian rhythms, drumming, and the cycles of nature. I remember walking down the Lakeshore Path by the not-yet-frozen waters of Lake Mendota during one of my first winters in Madison and I can still hear in my mind, so many decades later, the water pounding up against the light layer of ice. I thought then and now how it sounded like drums.

One of my favorite memories was at the Chamber in Madison in 1996. Clyde was playing with Luther Allison, a world-famous soulful blues guitar player. I've never heard anything so powerful before or since. After the set I experienced the graciousness of Luther's humble dignity, just a year before he died. I shook his hand and told him how moved I was by hearing him play. He looked at me wide-eyed as if no one had ever praised his musicianship and thanked me. I also had the honor of meeting several world-class musicians who lived quiet lives, away from east and west coast fame, in Madison. Blues master Luther Allison, Roscoe Mitchell from the Art Ensemble of Chicago, jazz musician Ben Sidran, and Primous Fountain, a world-class composer.

I'd personally walked, biked, or driven by a narrow, red-brick, "ugly" building for decades and never guessed the enormity of the musical history that was made there, in Smart Studios. It stood around the corner from where I once had an apartment and across the street from where many years later my best friend Bill cooked at the Friendly Bar. I never knew that Butch Vig would go over to the Friendly and pick up extra musicians or backup singers to fill in, including Marty, the bartender, who was the bartender when my friend was a cook there.

Watching the documentary *Soul of the Funky Drummers* made me smile to again see and hear Clyde. I got up and danced and pretended I was back on King Street on a cold Blue Monday night during a long Wisconsin winter. I watched it again and again, taken by the music and trying to understand just how it was that Clyde perfected his style.

I envisioned the feeling of freedom from both Clyde's funky rhythms and my favorite jam band musicians, the Grateful Dead. The Grateful Dead's unique drumming styles and their famous (among Deadheads) "Drums and Space." Ann Plata and David Stanoch conveyed the feeling of Clyde "going off to space" with his jamming styles. And the similarities of both Clyde and the Dead being open to merging of different styles of music; blues, rock, jazz, and country.

Rickey Vincent said, "You need to use terms that are somewhat in the abstract. George Clinton has a description when he talks about rhythm, and how the groove masters work around a beat. There's the expectation of exactly where the beat is, where the beat is supposed to be, and what time. A metronome or a computer can pinpoint it and tell you, but a master gives you something infinitesimal around that beat so that your mind, body, and soul must reconcile where that will be and where it belongs. The listener becomes an active participant."

Which made me think of being infinite and microscopic simultaneously. How universal the science is of nature mimicking each other in the orbits of the cell and the universe. I thought of the rhythms of nature, the seasons, the sounds of the river and the world around us, the grain elevator, the rolling wheels of steel on the train tracks, and the unrehearsed rhythms that were an intrinsic part of Clyde's being. How we are all active participants in the rhythm of the minute and galaxy at the same time. And how Clyde embodied that idea.

As I listened to music I love, a beautiful integration of melody, jamming, drums, psychedelia, poetry, and love that wrapped its melodies around community and freedom, I realized what I was missing, the rhythmic soul that Clyde showed me back in the '90s in the small, smoky club in Madison, Wisconsin. The pull of the beat with emphasis on the One, not the two and the four; the One that started you with the rhythm, didn't let you wait, didn't make you wonder, you were there right from the start. The funk, the groove, the guts of pure emotion that reach into one's soul. A place where emotion is raw and lets the blues and the pain loose until you smile when you dance, and you know this is where you want to be, where you have to be, to know something you never knew before—to something I never knew before. That to know myself, my depth, my pain, and its—antidote, I wish I had known it from the start, the moment I was born, to be reborn in the rhythm of myself and the planet—the drums leading the way with the first heartbeat of the earth.

He brought me rhythm
Timing the sounds beyond time
Stars shine clear tonight
—*D. Leah Steinberg*

ACKNOWLEDGMENTS

I owe my heartfelt gratitude to the following people, all friends, family, and musical collaborators and bandmates of Clyde's, for speaking with me and sharing their stories, photographs, and support: Joey Banks, Trevor Banks, Joe Burke, Pee Wee Ellis, Robert "Slim" Eppinger, Lenell Glass, Jody Hannon, Wally Ingram, John Medeski, Cris Plata, Ben Sidran, David Stanoch, Rickey Vincent, Fred Wesley, and last but certainly not least Kathie Williams.

To Steve Adams, for your guidance and writing coaching and direction. I couldn't have done this without you.

To John Anderson, for your feedback, input, and love.

NOTES

Chapter 1

1. Leadbelly, "'Midnight Special' by Leadbelly."
2. Oliver, *Songsters and Saints*, 247.
3. Seamons, "The Midnight Special."

Chapter 2

1. Kebede, *Roots of Black Music*, 94.
2. Kebede, *Roots of Black Music*, 46.
3. Montfort, *Ancient Traditions—Future Possibilities*, 1.
4. Jones, *Blues People*, 25.
5. Bowman, "Funk and James Brown," 258–68.
6. Bowman, "Funk and James Brown."
7. Sidran, *Black Talk*, 7.
8. Sidran, *Black Talk*.
9. Vincent, *Funk*, 5.
10. Vincent, *Funk*, 37.
11. Jones, *Blues People*, 19.
12. Bowman, "Funk and James Brown," 258–68.
13. Palmer, *Rock & Roll*, 45–47.

Chapter 3

1. "Historical Marker Database, "Congo Square."
2. Candy, "Black History."
3. Hoffman, "Mississippi Is the Birthplace of American Music."
4. Soul of America, "New Orleans."
5. Soul of America, "New Orleans."
6. Rowe, *Chicago Blues*, 40–49.
7. *Times of Malta*, "Leading R&B Drummer Earl Palmer Dead at 84."

Chapter 4

1. White, "Blues Culture and the Black Experience in the River City."
2. White, "Blues Culture and the Black Experience in the River City."
3. Wilkerson, *Warmth of Other Suns*.
4. Homan, "Know Your History!"

5. Travel Southeast Tennessee, "The Big 9."

6. Moss, "Lost Music Town of Tennessee."

7. Smith and McClane, "Rewriting a History."

8. World Population Review, "Chattanooga."

Chapter 5

1. The original Chattanooga African American Museum was opened in 1983 and renovated in 1996. It became the Chattanooga African American Museum and the Bessie Smith Performance Hall, renamed the Bessie Smith Cultural Center, in 2009, which is now on Ninth Street near Lindsay, the heart of the old Chattanooga music scene. It is named the Bessie Smith Cultural Center, African American Museum Performance Hall. It looks like a school and a church with its many long narrow windows—a sizeable five-sided bay on the second story in the center with long halls branching out on either side. Red bricks form a solid foundation and structure, giving the feel of holding its history and stories securely inside.

2. Travel Southeast Tennessee, "The Big 9."

3. Moss, "Lost Music Town of Tennessee."

4. Phil Walden, 66, began his career managing Otis Redding and booking shows for other R&B artists in the late '50s. He launched Capricorn Records in 1969, out of Macon, Georgia, which was home to Southern rock, the Allman Brothers, and the Marshall Tucker Band.

5. Fox, "Eddie Kirkland, 87, Known as the Gypsy of the Blues, Dies."

6. Stubblefield, "191: Clyde Stubblefield."

7. Stubblefield, "191: Clyde Stubblefield."

8. Dyer, "Eddie Kirkland, 'Hawg Man' and 'Gypsy of the Blues,' August 16, 1923–February 27, 2011."

Chapter 6

1. B. B. King was born on a plantation in Mississippi. His career began in 1947, when he hitchhiked to Memphis. A year later, he caught his first break when appearing on Sony Boy Williamson's radio show on KWEM.

2. DAHR Discography of American Historical Recordings, "Bill Doggett."

3. Ruth Alston Brown (1928–2006) was an American singer-songwriter and actress. She was known as "Miss Rhythm," and her rhythm and blues dominated the charts that helped establish Atlantic Records, the main rhythm and blues label during the 1950s. Atlantic became known as "the house that Ruth built."

4. Lenell Glass said: "If you go to the right store, Rose Records in Chicago, you can find just about anything you are looking for and probably get Ruth's albums. If they don't have it, they will get it. That's about the only way you can get those records now."

Chapter 7

1. Moss, "Lost Music Town of Tennessee."

2. Radlauer, "International Sweethearts of Rhythm." The International Sweethearts of Rhythm Jazz expanded to a band of seventeen women, with African American, Latina, Asian, Jewish, White, Native American, Hawaiian, and Puerto Rican musicians. They were active between 1937 and 1949. See Benjamin, "International Sweethearts of Rhythm Jazz Band."

3. PBS, "Lena Horne Documentary 1996."

4. Moss, "Lost Music Town of Tennessee."

5. See the Inclines, "The Atlanta Boogaloo."

6. The Inclines, "Pressure Cooker. Part II."

Chapter 8

1. Rhythms were demonstrated by the musician.

2. Matsumoto, *Soul of the Funky Drummers.*

3. Vincent, *Funk*, 70.

4. Stack Exchange, "Where Does 'Funk' and/or 'Funky' Come from and Why the Musical Reference?"

5. Zaferris, "The Etymology of 'Funk.'"

6. Urban Dictionary, "To Be in a Funk."

7. Zaferris, "Etymology of 'Funk.'"

8. Justman, *Standing in the Shadows of Motown.*

Chapter 9

1. Gibney, *Mr. Dynamite.*

2. O'Connor, "The History of Electronic Drum Sets."

Chapter 10

1. The original buck dance, or "buck and wing," referred to a specific step performed by solo dancers, usually men; today the term encompasses a broad variety of improvisational dance steps. See Baker, "Buck Dancing."

2. DeFrantz, "Thomas F. DeFrantz: Buck, Wing, and Jig."

3. Wallenfeldt, *Sounds of Rebellion*, 126.

4. Spellman, *Four Lives in the Bebop Business*, 43.

5. Vierkant, "James Brown and the Black Power," 20.

6. Brown, *Life of James Brown*, 206.

7. Ward, "Inspiration and Pioneer—Or Copycat?"

8. Davis, "James Brown on the Rock Icon Who Opened Doors for Him While Simultaneously 'Keeping Him From Being Number One.'"

Chapter 11

1. Remnick, "The Possessed."
2. Peeno, "The Biggest Mistake the Rolling Stones Ever Made."
3. Parker, *98 Percent Funky Stuff*, 67.
4. Gibney, *Mr. Dynamite.*
5. Parker, *98 Percent Funky Stuff*, 68.
6. Parker, *98 Percent Funky Stuff*, 68.
7. Parker, *98 Percent Funky Stuff*, 68.
8. Amorosi, "Drummer Clyde Stubblefield."
9. Amorosi, "Drummer Clyde Stubblefield," 65–66.
10. Smith, *The One*, 284.
11. Parker, *98 Percent Funky Stuff*, 119.
12. Vincent, *Funk*, 18.
13. Smith, *The One*, 78.
14. Gibney, *Mr. Dynamite.*
15. Gibney, *Mr. Dynamite.*

Chapter 12

1. Matsumoto, *Soul of the Funky Drummers.*
2. Amorosi, "Drummer Clyde Stubblefield."
3. Matsumoto, *Soul of the Funky Drummers.*
4. The Strad, "8 Ways to Increase Your Intonation."

Chapter 13

1. Weiner, "With One Raw, Irresistible Song, James Brown Found the Sound of the Racial Unrest of 1967."
2. Alesia, "Drummer Clyde Stubblefield."
3. Schaefer, "Give the Drummer Some!"
4. Smith, *The One*, 172.
5. Smith, *The One.*
6. Guralnick, *Sweet Soul Music*, 220.
7. Weiner, "With One Raw, Irresistible Song."
8. Vincent, *Funk*, 123.
9. Gibney, *Mr. Dynamite*, at 62:00.
10. Weiner, "With One Raw, Irresistible Song."
11. Brown, *James Brown The Godfather of Soul*, 173.
12. Gibney, *Mr. Dynamite*, at 59:00.
13. Brown, "James Brown Cold Sweat Live 1968."
14. Barry and Gianni, *The Drummer's Bible.*
15. Weiner, "With One Raw, Irresistible Song."

16. Weiner, "With One Raw, Irresistible Song."

17. Weiner, "With One Raw, Irresistible Song."

Chapter 14

1. Parker, *98 Percent Funky Stuff*, 112.

2. Sullivan, *The Hardest Working Man.*

3. Brown, *I Feel Good.*

4. Graham, "After Martin Luther King's Death, James Brown Calmed a Tense Boston."

Chapter 15

1. Hughes, *The Racial Mountain.*

2. Werner, "Black Music and Black Possibility," 172–93.

3. Werner, "Black Music and Black Possibility," 172–73.

4. Werner, "Black Music and Black Possibility," 182–83.

5. Smith, *The One*, 201.

6. Brown, *Life of James Brown*, 206.

7. The Martin Luther King Jr. Research and Education Institute, "Freedom Rides."

8. McGuire, *At the Dark End of the Street*, 109.

9. McGuire, 112.

10. McGuire, 191, 193.

11. McGuire, 192.

12. McGuire, 193.

13. McGuire, 194–95

14. Joseph, *Waiting 'Til the Midnight Hour*, 244.

15. Danielsen, *Presence and Pleasure*, 41.

16. Danielsen, *Presence and Pleasure*, 41.

17. Werner, "Black Music and Black Possibility," 184.

18. Vierkant, "James Brown and the Black Power Movement," 20.

19. Harris, "The Social Activist Side of James Brown."

20. Gilstrap, "A Trojan Horse of Funk and Soul."

21. Brown, James. "James Brown and the Civil Rights Movement."

Chapter 16

1. Smith, *The One*, 197–201.

2. Smith, *The One*, 197.

3. Stubblefield, "191: Clyde Stubblefield."

4. Stubblefield, "191: Clyde Stubblefield."

5. Stubblefield, "191: Clyde Stubblefield."

6. Smith, *The One*, 198–201.
7. Goodwin, "Black and White in Vietnam."
8. Smith, *The One*, 200.
9. Stubblefield, "191: Clyde Stubblefield."
10. Smith, *The One*, 198.

Chapter 17

1. Sisario, "Crimes Against Music."
2. *LA Weekly*, "The 20 Best Drummers of All Time."
3. Alesia, "Drummer Clyde Stubblefield."
4. Alesia, "Drummer Clyde Stubblefield."
5. *Total Drummer*, "The Funky Drummer/Clyde Stubblefield."
6. Gibney, *Mr. Dynamite*.

Chapter 18

1. McBride, *Kill 'Em and Leave*, 135.
2. Gibney, *Mr. Dynamite*.
3. McBride, *Kill 'Em and Leave*, 138.
4. Smith, *The One*, 232.
5. Smith, *The One*.
6. Smith, *The One*, 233.
7. Smith, *The One*, 234.
8. Sullivan, *Hardest Working Man*, 194.
9. Irwin, "Say It Loud."

Chapter 19

1. Weiner, "With One Raw, Irresistible Song."
2. Bobby Blue Bland was born in 1930 in Barretville, Tennessee. He played blues, R&B, and soul and was inducted into the Blues Hall of Fame in 1981, the Rock and Roll Hall of Fame in 1992, and the Memphis Music Hall of Fame in 2012.
3. Sidran, *Black Talk*, 147.

Chapter 20

1. Stubblefield, "Chick'n Pick'n."

Chapter 21

1. Williams, "Pee Wee Ellis Obituary": "Pee Wee Ellis was a composer, arranger, saxophonist and keyboard player, bandleader, musical director, writer and arranger, a musician whose repertoire encompasses all manner of music from jazz through soul and funk to rock. Pee Wee was born in Florida in 1941,

and raised in Lubbock, Texas, where he played his first public show in junior high school. His family moved to Rochester, New York, and he played professionally throughout High School. In 1965, he got 'the call' from his close friend Wayman Reed to join the James Brown Revue. He played alto sax and organ and in 1967 became Brown's bandleader. After leaving he was with Brown until 1969 and co-wrote twenty-six songs with him. He returned to playing jazz and became a respected arranger and conductor, playing concerts until his final years, when he passed away in 2021 at the age of eighty."

2. Concert Archives, "Still Black, Still Proud."

Chapter 22

1. Parker, *98 Percent Funky Stuff*, 192.
2. *Capital Times*, "Proves He's Number One," 34.
3. Jancelewicz, "The 'Whitewashing' of Black Music."
4. *Wisconsin State Journal*, "James Brown," 37.
5. Effigy mounds are sculptures that had deep meaning for the people who built them, but some were burial mounds and some represent their deep connection to the natural world.
6. Stubblefield, "191: Clyde Stubblefield."
7. *Capital Times*, "Stubblefield and Starks." March 10, 2000, p. 11.

Chapter 23

1. Stubblefield, "191: Clyde Stubblefield."
2. Stubblefield, "191: Clyde Stubblefield."
3. "The early days of the Nitty Gritty were turbulent ones that reflected the social and political unrest of the Vietnam War era. In the late '60s and early '70s, the 'Gritty' served as the informal headquarters for the campus subculture which led to many anti–Vietnam War protest demonstrations and marches. In fact, the 1970 bombings of Sterling Hall was planned by 4 anti-war activists within the walls of the Nitty Gritty. This event marked the pinnacle of the anti-war movement in Madison and a change in culture on the UW campus. During these years, the Nitty Gritty was a famous Midwest blues music venue, featuring live music 7 nights a week. The Gritty featured gigs by the likes of Muddy Waters, B. B. King, Luther Allison, Bonnie Raitt, Charlie Musselwhite, Buddy Guy, and Cheap Trick. The Nitty Gritty was home to nearly all regional bands at the time." From the Nitty Gritty website: https://www.thegritty.com/madison.
4. Black Star Drum Line, https://www.blackstardrumline.com/copy-of-media.
5. Marcy & the Highlights, http://marcyandthehighlights.com/meet-us/.
6. Tina and the Tigers, "Mr. Big Stuff."
7. Tina and the Tigers, "Bring it on Home."

8. Schneider, *Smart Studios Story.*

9. Schneider, *Smart Studios Story.*

10. Schneider, *Smart Studios Story.*

11. The album *Nevermind* was later finished in Sound City Studios.

12. Schneider, *Smart Studios Story.*

13. Stanoch, "Drummers on the Beat."

14. Justman, *Standing in the Shadows of Motown.*

15. Lee Roy Parnell, https://leeroyparnell.com.

16. Stubblefield, *Revenge of the Funky Drummer.*

17. "Come on in My Kitchen" on the *King of the Delta Blues Singers* in 1937 on Vocalion Records. Johnson sings the lyrics, "You better come on in my kitchen."

Chapter 25

1. Merlyn's was upstairs from a tiny gyros place on State Street in Madison and had hosted notable musicians such as Art Blakey with a nineteen-year-old Wynton Marsalis, Husker Du, the Art Ensemble of Chicago, and Joan Jett. It closed in 1982.

2. Their big hit after they moved to Austin, Texas, was "The Future's So Bright, I Gotta Wear Shades."

3. Genco, "Bandallamas."

4. Nominated for Best Rock Song and Rock Album of the year at the 53rd Annual Grammy Awards, which included, among others, UW professor and bassist Richard Davis, and Lisa Bethke (the Violent Femmes).

5. Tony Williams played with Miles Davis, John Coltrane, Thelonious Monk, Jimi Hendrix, and Bruce Springsteen and the Kronos Quartet.

6. Alesia, "Stubblefield Stays Upbeat as Cancer Survivor."

7. O'Cayz Corral was at 504 E. Wilson Street, Madison, Wisconsin.

8. Moore, "Fateful Flight."

9. Kovalic, "Singer's Death Left Indelible Mark on City."

10. Gibney, *Mr. Dynamite.*

11. Laskin, "Clyde Stubblefield."

12. Stubblefield, "191: Clyde Stubblefield."

Chapter 26

1. The author's first job while attending the UW was in the sheet music department at Ward-Brodt.

2. See Sabien, "About Randy Sabien."

3. You can see David Stanoch double drumming with Stubblefield on Stanoch's YouTube channel. See Stanoch, RhythmelodicMusic.

4. Stanoch, "On the Beat with David Stanoch."

Chapter 27

1. Wesley Jr., *Hit Me, Fred*, 191.

2. "The Masters of Groove, for all their current appeal to the acid jazz players, represent a style that has had longevity, reaching back to the urban blues of the 1940s and '50s. It was vitalized by the arrival of the jazz organ in the 1950s and '60s, and has been a jazz mainstay ever since. With players such as Wilson, Stubblefield and Green Jr. on the scene, the style won't be disappearing any time soon." See D. Heckman, "The Masters of Groove Set Rhythm on Fire," *Los Angeles Times*, March 7, 2003.

Chapter 28

1. HUSH Concerts, "SF Funk Festival." P-Funk album artists, including Pedro Bell, Overton Lloyd, Stozo the Klown, Tym Stevens, and George Clinton.

2. It had James Brown and Blind Boys of Alabama, Dr. John, Leela James, and Brian Setzer over two days on this incredible lineup, and the only original JBs in the band were James and Danny Ray and Fred Thomas on bass.

Chapter 30

1. Brown, *Star Time*.
2. Wood, "State of the Funk with the Funky 5."
3. Melamed, "Lettuce Dedicates Funky Capitol Theatre Performance."

Chapter 32

1. WBUR, "Call Him the Funk Doctor."
2. Franzen, *Copyright Criminals*.
3. Warnett, "How the Block Party Invented Hip-Hop."
4. Thomas, "How the Block Party Became an Urban Phenomenon."
5. Buruch, "DJ Kool Herc's Sister Cindy Campbell."
6. Thomas, "How the Block Party Became an Urban Phenomenon."
7. Sisario, "Crimes Against Music."
8. Franzen, *Copyright Criminals*.
9. Franzen, *Copyright Criminals*.
10. Wikipedia, "Pierre Schaeffer."
11. Franzen, *Copyright Criminals*.
12. Albertoni, "Clyde Stubblefield Gave DJ Kool Herc a Break."
13. Alesia, "Drummer Clyde Stubblefield."

Chapter 33

1. Worland, "Family: Prince Paid Off Medical Bills for Madison's 'Funky Drummer,' Clyde Stubblefield."

2. Payne and Stanoch, "Clyde Stubblefield."

3. Alesia, "Stubblefield Stays Upbeat," 45.

4. Alesia, "Battling the Blues," 9.

5. Black, "Shame on the Hall of Fame."

6. Amorosi, "Drummer Clyde Stubblefield."

7. Chipman, "Prince Donated Secretly to Support Louisville's Historic Western Branch Library in 2001"; Worland, "Family: Prince Paid Off Medical Bills"; Grow, "Prince, the Secret Philanthropist."

8. Hagerty and Audi, "Prince's Little-Known Life." Prince never spoke publicly about his charitable endeavors. The extent of his activism, philanthropy, and charity wasn't publicized until after his death. In 2015, he conceived and launched YesWeCode, paying for many hackathons (where people get together and write computer code) outright and performing musical acts at some of them. He also helped fund the Green for All initiative. When the Western Branch of the Louisville Free Public Library, the first full-service library for African Americans, was in danger of closing in 2001, he donated $12,000 to help keep it open, the same year he paid off Clyde's medical bills.

9. Alesia, "Stubblefield Stays Upbeat," 45.

10. Baik, "A Bench to Remember Long-time 'Funky Drummer' Clyde Stubblefield."

On the Drum Throne

1. Novak, "Clyde Stubblefield to Get Posthumous Honorary Degree from UW."

Final Notation

1. Rasmussen, "Mayor Presents Key to City: The King of Soul Reigns," 47.

2. Jacobson, "'Give the Drummer Some': Madison Pays Its Respects to the Legendary Clyde Stubblefield."

BIBLIOGRAPHY

Albertoni, Rich. "Clyde Stubblefield Gave DJ Kool Herc a Break." *Isthmus,* June 17, 2010.

Alesia, Tom. "Battling the Blues." *Wisconsin State Journal,* July 28, 2009.

Alesia, Tom. "Drummer Clyde Stubblefield: Keeping His Own Funky Beat." *Tom's Write Turns.* June 15, 1994.

Alesia, Tom. "Stubblefield Stays Upbeat as Cancer Survivor." *Wisconsin State Journal.* August 3, 2003.

Amorosi, A. D. "Drummer Clyde Stubblefield, Comes to Ardmore Music with James Brown Dance Party." *Philadelphia Inquirer.* December 27, 2016.

Baik, Michelle. "A Bench to Remember Long-time 'Funky Drummer' Clyde Stubblefield." WMTV-nbc15, August 17, 2019. https://www.nbc15.com/content/news/A-bench-to-remember-long-time-Madison-resident-Clyde-Stubblefield-550122231.html.

Baker, Bruce. E. "Buck Dancing." Encyclopedia of North Carolina. 2006. https://www.ncpedia.org/buck-dancing.

Barry, Mick, and Jason Gianni. *The Drummer's Bible: How to Play Every Drum Style from Afro-Cuban to Zydeco.* See Sharp Press, 2012.

Benjamin, Winston. "International Sweethearts of Rhythm Jazz Band (1937–1949)." *Black Past.* April 2, 2014.

Black Star Drum Line homepage. https://www.blackstardrumline.com/copy-of-media.

Black, Vistalite. "Shame on the Hall of Fame—Clyde Stubblefield." *Drumforum.* September 15, 2015.

Bowman, Rob. "Funk and James Brown: Re-Africanization, the Interlocked Groove, and the Articulation of Community." In *Music Traditions: Cultures and Contexts,* edited by Robin Elliott and Gordon E. Smith. Wilfrid Laurier University Press, 2010

Brown, Geoff. *The Life of James Brown: A Biography.* Omnibus Press, 2007.

Brown, James. *I Feel Good: A Memoir of a Life of Soul.* Penguin, 2005.

Brown, James. "James Brown and the Civil Rights Movement." Posted March 16, 2013. YouTube. https://www.youtube.com/watch?v=nsWWEcG-OrE.

Brown, James. "James Brown Cold Sweat Live 1968." Posted August 5, 2015. YouTube. https://www.youtube.com/watch?v=tvltTXEg5kI.

Brown, James. *James Brown: The Godfather of Soul.* Thunder's Mouth Press, 1986.

Brown, James. *Star Time.* 1991. Four-CD disc compilation of James Brown's 1954–84 hits. Polydor Records.

Buruch, Yolanda. "DJ Kool Herc's Sister Cindy Campbell Talks the Birth of Hip Hop Christie's Auctions." *Forbes.* August 11, 2022.

Candy, Eye. "Black History: Congo Square, New Orleans—The Heart of American Music." *Afropunk*, February 26, 2018. https://afropunk.com/2018/02/black-history-congo-square-new-orleans-heart-american-music/.

Charters, Samuel. *The Roots of the Blues: An African Search.* Da Capo Press, 1981.

Chipman, Melissa. "Prince Donated Secretly to Support Louisville's Historic Western Branch Library in 2001." *Insider Louisville.* Retrieved April 22, 2016.

Crimes Against Music. "Questlove on Clyde Stubblefield." March 29, 2011. http://charmicarmicat.blogspot.com/2011/03/questlove-on-clyde-stubblefield.html.

Concert Archives. "Still Black, Still Proud—African Tribute to James Brown Concert History." https://www.concertarchives.org/bands/still-black-still-proud-african-tribute-to-james-brown.

DAHR Discography of American Historical Recordings. "Bill Doggett." UC Santa Barbara Library. https://adp.library.ucsb.edu/index.php/mastertalent/detail/106060/Doggett_Bill?Matrix_page=2.

Danielsen, Anne. *Presence and Pleasure: The Funk Grooves of James Brown and Parliament.* Wesleyan University Press, 2006.

Davis, Melaine. "James Brown on the Rock Icon Who Opened Doors for Him While Simultaneously 'Keeping Him From Being Number One.'" *American Songwriter*, October 2, 2025.

DeFrantz, Thomas F. "Thomas F. DeFrantz: Buck, Wing, and Jig." *Duke Today*, March 28, 2012. Duke University. https://today.duke.edu/2012/03/thomas-f-defrantz-buck-wing-and-jig.

Dyer, Candice. "Eddie Kirkland, 'Hawg Man' and 'Gypsy of the Blues,' August 16, 1923–February 27, 2011." *Candice Dyer's Writing*, April 19, 2011. https://anticsincandyland.wordpress.com/2011/04/19/eddie-kirkland-august-161923-february-27-2011/.

Franzen, Benjamin, dir. *Copyright Criminals.* 2009. Copyright Criminals, LLC, and Alphabet Entertainment.

Fox, Margalit. "Eddie Kirkland, 87, Known as the Gypsy of the Blues, Dies."
New York Times, March 6, 2011. https://www.nytimes.com/2011/03/07/arts/music/07kirkland.html.

Fox, Ted. *Showtime at the Apollo.* Da Capo Press, 1993.

Genco, Emily. "Bandallamas." *Maximum Ink: Madison's Music Magazine*, November 2011.

Gibney, Alex, dir. *Mr. Dynamite: The Rise of James Brown*. 2014. Jagged Productions.

Gilstrap, Peter. "A Trojan Horse of Funk and Soul: The Story of the Black Panthers House." *California Report Magazine*, KQED, July 10, 2020.

Goodwin, G. F. "Black and White in Vietnam." *New York Times*, July 18, 2017.

Graham, Renee. "After Martin Luther King's Death, James Brown Calmed a Tense Boston." *Boston Globe*, April 3, 2018.

Grow, Kory. "Prince, the Secret Philanthropist: His Cause Was Humanity.'" *Rolling Stone*, April 25, 2016.

Guralnick, Peter. *Sweet Soul Music: Rhythm and Blues and the Southern Dream of Freedom*. Little, Brown, and Company. 1986.

Hagerty, James R., and Tamara Audi. "Prince's Little-Known Life." *Wall Street Journal*, April 24, 2016.

Harris, Aisha. "The Social Activist Side of James Brown You Won't See in *Get On Up*." *Slate*, August 1, 2014. https://slate.com/culture/2014/08/james-browns-social-activism-a-brief-history-of-the-singers-politics-not-found-in-get-on-up.html.

Harris, Robert L., and Rosalyn Terborg-Penn, eds. *The Columbia Guide to African American History Since 1939*. Columbia University Press, 2006.

Hentoff, Nat. "The New Jazz: Black, Angry, and Hard to Understand." *New York Times*, December 25, 1966.

Historical Marker Database. "Congo Square." https://www.hmdb.org/m.asp?m=20954

Hoffman, Anne. "Mississippi Is the Birthplace of American Music, Here's Proof." *Matador Network*, June 7, 2016. https://matadornetwork.com/nights/mississippi-birthplace-american-music-heres-proof/.

Homan, Spencer. "Know Your History! John Coltrane's Strawberry Mansion Home." *The Spirit of Penn's Garden*, April 29, 2016. https://spiritnews.org/articles/know-your-history-john-coltranes-strawberry-mansion-home/.

Hughes, Langston. *The Racial Mountain*. 1926.

HUSH Concerts. "SF Funk Festival." *HUSH concerts*. https://www.hushconcerts.com/hushoffices/sf-funk-festival/.

Irwin, Corey. "Say It Loud—I'm Black and I'm Proud: How James Brown Delivered His 'Rallying Cry.'" *Classical Rock and Culture*, August 20, 2020. https://ultimateclassicrock.com/james-brown-say-it-loud-im-black-and-im-proud/.

Jacobson, Bob. "'Give the Drummer Some': Madison Pays Its Respects to the Legendary Clyde Stubblefield." Isthmus, September 10, 2015. https://isthmus.com/arts/music/give-the-drummer-some-clyde-stubblefield/.

"James Brown: 'Say It Loud—I'm Black and I'm Proud.'" *BlackConsumers*.

Jancelewicz, Chris. "The 'Whitewashing' of Black Music: A Dark Chapter in Rock History." *Global News*, January 30, 2019. https://globalnews.ca/news/4321150/black-music-whitewashing-classic-rock/.

Jones, LeRoi. *Blues People: Negro Music in White America and the Music That Developed from It*. Willam Morrow and Company, 1963.

Joseph, Peniel E. *Waiting 'Til the Midnight Hour: A Narrative History of Black Power in America*. Henry Holt and Company, 2006.

Justman, Paul, dir. *Standing in the Shadows of Motown: The Soul Behind the Sound*. 2002. Artisans Entertainment.

Kebede, Ashenafi. *Roots of Black Music: The Vocal, Instrumental, and Dance Heritage of Africa and Black America*. Prentice Hall Inc., 1982.

Kovalic, John. "Singer's Death Left Indelible Mark on City." *Wisconsin State Journal*, December 6, 1992.

Knutson, Kari. "UW to Award Clyde Stubblefield Posthumous Honorary Degree."

University of Wisconsin News, February 21, 2017. https://news.wisc.edu/uw-madison-to-award-clyde-stubblefield-posthumous-honorary-degree/.

LA Weekly. "The 20 Best Drummers of All Time." November 11, 2014. http://www.laweekly.com/music/the-20-best-drummers-of-all-time-5199372.

Laskin, Tom. "Clyde Stubblefield the Hardest Working Man in Madison." *Isthmus*, April 7, 2011. https://isthmus.com/archive/from-the-archives/clyde-stubblefield-the-hardest-working-man-in-madison/.

Leadbelly. "'Midnight Special' by Leadbelly." Song Facts. https://www.songfacts.com/facts/leadbelly/midnight-special.

Marcy & the Highlights. Homepage. http://marcyandthehighlights.com/meet-us/.

The Martin Luther King Jr. Research and Education Institute. "Freedom Rides." Stanford University. https://kinginstitute.stanford.edu/freedom-rides.

Matsumoto, Chiaki, dir. *Soul of the Funky Drummers*. 2004. Rittor Music, Hal Leonard Corp.

McBride, James. *Kill 'Em and Leave: Searching for James Brown and the American Soul*. Random House Publishing Group, 2016.

McGuire, Danielle L. *At the Dark End of the Street: Black Women, Rape, and Resistance-a New History of the Civil Rights Movement from Rosa Parks to the Rise of Black Power*. Vintage Books, 2010.

Melamed, Dave. "Lettuce Dedicates Funky Capitol Theatre Performance to Clyde Stubblefield (Full Audio)." Live for Live Music, February 21, 2017. https://liveforlivemusic.com/news/lettuce-dedicates-funky-capitol-theatre-performance-clyde-stubblefield-full-audio/.

Montfort, Matthew. *Ancient Traditions—Future Possibilities: Rhythmic Training Through the Traditions of Africa, Bali, and India*. Panoramic Press, 1985.

Moore, Andy. "Fateful Flight." *Wisconsin State Journal*, December, 2, 2007.

Moss, Charles J. "The Lost Music Town of Tennessee." *Medium*, January 9, 2015. https://medium.com/@charlesjmoss/the-lost-music-town-of-tennessee-2b4593a08e02.

The Nitty Gritty website. https://www.thegritty.com/madison.

Novak, Bill. "Clyde Stubblefield to Get Posthumous Honorary Degree from UW." *Wisconsin State Journal*, February, 21, 2017.

O'Connor, Mike. "The History of Electronic Drum Sets: 1960s to the 2020s." *Electronic Drum Advisor*, March 7, 2022.

Oliver, Paul. *Songsters and Saints: Vocal Traditions on Race Records*. Cambridge University Press, 1984.

Palmer, Robert. *Rock & Roll: An Unruly History*. Harmony Books, 1995.

Parker, Maceo. *98% Funky Stuff: My Life in Music*. Chicago Review Press, 2013.

Parnell, Lee Roy. https://leeroyparnell.com.

Payne, Jim, and David Stanoch. "Clyde Stubblefield: April 15, 1943–February 18, 2017." *Modern Drummer*, August 2017. https://www.moderndrummer.com/wp-content/uploads/2017/06/1708_Md._August_453.pdf.

PBS. "Lena Horne Documentary 1996." *American Masters*, 1996. YouTube. https://www.youtube.com/watch?v=AErWqNBhawI&t=16s.

Peeno, Jeffrey. "The Biggest Mistake the Rolling Stones Ever Made." *Far Out*. November 26, 2021.

"Pierre Schaeffer." Wikipedia. https://en.wikipedia.org/wiki/Pierre Schaeffer.

The Inclines. "The Atlanta Boogaloo – The Inclines." Posted December 27, 2012, YouTube. https://www.youtube.com/watch?v=Nkup8eWRFh4.

The Inclines. "Pressure Cooker. Part I." Music Outside the Box Channel. ATCO Records. Fame Recording Studios, Muscle Shoals, Ala. 1969. https://www.youtube.com/watch?v=RBrjxbSqMKY.

The Inclines. "Pressure Cooker. Part II." Music Outside the Box Channel. ATCO Records. Fame Recording studios, Muscle Shoals, Ala.. 1969. https://www.youtube.com/watch?v=vBqM6Qu-cFQhttps://www.youtube.com/watch?v=9nM3TYtB7Co.

Radlauer, David. "The International Sweethearts of Rhythm: Exploring the World of Hot Jazz, Ragtime, and Swing." *The Syncopated Times*, November 30, 2022. https://syncopatedtimes.com/the-international-sweethearts-of-rhythm-1937-49/.

Rasmussen, Lynne. "Mayor Presents Key to City: The King of Soul Reigns." *Wisconsin State Journal*, July 9, 1969.

Remnick, David. "The Possessed: James Brown in Eighteen Minutes." *The New Yorker*. July 30, 2014.

Robinson, Charlotte. "Proves He's Number One: James Brown Revue Rocks Coliseum's Soul." *The Capital Times*, July 9, 1969.

Rowe, Mike. *Chicago Blues: The City and the Music*. Da Capo Press, 1975.

Sabien, Randy. "About Randy Sabien." https://www.randysabien.com/about.html.

San Francisco Funk Festival. HUSH concerts. https://www.hushconcerts.com/hushoffices/sf-funk-festival/.

Schaefer, John. "Give the Drummer Some!" *Soundcheck*, WNYC Studios, February 9, 2010. https://www.wnycstudios.org/podcasts/soundcheck/articles/13145-give-drummer-some.

Schneider, Wendy, dir. *The Smart Studios Story*. 2016. Coney Island Studios. https://thesmartstudiosstory.com.

Seamons, Joe. "The Midnight Special: Origins and Sources." *The Rhapsody Project*, August 31, 2021. https://therhapsodyproject.org/the-midnight-special-origins-sources/.

Shteamer, Hank. "Architecture and Explosion: Cecil Taylor, the Composer." Dark Forces Swing Blind Punches (blog), April 29, 2016. Darkforcesswing.blogspot.com/2016/04/architecture-and-explosion-cecil-taylor.html.

Sidran, Ben. *Black Talk*. Da Capo Press, 1971.

Sisario, Ben. "Crimes Against Music." Questlove on Clyde Stubblefield. March 29, 2011. http://charmicarmicat.blogspot.com/2011/03/questlove-on-clyde-stubblefield.html.

Smith, RJ. *The One: The Life and Music of James Brown*. Penguin Random House, 2012.

Smith Lukachick, Joy, and Joan Garrett McClane. "Rewriting a History, Recasting a Future." *Chattanooga Times Free Press*. https://projects.timesfreepress.com/2017/08/thelostway/day3.html.

Soul of America. "New Orleans: Birthplace of Jazz." *Soul of America and World of Black Travel*. https://www.soulofamerica.com/us-cities/new-orleans/no-birthplace-of-jazz/.

Spellman, A. B. Four Lives in the Bebop Business. Limelight Editions, 1966.

Stack Exchange. "Where Does 'Funk' and/or 'Funky' Come from and Why the Musical Reference?" 2011. https://english.stackexchange.com/questions/17228/where-does-funk-and-or-funky-come-from-and-why-the-musical-reference.

Stanoch, David. "On the Beat with David Stanoch: Where Old School Meets New—The Timeless Rhythm of Clyde Stubblefield." *Modern Drummer*, July 2, 2017. https://www.moderndrummer.com/2017/07/beat-david-stanoch-old-school-meets-new-timeless-rhythm-clyde-stubblefield/.

Stanoch, David. RhythmelodicMusic. YouTube channel of David Stanoch. https://www.youtube.com/@rhythmelodicmusicdavidstanoch.

"Still Black, Still Proud: African Tribute to James Brown Concert & Tour History." Concert Archives. https://www.concertarchives.org/bands/still-black-still-proud-african-tribute-to-james-brown.

The Strad. "8 Ways to Increase Your Intonation." September 13, 2022.

Stubblefield, Clyde. "191: Clyde Stubblefield." Interview by Leo Sidran. *The Third Story*, WBGO Studios, April 19, 2020.

Stubblefield, Clyde, drums. "Chick'n Pick'n." Donald Segar, bass; guitar; Johnn Davis, piano; Fred Wesley, horns; John "Jabo" Starks, claves. Posted March 19, 2023. YouTube. https://www.youtube.com/watch?v=71H-i3_8wwU.

Stubblefield, Clyde. "The Clyde Stubblefield Interview." Interview by Jake Feinberg. *Jake Feinberg Show*, December 15, 2020. https://www.youtube.com/watch?v=xwUibtapRxU&t=633s.

Stubblefield, Clyde. *Revenge of the Funky Drummer*. 1997. United Kingdom, Interaction Records. Produced by Richard Mazda.

Sullivan, James. *The Hardest Working Man: How James Brown Saved the Soul of America*. Gotham Books, 2008.

Thomas, Briana A. "How the Block Party Became an Urban Phenomenon." *Smithsonian*. August 10, 2022.

Times of Malta. "Leading R&B Drummer Earl Palmer Dead at 84."
September 20, 2008. https://timesofmalta.com/article/leading-r-b-drummer-earl-palmer-dead-at-84.225440.

Tina and the Tigers. "Bring it on Home." Recorded August 29, 1984, at WHA tv in Madison, Wis. Posted February 26, 2017. YouTube. https://www.youtube.com/watch?v=m1wIEGs2Psc.

Tina and the Tigers. "Mr. Big Stuff." Recorded August 29, 1984, at WHA tv in Madison, Wis. Posted February 26, 2017. YouTube. https://www.youtube.com/watch?v=P5py-Yk2DdA.

Total Drummer. "The Funky Drummer/Clyde Stubblefield: The Funky Drummer Drum Beat." https://www.totaldrummer.com/the-funky-drummer/.

Travel Southeast Tennessee. "The Big 9: Chattanooga's Vibrant Musical Past." September 2, 2020. https://www.southeasttennessee.com/big-nine/.

Urban Dictionary. "To Be in a Funk." March 14, 2017. https://www.urbandictionary.com/define.php?term=to%20be%20in%20a%20fun.

Vierkant, Paul, "James Brown and the Black Power Movement or Was America's Soul Brother Number One a Black Nationalist?" Seminar paper. GRIN Publishing. 2007.

Vincent, Rickey. *Funk: The Music, the People, and the Rhythm of the One*. St Martin's Griffin, 1996.

Wallenfeldt, Jeff, ed. *Sounds of Rebellion: Music in the 1960s*. Britannica Educational Publishing, 2013.

Ward, Brian. "Inspiration and Pioneer—Or Copycat? Elvis Presley's Ambiguous Relationship with Black America." *Independent*. August 16, 2017.

Warnett, Gary. "How the Block Party Invented Hip-Hop." *Mr Porter: The Journal*. July 13, 2016.

WBUR. "Call Him the Funk Doctor." *Here & Now*, February 16, 2012. https://www.wbur.org/hereandnow/2012/02/16/funk-george-clinton.

Weiner, Natalie. "With One Raw, Irresistible Song, James Brown Found the Sound of the Racial Unrest of 1967." *Timeline*, June 26, 2017. https://medium.com/timeline/with-one-raw-irresistible-song-james-brown-found-the-sound-of-the-racial-unrest-of-1967-18017dbce903.

Weingarten, Christopher R., Jon Dolan, Matt Diehl, et. al. "100 Greatest Drummers of All Time." *Rolling Stone*, March 31, 2016. http://www.rollingstone.com/music/lists/100-greatest-drummers-of-all-time-20160331/clyde-stubblefield-and-john-jabo-starks-20160325#ixzz45LMzSCd1.

Werner, Craig. "Black Music and Black Possibility: From Be-bop to Hip-Hop." In *The Columbia Guide to African American History Since 1939*, Robert L. Harris Jr. and Rosalyn Terborg-Penn. Columbia University Press, 2006.

Wesley Jr., Fred. *Hit Me, Fred: Reflections of a Sideman*. Duke University Press, 2002.

White, Clark. "Blues Culture and the Black Experience in the River City." *the pulse*, February 6, 2014. https://www.chattanoogapulse.com/features/blues-culture-and-black-experience-in-the-river-city.

Wilkerson, Isabel. *The Warmth of Other Suns: The Epic Story of America's Great Migration*. Random House, 2010.

Williams, Richard. "Pee Wee Ellis Obituary." *The Guardian*, September 30, 2021.

Wiltz, Allison. "How a Creole Man Became the Test Case for Segregation." *Momentum*, December 12, 2021.

Wisconsin State Journal. "James Brown: Poor Boy Makes It." July 24, 1970, p. 37.

Wood, Jake. "The State of the Funk with the Funky 5." *Drum!*, 2018. https://drummagazine.com/the-state-of-the-funk-with-the-funky-5/.

Worland, Gayle. "Family: Prince Paid Off Medical Bills for Madison's 'Funky Drummer,' Clyde Stubblefield." *Wisconsin State Journal*, April 27, 2016.

World Population Review. "Chattanooga." https://worldpopulationreview.com/us-cities/chattanooga-tn-population.

Zaferris, Jess. "The Etymology of 'Funk.'" Useless Etymology, November 25, 2017. https://uselessetymology.com/2017/11/25/the-etymology-of-funk/.

INDEX

MUSIC OF THE AMERICAN SOUTH

Whisperin' Bill Anderson: An Unprecedented Life in Country Music
by Bill Anderson, with Peter Cooper

Party Out of Bounds: The B-52's, R.E.M., and the Kids Who Rocked Athens, Georgia
by Rodger Lyle Brown

Widespread Panic in the Streets of Athens, Georgia
by Gordon Lamb

The Philosopher King: T Bone Burnett and the Ethic of a Southern Cultural Renaissance
by Heath Carpenter

The Music and Mythocracy of Col. Bruce Hampton: A Basically True Biography
by Jerry Grillo

An OutKast Reader: Essays on Race, Gender, and the Postmodern South
edited by Regina N. Bradley

Straight Into Darkness: Tom Petty as Rock Mystic
by Megan Volpert

Kill Your Masters: Run the Jewels and the World That Made Them
by Jaap van der Doelen

Chet Atkins: Mr. Guitar
by Don Cusic

Hacking Hip Hop: Design Remix Logic in Research, Method, and Practice
by Joycelyn Wilson

Clyde Stubblefield: Rhythms of the Funky Drummer
by D. Leah Steinberg

www.ingramcontent.com/pod-product-compliance
Lightning Source LLC
LaVergne TN
LVHW091246030926
847199LV00026B/93